Praise for *Raising Res*t *.* *Kids in a Rude World*

"Highly recommended. Plain-spoken, loaded with examples, and organized so you can get the guidance you need now. This is all parenting books rolled into one."

—Jane Griffith, counselor, professor, and past president,
North American Society of Adlerian Psychology

"This book acknowledges the responsibility of parents to provide children healthy and respectful role models for interpersonal relationships, and gives concrete examples of how to develop mutual respect in the family as well as methods for handling rudeness."

—Oscar C. Christensen, Ed.D.,
professor emeritus, University of Arizona

"A terrific manual and reference book for parents as they deal with these vitally important issues."

—Francis X. Walton, Ph.D., international consultant,
child and adolescent psychology

Raising Respectful Kids in a Rude World

Teaching Your Children the Power of Mutual Respect and Consideration

Gary D. McKay, Ph.D.

Joyce L. McKay, Ph.D.

Daniel Eckstein, Ph.D.

Steven A. Maybell, Ph.D.

PRIMA PUBLISHING
3000 Lava Ridge Court • Roseville, California 95661
(800) 632-8676 • www.primalifestyles.com

The authors are grateful to Dr. John F. Newbauer for his invaluable contributions to chapter 2.

Library of Congress Cataloging-in-Publication Data
McKay, Gary D.
   Raising respectful kids in a rude world : teaching your children the power of mutual respect and consideration / Gary McKay . . . [et al.].
      p.   cm.
   Includes bibliographical references and index.
   ISBN 0-7615-2811-3
   1. Respect for persons. 2. Etiquette for children and teenagers. 3. Child rearing.
I. McKay, Gary D.

BJ1533.R42 R35 2001   00-068690

01 02 03 04 HH 10 9 8 7 6 5 4 3 2 1
Printed in the United States of America

HOW TO ORDER

Single copies may be ordered from Prima Publishing, 3000 Lava Ridge Court, Roseville, CA 95661; telephone (800) 632-8676 ext. 4444. Quantity discounts are also available. On your letterhead, include information concerning the intended use of the books and the number of books you wish to purchase.

Visit us online at www.primalifestyles.com

To our teachers:
Oscar C. Christensen, Don Dinkmeyer Sr.,
Rudolf Dreikurs, Jane Griffith,
Bernice Bronia Grunwald,
Bill W. Hillman, Harold Mosak,
Robert L. Powers, and Frank Walton.

CONTENTS

ACKNOWLEDGMENTS

WRITING *Raising Respectful Kids in a Rude World* has been both challenging and rewarding. Several people from our past and present have made this book possible. We'd like to acknowledge the following people with appreciation:

The late Rudolf Dreikurs—his persistent spreading of Alfred Adler's work throughout the world gave each of us the foundation for our philosophies of life and our careers.

A special thanks goes to John F. Newbauer, friend and colleague, for his contributions and encouragement.

Joyce and Gary McKay wish to acknowledge their friends and mentors Harold Mosak, Oscar C. Christensen, Bill W. Hillman, Sally Laufketter, and Bernice Bronia Grunwald. They give a special acknowledgment to Don Dinkmeyer Sr., their friend and writing partner for more than thirty years. They also acknowledge their son and stepson Robert F. Binz, grandson Michael Binz, and nieces Jennifer and Kristin Wessel. These special people gave the McKays ample opportunity to practice respectful parenting. Special thanks to Jennifer for her secretarial assistance.

Daniel Eckstein would like to acknowledge the 28-year Adlerian-psychology mentoring and friendship of Frank Walton and Don Dinkmeyer Sr. and the manuscript assistance of Amy Zimmerman. Special thanks to his father, the late Oscar Gotlieb Eckstein, and his mother, Frances Lilian Eckstein, who did an outstanding job raising four creative and challenging children. Thanks, too, to his siblings, Donna, David, and Doug, who successfully survived the unique challenge of a first-born son left in charge when the parents were away. He also extends appreciation to the many colleagues who have volunteered their time and energy in support of the governance of the North American Society of Adlerian Psychology.

Steven A. Maybell wishes to acknowledge Robert L. Powers and Jane Griffith, his mentors and friends, for their years of support to his career and to the development and growth of Adlerian psychology. Warmest appreciation goes to Steve's wife and partner in parenting, Debbie Gregson, for her grace and encouragement every single day. He thanks their sons, Sean and Jason, for enriching their lives and providing so many lessons in parenting. To all his Y.E.S. colleagues, thanks for their inspiration—especially Debbi Halela, Belinda Lafferty, and Ken Wong, who made valuable contributions to this book. Heartfelt thanks to Ben Wisckol, Shirley Cole, and Patti Skelton for the leadership they have provided over the years and for their contribution to Steve's own leadership skills.

Finally, all of us give our appreciation for the encouragement and support for this project by fellow author Jane Nelsen, our editor Jamie Miller, and to all the personnel at Prima Publishing without whose dedication and work this book would not be a reality.

INTRODUCTION

PARENTS AND TEACHERS throughout the country today complain about the lack of civility among children. Kids talk back to their parents, shove other students in the hallways, and are rude to their teachers. Most parents agree that they would like their children to grow up respecting others, but there is some confusion about how to accomplish that. Some believe they are teaching respect by using an attitude of, "Do what I say, when I say it, and don't give me any lip!" That may have worked fifty years ago, but not today. Other parents think that if they expect less from their children they will earn more respect, and they end up overindulging them. True respect means caring, courtesy, consideration, and cooperation, and it must go *both* ways. What parents often don't realize is that in order for today's kids to respect others, they need to feel respected.

Because some parents don't fully understand this concept, many of their parenting practices actually model disrespect. That's what *Raising Respectful Kids in a Rude World* is all about— how to show respect to kids so they will respect others. Mutual respect is the foundation for effective human relationships.

In addition, the book shows you how to help kids develop civility skills. Manners, politeness, and courtesy are a lost art for many kids—and adults. Finally, we discuss the ultimate rudeness in our society—violence—and how you can help your kids be safe and nonviolent.

The book is divided into three parts. In Part I, "Respectful Parents—Respectful Kids," you learn the skills of respectful parenting, how to teach respect to your children, how to encourage and communicate with them, and anger management for the whole family. Part II, "Respectful Kids Learning to Operate in the World," shows you how to respectfully discipline in order to teach life skills, and how to help your kids develop civility skills. In Part III, "Dealing with the Ultimate Rudeness: Violence," you learn what you can do about violent influences in our society and how you and your kids can deal with violence they may encounter.

You'll be learning many skills in this book. Give yourself time to practice and develop your new skills. Don't expect them to "jump from the pages of the book" and perform magic. Good parenting is hard work. Also, realize that your kids won't automatically respond in a more positive, respectful way when you begin to use these skills. They will need time, as well, to get accustomed to the new you. With patience and persistence you'll develop a more positive relationship with your kids.

PART I

Respectful Parents— Respectful Kids

1

Parenting with Respect

How can we raise respectful kids in our world today? Schools use metal detectors to keep out dangerous weapons, popular entertainment grows increasingly vulgar and crude, sports heroes talk trash, the Internet is littered with pornography, and political campaigns resemble food fights. Add to that the complete erosion of civility and manners and you have what some have referred to as today's "American Uncivil War,"[1] where rudeness begets rudeness until it eventually leads to the ultimate rudeness: violence. How can we, as parents and teachers, withstand the mean-spirited tide of the past decade and nurture kindness, tolerance, and respect in our growing children?

The solution is not a simple one, and no one person can change the coarsening of an entire country, but there are steps that can safely steer you and your family in the right direction to stem the tide. Because mutual respect is the foundation of all effective relationships, it is perhaps the most essential value we can teach our children. When we establish an atmosphere of mutual respect in our families, we give our kids a model of how to relate to others. Respect in the family translates to respect in the world.

The Elements of Respect

RESPECTFUL KIDS ACCEPT responsibility. They learn to be encouraging. These kids possess healthy self-esteem and esteem for others, or "people-esteem." They learn empathy for others and are more cooperative and thoughtful. These are the things you will be learning in this book for yourself, your child, and your family.

> Because mutual respect is the foundation of all effective relationships, it is perhaps the most essential value we can teach our children.

If we're going to raise children to be more respectful, then we first have to look at ourselves as parents and as role models for respect. In the autocratic past, parents were able to operate in a superior manner and to practice the traditional principle that kids should do as we say and not as we do. No longer! In our democratic world, kids learn far more by what we do as parents and as people. If we wish to have more respectful kids, we need to become more respectful parents.

We'll begin our discussion of respectful behavior by looking at what constitutes rude behavior. Then we'll examine traditional disrespectful parenting roles and the new roles we can choose that are based on mutual respect.

The Many Faces of Rude Behavior

RUDENESS IS NOT just what we say or the lack of good manners. Rudeness takes many forms from the simple put-down remark to rage and violence—the ultimate form of rudeness.

> Eight-year-old Tonya sassed her mother in front of her mother's friends. Mom swatted Tonya on the bottom.

Here we have two examples of rude behavior or disrespect—one verbal and one physical. Of course, no parent wants to be sassed, but responding in the way Mom did doesn't model respect. What could Mom do instead? She could ignore the outburst for the present and later discuss her feelings with Tonya. Later in the book you'll learn how to respectfully confront your child's misbehavior.

How Did We Get This Way?

IN THE PAST couple of generations, we've had much activity and progress toward equality. Racial minorities demand their rights. Workers demand better treatment and better pay. Women are no longer willing to be subservient to men. It's no longer "father knows best." Equality is in the air, and whether we like it or not, our children breathe the same air. Today's children are raised in a different social environment than we were. They are raised in an environment where social equality is a given expectation. They are a generation who pictures themselves as equals to their parents. The sum total of these changes and their momentous impact on society we call the "democratic revolution."

Since the beginning of civilization, human relationships have been organized in the same manner. In every human relationship there has been a built-in structure defining one member of the relationship as occupying the "superior" position and

Rude Kids

Child leaves toys strewn around the house, creating a
possibility of someone falling and getting hurt.
Teen violates curfew, unconcerned about parents' fear
that something might have happened to him.
Child teases another child in school, using verbal
put-downs.
Kids belong to fight clubs.
Students bring guns to school and threaten, wound, or
kill other students and teachers.

Rude Parents

Mom compares one child to a sibling, holding the
"good" sibling's behavior over the "bad" child's head.
Dad treats door-to-door salesman with disrespect.
Mom stops a fight between siblings and automatically
punishes the older one.
Dad gets angry and calls a child names.
Parents argue and fight disrespectfully with each other.

These examples show that anything that violates
mutual respect—on the part of child or adult—can be
classified as rude behavior.

other the "inferior" position. Society was always structured in
this way and this consistency resulted in general acceptance and
compliance. Some of the obvious examples are shown in table 1.

People in society who occupy the superior position have all
the power, and those occupying the inferior position are re-

PARENTING WITH RESPECT • 7

Table 1 Traditional Positions in Society

Area of social life	The superior position	The inferior position
Government	Dictatorial leaders	The citizens, the people
The workplace	Boss, owners, management	The workers
Race relations	Caucasians	People of color
Gender relations	Males	Females
Parent-child relations	Parents (fathers then mothers)	Children

stricted to adapting to this power. The essential methods applied by the superiors to maintain order (and power) include the following "coercive" tactics:

1. Imposing rules.

2. Rewarding those who obey the rules.

3. Punishing those who violate the rules.

Looking at social institutions and the hierarchy that was traditionally established in all of them—it is interesting to note the vast changes that have occurred. In government, there has been a worldwide trend toward democracy. In the workplace, the union movement has prompted progressive workplace legislation (the 40-hour workweek, minimum wage, profit sharing). The civil rights movement has brought the races closer to equality. In gender relations, the women's movement has empowered women in the workplace, in marriage, and in government.

These developments are what we mean by the "democratic revolution." It's as if, en masse, during the latter part of the twentieth century, the human community declared that all human beings have value, must be treated with respect, and therefore are entitled to take part in matters that affect their lives regardless of position, race, gender, or even age.

Today's parents were raised on the tail end of the period when parents occupied the traditional superior role and children were expected to comply. Quite naturally we learned this way of parenting from our own parents and often attempt to create this same relationship with our kids. Like other traditionally oppressed groups, however, our kids living in the pervasive atmosphere of equality have a very different reaction than we did as children. This is what happens when:

> We impose rules—Kids rebel to demonstrate their equality.
>
> We use a reward system—Kids expect a reward for all desirable behavior.
>
> We punish—Kids, in their effort to be equal, punish us back.

> **Rudeness can be prevented only to the extent that parents practice mutual respect and equality in all areas of family life.**

The "clash of forces" between the outmoded, traditional model of parenting and today's youth often results in rudeness in all its forms, including conflict and violence. The remedy is not to go back in time and attempt to make the "coercive" model work, anymore than it is to expect citizens, employees, minorities, or women to once again accept a position of inferiority.

The remedy is to develop a new tradition in relationships where parents, as leaders in the family, incorporate methods of communication, problem solving, and discipline that take the child's value into account. Rudeness can be prevented only to the extent that parents practice mutual respect and equality in all areas of family life. In this way they teach their children the value of all human beings.

But equality can be misunderstood and not just by kids. Equality does *not* mean everyone is the same. We all have different responsibilities and abilities. Equality *does* mean that everyone is entitled to respect and dignity. In an equal relationship, between adults or between adults and kids, no one tries to be superior, seize power, get even, or talk down to the other. In an equal relationship, people value each other. Equality means that no one should be subservient to another and that we all have rights.

Those who misunderstand equality also misunderstand rights. They believe equality means, "I have the right to do whatever I want." This misconception leads to insensitive and uncivil behavior. To these people, rights mean "my rights." They forget about others' rights.

Parenting Roles

THERE ARE SEVERAL roles we can play with our kids, some are respectful, some disrespectful. The roles we play influence our children—sometimes the influence is not what we want. We'll begin by looking at disrespectful roles.

Disrespectful Parenting Roles

There are basically three disrespectful parenting roles: The "boss"—a parent who gives orders; the "doormat"—a parent who gives in; and the "servant"—a parent who gives special service. Many parents alternate between roles, but most of us have a predominant one.[2]

The Boss

Many parents are autocratic and focus on controlling their children. They tell their kids what to do, reward them if they do it, and punish them if they don't do it. Controlling parents give kids a model of disrespect. Yelling, threatening, hitting, or manipulating show a child or teen discouraging ways of relating to others.

Teaching our kids respect for others doesn't mean asking for blind obedience. Trying to force children to obey has consequences. Parents may get some kids to be dependent on them and others who try to please them, but the kids don't learn to think for themselves. Kids who are dependent or learn to please may look to their peers for direction as they go into the preteen and teenage years. If the influence from peers is negative—such as engaging in sex or taking drugs—then dependency or pleasing has serious consequences.

> Connie, a charming 15-year-old, was the delight of her parents. She always did what they asked. That's why they were so shocked when they found out she was pregnant. It turned out she'd chosen a boyfriend who liked to tell her what to do, and she followed his wishes.

Some kids of bossy parents become afraid of their parents. As they grow up, this fear can be transferred to any authority figure and hamper their development.

> Rory was a bright young man who wanted to work with computers. He took courses at the local community college and got a job with a software support company. After being on the job for a while, Rory noticed that some of the policies in his department were inefficient. He had some ideas he believed would improve the situation. Yet he was afraid to mention them to his boss for fear the boss might be angry with him for criticizing. He did mention them to a coworker with whom he'd become friendly. The coworker

went to the boss with the ideas as if they were his own. The boss liked the ideas and passed them up the line. The policies were implemented and the coworker was promoted.

Other kids rebel against their parents and seek to get even. They resist being controlled and seek revenge if they think the parent has the upper hand. These kids also don't learn to think for themselves. Their behavior is dependent on having someone to rebel against.

Ten-year-old Tom had behavior problems in school. His parents dreaded going to parent-teacher conferences. Tom's teachers would tell his parents that Tom constantly did the opposite of what was expected of him. He was a rule breaker. Tom's parents lectured and punished him. One time they grounded him for two weeks. The next day Tom didn't come home after school. Finally the parents had to call the police to try to find out where Tom was.

Respecting kids doesn't mean that we give in to their demands, which would be a violation of respect for both the child and parent. It does mean we take their ideas and feelings into consideration. It means we treat them as valued human beings. We give them the same respect we would give anyone else. We don't talk down to them, threaten them, or hit them. While we must discipline, there are other ways to discipline than verbal and physical punishments. You'll learn respectful discipline in this book.

> **Respecting kids doesn't mean that we give in to their demands, which would be a violation of respect for both the child and parent.**

It's the parent's job to provide limits for children. But limits without any freedom do not teach kids how to function in a world where they are expected to make decisions. Some bosses express their control through perfection. They believe that a less than perfect performance is a bad performance. They are just as hard on themselves as they are on their kids. Expecting perfection is discouraging to the adult and the child.

> Limits without any freedom do not teach kids how to function in a world where they are expected to make decisions.

While they want their children be perfect, they don't want them to be *too* perfect. If the children were as perfect as the perfectionistic parent, the parent would be in an inferior position. These parents are quick to point out mistakes. In effect they are telling their kids, "You're not good enough."

> Twelve-year-old Nancy brought home her report card. She had several A's and one B. Instead of commenting on the A's, her parents chose to focus on the B and asked her to explain why she didn't get an A in that subject. Nancy felt discouraged. She thought she couldn't please her parents so she didn't try as hard. The next report card showed she'd slipped. Now she had a couple of C's.

Other bosses believe they must be superior. Like perfectionistic parents, superiority seekers have excessively high standards—for themselves and their kids. But parents who believe they must be superior don't have to be perfect, just better. Their motto is: "Those of you who think you know everything are particularly irritating to those of us who do!"[3]

These folks are often creative, competent, and helpful, but they, like perfectionists, can burn out always striving to do better. They frequently suffer guilt because they can't get everything done—they're always short of time. These parents push their children to do better. The kids often find that if they're not superior, they're not acceptable. Pushing kids to do better may induce inferiority feelings.

> Sean, 13, was a talented tennis player. At one match, he met his match. The other kid had a deadly serve. Sean played hard but he lost. He felt down. Instead of recognizing his efforts, Mom told him he needed to practice more, that he should have beaten his opponent.

Then there are bosses who have to be right. There's no middle ground with these parents—everything is black and white or right and wrong. They fear being wrong and may frequently argue, trying to prove their point. If their children don't agree with them, the kids don't just have a different opinion—they're wrong!

These parents can be highly critical of their kids, pointing out what they consider wrong behavior or thinking. Their motto is, "I'm right; I'm always right. I thought I was wrong once, but I was wrong!"

> Like many teenagers, Jay, age 16, challenged his father's opinions. They would frequently argue, leaving both feeling angry. Father constantly pointed out the "errors" in Jay's thinking. Jay would stomp out, go to his room, and slam the door. At other times it seemed Jay would deliberately say or do things to provoke his dad.

The Doormat

Some parents are permissive and let the kids walk all over them. They set few or no limits. These parents often produce children who do as they please and lack respect for others. If parents let kids do as they please, the kids may have difficulty learning how to function in the world. They probably won't learn responsibility and most likely will have trouble relating to others.

> When three-year-old Jason entered preschool he wouldn't follow the teacher's rules and refused to share with the other kids. At a parent-teacher conference, the teacher explained the problem to Jason's mother. Mom just couldn't understand why Jason was having trouble, he was an "angel" at home. As the teacher explored what went on at home, she discovered the reason Jason didn't have trouble at home was because his mother let him do whatever he wanted to do.

Parents may be permissive because they think it's easier to let kids do what they want than to try to impose discipline. Eventually parents get sick of unruly behavior and try to lay down the law. Being used to doing whatever they want, kids of permissive parents fight back. Permissive parents often back down and give in.

Kids need limits because the world they're growing up in has limits. For example, if you drive down a street breaking the speed limit, there are several possible consequences. Freedom without limits doesn't work in the real world.

The Servant

Some parents pamper their kids by providing special service. If the parents do what kids can do for themselves, kids may operate on the idea that success and security are obtained by getting service from others. Kids may believe, "While I can't do too many things for myself, I'm very important around here, and therefore I'm entitled to special service." This can result in pampered, self-centered, and spoiled kids.

It's tempting for parents to support this position as it helps them feel important and minimizes the child's unhappiness.

When parents do this they may be guaranteeing their children's eventual unhappiness. This unhappiness stems from the kids' lack of belief in themselves, their disappointment when parents try to stop giving service, and the discovery that the rest of the world refuses to provide special service.

Servants are often pleasers who deny their own rights and lack self-regard. They will go out of their way to please others, including their children. Sometimes pleasing their children is not helpful to the kids. By trying to buy the kids' love and approval, these parents end up spoiling their children. The result is often selfish children.

Kids who expect service can be rude, angry, and even violent when they don't get their way.

> Twelve-year-old Vicki, an only child, was raised with an abundance of love from parents who never wanted her to be unhappy. They did everything they could to please her. Whenever she felt challenged by any task, her parents were there to help her or do it for her. Vicki had a hard time making friends, as they would not always give in to her. As she grew older, she felt more overwhelmed with responsibilities at school and frequently acted helpless. Whenever her parents decided not to give in to her wishes, Vicki would sulk and pout, and if her parents persisted, call them names and throw a temper tantrum.

It's important to let children do for themselves what they are capable of doing. Even young children can learn to do things for themselves. For example, a three-year-old can learn to dress himself.

Respectful Parenting Roles

There are two roles you can play that help you raise respectful children. These roles work together in your efforts to provide positive experiences.

The Leader

Unlike bosses who give orders, or doormats and servants who give in, leaders give choices. Also called the democratic role, giving choices and letting children learn from the consequences of their choices, helps kids learn responsibility for themselves and their responsibility to others. Kids aren't given unlimited choices as no one has unlimited choices. The choices are given within limits: limits of age and development and limits of a particular situation (more on this in chapter 6, "Respectful Discipline and Life Skills").

> Giving choices and letting children learn from the consequences of their choices, helps kids learn responsibility for themselves and their responsibility to others.

Here's an example of learning responsibility for oneself.

Nine-year-old Matt was given an allowance on Friday. His parents discussed the purpose of the allowance and that it was to last until the next Friday. Shortly after receiving the allowance, Matt spent it on candy. He asked his dad for more money. Dad reminded Matt that the money was to last until the next Friday. "But I'm supposed to go to the movies tomorrow with Bryan and Bill," cried Matt. "I'm sorry you chose to spend your money," Dad replied. "Can't you loan me the money, Dad, please?" pleaded Matt. "No, I'm sorry, Matt. I don't give loans," said Dad.

Dad set the limits of the allowance. Matt chose to violate the limits and therefore experiences the consequences of his choice. Dad showed respect for Matt by letting Matt be responsible for his choice and respect for himself by refusing to be manipulated into a loan to get Matt off the hook. Matt has a future opportunity for making another decision about spending his allowance—he can learn to budget. Dad can help Matt plan his budget if Matt is willing. Parents can use choices to help children learn responsibility toward others.

> Elizabeth, 15, is in her room playing music. The volume is very high. Mom knocks on the door loudly, so as to be heard over the music volume. Elizabeth comes to the door. "Elizabeth," Mom says, "the volume of the music is disturbing us. Please turn it down, use your earphones, or turn it off; you decide."

If Elizabeth turns the volume down to an acceptable level or uses her earphones, fine. But if she continues to play the music loudly on her speakers, her behavior tells Mom that Elizabeth has chosen to turn off the music. Either way, Elizabeth has an opportunity to practice being sensitive to others' rights.

Democratic parenting is characterized by giving children freedom. But unlike permissive parenting, democratic parenting is freedom *within* limits. This helps kids develop self-discipline.

The Encourager

Encouragers are also democratic in their approach to their children. They look for what's good about a performance rather than what's bad. They have faith in their kids and accept them as they are despite behavior they find unacceptable. They don't accept misbehavior, but they do accept the child as a worthwhile human being. They are interested in building their children's self-esteem and people-esteem (more on this in chapter 3, "Teaching Kids to Value Themselves and Others").

> Eight-year-old Jake liked to show off when Mom and Dad had company. Dad told Jake his boss was coming to dinner

and that he'd appreciate it if Jake would be on his best behavior. "If you decide to clown around, I'll ask you to go to your room and stay there until you're ready to cooperate." That evening, Jake began to show off. Dad excused himself and calmly took Jake by his hand and led him to his room. Dad told Jake he could come back when he was ready to cooperate. Jake came out of the room, but shortly decided to show off again. Dad led Jake back to his room, telling him he'd check with him in a few minutes to see if he was ready. The next time Jake came out of his room, he cooperated for the rest of the evening. When the company left, Dad thanked Jake for his cooperation.

Encouragers are quick to "catch the child being good." They look for positive behavior and recognize it.

Susan, age five, and Debbie, age three, are sisters. Usually when they play together, they argue and take toys from each other, and at least one of them ends up crying. One day, Mom sees them playing nicely together. She comments, "I see you're playing nicely. You two look like you're really enjoying yourselves!"

Changing Your Role

YOU MAY BE wondering how you can move from being a boss, doormat, or a servant to being a leader and encourager. Following are some suggestions.

Letting Go of the Boss Role

If you believe you must be in control, you are probably very good at organizing and orderliness. You can use this talent to set guidelines or limits and let the kids choose within the limits. In this way, you take control of the situation instead of focusing on controlling the child.

You can learn to let go and trust the kids to learn from the consequences. Take the case of Joan as an example.

Single mom Joan had two children, ages seven and five. Whenever she took them in the car, the kids would fight. She would usually yell at them to stop and they would for a short while. This was a constant problem. Then Joan attended a parenting class and learned a different method.

Before they got into the car the next time, Joan calmly explained to her kids, "It's dangerous to drive when there's fighting because it distracts me. So, if you decide to fight, I'll just pull to the side of the road until you're finished." The kids began to fight after Joan had driven a few blocks; she pulled to the side of the road and didn't say a word. After a couple of minutes, the kids stopped. This happened three more times. On the next trip, it happened once. From then on, only occasionally did the kids fight.

If you are a perfectionist, you may have forgotten that making mistakes or being imperfect is part of the human condition. Sometimes it takes courage to admit one is not perfect—especially for one who believes, "I must be perfect."

Hard as it is, you need to freely acknowledge your errors and acquire a sense of humor about your mistakes. Concentrate on your own and the kids' efforts and improvements rather than expecting perfection. Let's see how Tim worked on his perfectionism.

Tim was a reforming perfectionist. He decided that he would deliberately make a mistake and point it out to his kids. One day he was hanging a picture and the nail slipped out of his hand and rolled beneath the couch. This was not one of Tim's planned mistakes. He got upset with himself. Six-year-old Gretchen said to her dad, "That's okay, Dad, everybody makes mistakes." Tim found himself laughing, not at Gretchen, but at himself. He thanked his daughter for her encouragement.

A few days later Gretchen was drawing a picture. Tim asked her to tell him about her picture. "It's not very good," she sighed. "I can see you're not pleased with it," said Tim, "but it looks like you worked hard on it." "Yeah, but I just can't get the house right." Tim looked at the picture and noticed how well she'd drawn a tree for a child her age. "I know, that's difficult, but look at the tree," Tim said, and began to point out the positive aspects of the tree.

Maybe you're not a perfectionist, but you want to constantly improve yourself and expect the same from your kids. In other words, you seek superiority for yourself and your kids. If you strive for superiority, you are most likely a creative person. You can use this creativity in a positive way. You can set up situations where kids are encouraged to use their strengths. Look what Mom did with John.

> You can use this creativity in a positive way. You can set up situations where kids are encouraged to use their strengths.

Eleven-year-old John was by no means the perfect child, but he did have some talents. He was good at math. Mom acknowledged his skill and asked if he would help her balance the checkbook.

You also need to give yourself a break. Instead of trying to be all things to all people, take time for yourself. Believe it or not, the world won't fall apart!

If being right is important to you, instead of trying to enforce the "right," you can give your kids opportunities to learn acceptable behavior. You can give choices and let the kids experience the consequences of their choice. Here's how one father handled his tendency to want to be right.

> Fifteen-year-old Bart was a stubborn teen. He insisted he knew the right way to do things. His dad felt the same way. They had constant conflicts over who was right. One day Bart had a science project. Dad suggested he check the Internet to see if there was any up-to-date data on his topic. Bart resisted, saying he knew enough about the topic. This time, Dad decided not to get into an argument and let Bart be responsible for his project. Bart's teacher felt Bart had not fully researched the subject and gave him a low grade. Bart was angry, but Dad resisted the temptation to say, "I told you so."

Listen and respect your kids' ideas and realize that if your child or teen doesn't agree with you, it doesn't mean the kid is wrong. It simply means the youngster has a different opinion. One mother handled a difference of opinion this way.

> Mom and 10-year-old Susan were shopping in the mall for school clothes for Susan. Mom saw an outfit that she particularly liked. Susan didn't like it. Mom was tempted to tell Susan that this was the perfect outfit, she was going to buy it, and Susan was going to wear it. But she didn't; she listened to Susan's objections and continued shopping for clothes that Susan would feel more comfortable wearing and that fit within the school's dress code.

Refusing to Be a Doormat

When you let your child walk all over you, you not only do your child a disservice, you do yourself one as well. Stand up for your rights. Have the courage to say no to unreasonable requests. Here's what one father did.

Peter, 13, was invited to a party. Dad found out the party was not going to be supervised, so he said no. Peter whined and complained that all the other kids in his class were going. Dad stood firm. Peter called Dad names and claimed that Dad didn't love him. Dad replied, "I can see you're angry, but I don't appreciate your comments. I'm going to the garage to do some work. When you decide to calm down, we can talk about alternatives for Saturday night if you want to."

Dad was wise not to get angry and fight with Peter. Taking himself out of the situation was a smart move on Dad's part—he refused to be intimidated. If he'd tried to remove Peter to his room, given Peter's age, he could have been in for a struggle. Instead, Dad left the door open for a civil discussion on what Peter could do instead of going to the party.

If you've been permissive, don't expect your kids to readily accept your decisions or their responsibilities. They've had it made. It will take a while for them to realize the game is over.

Giving Up the Servant Role

If you've allowed yourself to be pressed into service, begin to transfer to your kids those responsibilities that they are capable of handling. In other words, let them "own" their own problems (see "Who Owns the Problem?" on page 48). You can allow your kids to accept the consequences of irresponsible behavior. This mom transferred some responsibility to her son.

Five-year-old Hayden refused to learn to tie his shoes; he complained, "I can't." Mom told him he was old enough to handle it on his own, but Hayden played helpless. At a relaxed time, Mom attempted to teach him. Hayden refused. So Mom decided to let Hayden run around with untied shoes. After tripping over himself a few times, Hayden asked Mom to show him how to tie his shoes.

Since children of servants are often self-centered, you need to encourage your kids to give rather than just receive. You can set up situations where kids can contribute, for example, encouraging them to collect food for the homeless.

The role you play will determine whether you encourage mutual respect or promote disrespect. Mutual respect is what this book is all about. Throughout this book, you'll learn ways to help your kids take a respectful approach to life and relationships.

Looking Ahead: How Do We Teach Children Mutual Respect?

HERE'S AN OVERVIEW of what it takes to raise kids for parents who base their actions on mutual respect.

Being a Good Model

Kids learn more from what they see than what they hear. Parents can lecture on what they expect from their children, but if the parents' behavior violates what they say, the kids will learn by the behavior. A parent was observed in a supermarket trying to teach her kids not to fight. She grabbed the older one, slapped him on the bottom, and said, "I told you not to hit people smaller than you!"

Building Self-Esteem

When kids feel good about themselves and others, they behave in positive and respectful ways. Parents build self-esteem by:

- Accepting the child or teen.

- Having positive and realistic expectations.

- Focusing on the positive.

- Recognizing contributions.

- Focusing on effort and improvement.

- Recognizing and understanding the child's or teen's feelings.

- Having faith and confidence.

- Letting the child do what the child or teen is capable of doing.

- Giving choices and letting the child or teen learn from the consequences

- Instilling the courage to be imperfect.

- Developing people-esteem: teaching kids to care about others, to have good manners, to help out.

Encouraging Cooperation and Contribution

Kids who cooperate and contribute through helping out, feel good about themselves and others. They develop confidence and a feeling of self-worth. We live in a world where cooperation is required and contribution is expected. You can help your children develop these qualities by giving them opportunities to participate. Even toddlers can cooperate and contribute by learning to pick up their toys, for example.

Teaching Tolerance

Intolerance breeds disrespect. Racial tension, gender inequalities, disrespect of people with physical or intellectual challenges, hatred of sexual minorities, all fuel incivility and violence. We have laws about equality, but these don't necessarily filter down to actual day-to-day living in our communities. Even in integrated schools, kids tend to hang out with their own race. While we talk about gender equality, there are often different expectations for boys and girls. Intolerance of differences results in stereotyping, prejudice, discrimination, and alienation.

Our society is increasingly multicultural. Unless we learn to accept and respect cultures different from ours, we may see an increase in hatred.

The more understanding and tolerant our children are of differences, personal and cultural, the more they will be able get along with others and the less conflict and disrespect they are likely to bring into their lives. Kids' levels of tolerance are learned primarily from the modeling of their parents. What is your attitude toward people who are different from you? How do you treat people who are physically, intellectually, or emotionally challenged? Do you have friends of different races? What about your kids: Are they involved with children who are different from them?

> The more understanding and tolerant our children are of differences, personal and cultural, the more they will be able get along with others.

You'll find many suggestions in this book for helping your kids appreciate and value the uniqueness of others. For example, you can model accepting and celebrating the cultural differences in your community. Take a stand against stereotyping, prejudice, and discrimination. You can limit biased and violent TV. You can also watch TV with your kids and talk about what they're seeing. We will give specific guidelines for these discussions.

Resolving Conflicts and Administering Discipline Respectfully

Conflicts don't have to have winners and losers. Parents and children can learn to talk things over and reach an agreement that respects everyone. Discipline doesn't have to mean hitting or verbal confrontations. There are alternatives that respect everyone's rights. For example, if your children are fighting at the dinner table, you don't have to spank or lecture. You can simply give them a choice. "Either settle down and eat your dinner or leave the table until you're ready to settle down. You decide." Then, you simply act on their decision. If they continue to fight, they've chosen to leave the table.

Remember that the way you relate to your kids is a primary influence in their lives. A recent poll of almost 1,200 kids ages 6 to 14 showed that 72 percent see their parents as role models,[4] so even though there is rudeness in the world, your model of respect will help your kids develop civility.

The Dalai Lama gives his "3 R's" of life. If we follow these guidelines and teach them to our children, respect will return to our relationships.

Respect for self

Respect for others

Responsibility for all of your actions

In this chapter we've discussed respectful and rude behavior. We've pointed out disrespectful and respectful parenting roles and how you can change your role. In chapter 2 we'll focus on better understanding the purposeful goal-directed nature of children's behavior, how you can help your children develop positive goals, and "who owns the problem."

2

Understanding Kids' Behavior

*Discouragement is at the
root of all this behavior.*
—RUDOLF DREIKURS

W HY DID SHE do that?" "I just don't understand him;
he has more opportunities than most kids his age." "I
can't believe she spoke to me that way; after all the sac-
rifices I've made for her!"

Kids' behavior can be puzzling at times. If we're going to
raise respectful kids, we need to know what motivates them.
There is no parent academy where parents learn why kids do
what they do, let alone how to respond when they behave in
ways that require corrective action. So we'll begin with how to
understand kids' behavior.

Basic Motivations

CHILDREN ARE BORN small and helpless. They would die without adult care. They are legally blind, don't understand language, and need to be fed. They depend on others for warmth and comfort. It's no accident that parents are usually attracted to their children at birth; it's necessary for survival. Parents of newborns usually spend lots of time holding them, feeding them, playing with them, and changing their diapers. These acts stimulate the child's developing nervous system and provide a sense of security. Providing for the child's needs during these first few years of life encourages a sense of belonging.

During these first few years, children are very observant and curious. They see, hear, and experience many things. They notice how adults behave toward them. "What happens when I cry, laugh, or try to do things for myself?" Out of these observations and experiences, they develop some basic unique beliefs about what it takes to belong and feel significant in their families. The most basic of these beliefs are about who they are, what other people are like, what the world is like, and what they must do in order to find a place in the world.

Developing Competence

Kids are very observant but often make distorted interpretations. They see themselves as smaller, less knowledgeable, and less capable. They tend to conclude they're inferior. Inferiority feelings are present in all children. The natural process of development results in children's determination to overcome this felt sense of inadequacy. Children can compensate for these feelings by striving toward greater competence and mastery, significance, and belonging (or in other, negative ways). A genuine belief in self occurs when the child succeeds in this effort. The child develops self-esteem. Parents are a major influence on children feeling more inferior, or more competent, as they develop through life.

Courage and Natural Striving

Child psychologist Dr. John F. Newbauer tells us: "Children usually proceed with great courage. They have little fear of failure. They try to walk and fall down. They get up again and try it over and over until they learn how to do it. This willingness to proceed in the face of uncertainty is as natural for a child as drinking mother's milk. They show persistent courage!"[1]

Efforts of young children, to learn new things and become competent like the adults they see around them, are sometimes awkward. Often it's more work to have little Emily and Eric help with the dishes or tie their own shoes than it is for adults or older siblings to do it for them. But, only through doing it for themselves do Emily and Eric gain self-esteem.

When parents doubt children's ability to learn, or interfere with their learning by doing for children instead of letting the children do, they *rob* the kids of an opportunity to gain self-esteem. In other words, they show disrespect for their children. They undermine the child's natural courage. Kids parented in this way develop a view of themselves as incompetent and dependent on others. These parents teach children that the world is too big or too complex for a child to master. Pampered, spoiled kids grow up to be afraid, doubt their abilities, demand that others do for them, and end up angry and depressed as teens and adults.

> Sixteen-year-old Matthew was the youngest in a family of three children. He occupied the baby position of the family and everyone treated him that way. From an early age, he was used to being served. If his wishes or demands were denied, he'd lash out—sometimes verbally, sometimes physically.

Matthew was dating Beth. He expected Beth to cater to his wishes, just like others had done all his life. Beth got sick of it and tried to break off the relationship, but Matthew wouldn't hear of it. One day Beth told him she wanted nothing more to do with him. Matthew got angry and hit Beth, bloodying her nose.

Developing a Sense of Belonging

As children grow, many people play an important part in their developing sense of belonging. If the child has sisters or brothers, the child learns to relate to them in a way that provides a sense of belonging as well. Each child develops a unique place in the family, a place the child believes will provide a sense of belonging and significance. This striving for a significant place in the family stems from the child's feelings of inferiority that are very natural and very strong.

> Each child develops a unique place in the family, a place the child believes will provide a sense of belonging and significance.

It's essential that parents avoid comparing a child to siblings. Comparisons such as, "Why aren't you like your brother?" tend to discourage kids.

One of the major influences on a child's personality is the sibling most different from him or her. It's with this sibling that we compete for a place in the family. When you accept each of your children's unique qualities and build on their strengths, each child has the opportunity to develop positive attributes.

Other influences on children's development could include grandparents, uncles and aunts, cousins, children in the neighborhood or the day-care center, and eventually classmates at school and playmates in the community. From each of these people, the child learns something about life and living with others.

Psychiatrist Alfred Adler said a child has motivation to move from a feeling of inferiority or a "felt minus" to what the child views as potentially a positive place, or a "perceived plus."[2] This motivation is strong and continues to influence kids into adulthood. Adults, too, strive to move from a "felt minus" to a "perceived plus" in any given area of life.

The Power of Perception

Children are active, creative individuals who are constantly perceiving and interpreting everything that happens. They are not simply recorders (like video recorders or tape recorders) that take in exactly what happens. Instead, they are creative recorders that pay attention to some parts of an event and ignore other parts of that same event. What they pay attention to is shaped by their experience and creative power. As they have more and more experiences, the lenses through which they perceive the world change.[3]

Parents may provide encouraging, positive experiences for their children, yet they cannot determine what their kids will make of these experiences. They also cannot determine what conclusions the children will draw from their life experiences about themselves, about others, and about life in general and what they need to do to feel successful and significant. What the child learns from others is not always what those people want to teach. However, the more positive a child's experiences, the more likely he or she will develop a positive outlook on life.

Developing Community Feeling

Basic ideas about what the world is like, what other people are like, and who you are yourself are learned and established between the ages of four and six. By that age, kids develop an idea about what they need to do to belong and feel significant. Positive early-childhood experiences encourage children to develop a strong sense of community feeling. "Community feeling" is a phrase that Alfred Adler used that reflects a strong sense of belonging as well as value of and a concern for others. Community feeling acknowledges, "I care for you and I believe you care for me."

For kids who grow up in a family where there is a lack of emotional stimulation, a sense of belonging and a feeling of attachment may be missing. If parents haven't developed closeness with their children, their children may have difficulty feeling close to others. A sense of community feeling is lacking because children feel insignificant, striving to prove they have a place rather than knowing they have a place just because they are here.

> Fourteen-year-old Jill grew up in a family with a cold atmosphere. Jill never felt sure of herself and had difficulty relating to others. She didn't feel she fit in at school, had no friends, and was frequently in trouble with teachers and peers. She was devious, always trying to put one over on others. Then she discovered a girl gang. Finally she felt she had the family she'd never experienced. The gang was involved in stealing and drug dealing. After a few months in the gang, Jill was arrested along with other gang members and ended up in a juvenile facility.

"They'll Grow Out of It"

There's a common belief that kids grow out of misbehavior. This is not always true. Kids who are irresponsible, rude, or violent don't necessarily discontinue the misbehavior as they mature. The behavior may change in form as they get older, but the pattern usually remains the same. Kids who haven't learned about mutual respect as younger children probably won't develop it simply because they age—not without intervention. Research has demonstrated that disrespect and violence are learned at an early age. Forceful parental discipline, viewing of negative TV, misconduct at home and in the community, and fighting seem to be directly related to rudeness and violence in childhood and adulthood.

Behavior Has Goals

CHILDREN BEGIN TO interact with the world at birth. Their movements have a purpose, or goal, even though the purpose is not always recognized by adults. They spend many hours learning about their new environment, learning to coordinate their muscles and to speak and understand language. For kids, play is a form of work in which they learn how people and things in the world behave.

The goals of children's behavior are to become competent and to attain a place in the family. Belonging and competence are the primary ways in which children develop a sense of significance. This is one way they can move from the "felt minus" to a "perceived plus" position. If children do not feel accepted by their family, they often engage in behavior that is misguided. Adults call such behavior "misbehavior." The children are not "bad" but are acting in rude ways that reflect misunderstandings about themselves, other people, or what it means to belong.

When kids believe that they are accepted and recognized as part of the family or group they are in, they try to develop skills they believe will contribute to the family or to the welfare of the group.

Four-year-old Scott loved to help. His father let Scott do what Scott was capable of doing. For example, when it was time for dinner, he handed Scott plastic plates and let him help set the table. Dad also made sure he thanked Scott for his help and encouraged his efforts. "Thanks for helping, Scott. Your help makes setting the table easier."

If kids feel they don't belong, it may be because they haven't been accepted by parents or siblings. More frequently, the parents have tried hard to show their love and acceptance but the child *feels* she doesn't belong despite these efforts. No one can make a child feel a sense of belonging. We can only offer her a place and value her presence.

The Four Goals of Misbehavior

PSYCHIATRIST RUDOLF DREIKURS discovered that if children feel they don't belong by being cooperative, they will develop mistaken ideas about what it means to belong. These ideas result in misbehavior. Misbehavior is often self-centered and disrespectful. Dr. Dreikurs observed that children's misbehavior can be related to goals of attention, power, revenge, and displaying inadequacy.

We'll discuss each of these four goals, followed by an example and ideas on what you could do if you were the parent in the situation. These ideas may be new to you, and you may not fully understand them or may be skeptical. As you continue to read this book, the ideas will become clearer.

1. Attention

When attention is the goal, the child behaves in ways that attract attention from adults. This may be by doing things that seem to please or entertain adults or by things that they find annoying. Either way, parents show that they have noticed the child and the child feels he belongs, at least for the moment. Unfortunately, if the belief that guides the child's behavior is something like, "I am only significant if I am noticed," the child will continue to engage in behaviors that get him noticed over and over again—frustrating for the parents and others, for sure.

Some children will use violence to gain attention as in the case of Sara.

Six-year-old Sara wanted to be noticed in the worst way. Her mom, Mitzy, was talking on the phone. Sara tugged at Mitzy's slacks. Mitzy said, "Please don't bother me now, Sara, I'm on the phone. I'll be with you in a minute." Sara stopped the tugging for about a minute and then resumed. Mitzy ignored her and continued her phone conversation. Another minute went by and frustrated Sara slapped her mother on the bottom. This got her mom's attention.

If you were this child's parent, what could you do? Many attention-getting behaviors can be ignored. When the behavior is ignored, the bids for attention don't work and the child eventually gives up the misbehavior. It's important to replace the withdrawn attention by attending to the child in other ways, when he or she is *not* asking for attention. Don't constantly respond to demands for attention, even for positive behavior—this just reinforces the child's belief that in order to belong, the child must have attention. Instead, as we discussed in chapter 1, "catch the child being good." For example, show appreciation for helping out. "Thanks for helping me clean out the garage. It goes much faster with two people working on it."

However, in cases like the example of Sara, a different approach is needed. The best action in this situation is to remove yourself. If you have another phone in a room where you can close the door, go there. If not, you could give her a choice of remaining in the room or going to her own room. "Sara, I'll be with you after I finish my phone conversation. You can choose to wait here for me or go to your room and wait. Which would you rather do?" If she chooses to stay in the room with you, but tugs at your slacks again, you could say, "I see you've chosen to wait in your room." You would then put your phone call on hold and tactfully usher Sara to her room. At other times, make an effort to notice the positive things Sara does.

2. Power

Children sometimes develop the belief that they belong only if they are seen as having power. This leads them to engage in power struggles with adults. Power struggles end up angering parents who feel challenged and offended by the child's behavior. The child is saying, "I'll do what I want and you can't stop me." This usually results in parents or other adults responding with more force until the child becomes submissive. In the end, the child learns how important power is and seeks more of it. In some cases, the parent gives in to the child's demands. Again the child is impressed with his power.

> Even if you win a power struggle, it's a temporary victory.

> Fourteen-year-old Ted, an only child, was in constant power struggles with his single father. Dad needed help around the house to make the family function. Whenever Dad assigned Ted a task, Ted would respond with anger and complain that his father expected too much of him. Arguments followed these encounters—usually ending up with Dad grounding Ted. The boy would respond by sneaking out at night.

If you were this child's parent, what could you do? Even if you win a power struggle, it's a temporary victory. The child will pick other fights or seek revenge. It's best, as Rudolf Dreikurs said, to sidestep the power struggle and win cooperation instead of trying to force it. In the case of Ted, you could ask him what he's willing to do. At a relaxed time—when there's no conflict—you could discuss with him what needs to be done around the house. Don't just list the tasks, involve him in the discussion. Ask him what he thinks needs to be done. Together, make a list. Then ask Ted what he's willing to do on the list. Or, if Ted agrees, tear the list up into slips, put them in a jar, and have a drawing. Each person does the task he draws. Most kids are more committed to chores they select. You may be wondering, "What if Ted chooses a task and doesn't do it?" That's another issue. Later in the book, we'll discuss logical consequences—an effective approach to discipline. For now, let's assume we can win Ted's cooperation by taking a different approach to task selection.

3. Revenge

If the battle rages on, both the child's and the parents' behavior escalate until the child feels hurt. At this point, the child's belief is that she is significant only if she gets even. In turn, she strikes out against her parents in a way that touches them in a vulnerable spot. She behaves in a rude way that will hurt them as much as the child feels hurt. The goal becomes revenge.

> Dad and Brenda were arguing about Brenda's grades. Dad grounded 11-year-old Brenda "until further notice." Brenda scowled, ran to her room, and slammed the door.
>
> Mom and Dad went out to dinner. Upon returning home, they noticed a strange odor coming from the kitchen. Smoke was pouring out of the oven. Dad opened the oven to find his cherished record collection melting in the heat of the oven.

If you were this child's parent, what could you do? If you have a child bent on revenge, you need to work on the relationship. Any disciplinary action with the vengeful child will be seen as reason to continue the revenge. In this case, you would have been better off not setting up the conflict in the first place. Arguing about grades is usually futile because there's no way you can *make* a child learn. And grounding, though common, is so resented by children that the parent sets himself up for revenge. What about the record collection? There's really nothing that can be done—it's gone. Trying to make Brenda pay for the damage or withholding money from her allowance won't replace the collection. Besides, with kids seeking revenge, trying to get them to make retribution usually backfires—they see it as punitive. So, it's best to cut your losses at this point and build the relationship. Encourage Brenda; show appreciation for any cooperation you get. Make sure you approach her in considerate ways, not giving her cause to feel hurt. Realize, though, that building the relationship takes time and you can't be responsible for how she interprets your actions. You can monitor only your own behavior, you can't be responsible for her responses.

4. Displaying Inadequacy

Some kids feel so overwhelmed with the power of the adults in their lives and the demands that are placed on them that they simply give up. Their goal becomes displaying inadequacy; they want to be left alone. One of the easiest ways to be left alone and not have any expectations placed on you is to demonstrate that you are incompetent. The perceived inadequacy is usually not total, but more often in a particular area of expectation.

> Marty, nine, had trouble in math. Yet Marty wasn't dumb. He'd showed competence in other school subjects, but math seemed too much. Whenever his parents or his teacher would try to help him, Marty would simply shrug and say, "I can't do it." The adults felt as discouraged as

Marty. Both his parents and his teacher felt Marty just had no "head" for math, so they gave up.

If you were this child's parent, what could you do? First of all, don't give up on Marty. This doesn't mean trying to force him to do math, it simply means recognizing the discouragement—his *belief* that he just can't do math. The way to encourage him is to recognize his assets in other areas of his life. As he feels confident in general, he'll probably eventually discover math isn't so overwhelming. A person, child or adult, who's discouraged and fails to recognize the things she or he does well, is too focused on inadequacy—perceived or real. Focusing on the inadequacy causes further discouragement.

Some of the most discouraged kids in our society respond to everything with, "I don't know," or, "I don't care." They convey to adults, "You can't hurt me." This is a very discouraged position in life that reflects their feeling and belief that others want to hurt or control them.

All misbehavior is related to feelings of discouragement. At the root of misbehavior is a belief in never being able to find a place of belonging, of significance in a positive way.

Attention, power, and revenge reflect rude behavior. As the examples above show, the kids who pursue these goals can act in ways that violate mutual respect. Displaying inadequacy, however, is not rude, but indicates the child or teen is so discouraged that she or he lacks self-respect. It is more a disrespectful attitude toward the self. Kids who display inadequacy really believe they can't do what's expected.

The Progress of Misbehavior

Children may progress through the goals of misbehavior with some predictability. They may start out with simple attention-getting behaviors and progress to power struggles followed by revenge or a display of inadequacy when those don't work.

Sometimes this progression takes years, while other children seem to arrive at the very discouraged positions in a shorter period of time. However, this is not always the sequence. For example, some children—especially those with very perfectionistic or demanding parents—may proceed directly from attention getting to displaying inadequacy.

Behavior is related to the goal of feeling a sense of belonging. The feeling of belonging is based on the child's perception and interpretation of events. It is a process that occurs in the child. It may or may not reflect the efforts of others in trying to help the child develop a sense of significance and belonging.

While parents don't cause children to misbehave, they do reinforce children's negative goals. By responding in ways their children expect, parents show the kids such misbehavior pays off.

> Charlie, 10, liked to have his own way. Whenever his parents denied one of Charlie's demands, Charlie would cry and accuse them of not caring about him. His parents would feel hurt and give in. Through crying and accusations, Charlie got his way by demonstrating his power and getting even.

> **Kids aren't usually aware of the goals of their misbehavior, but they are aware of the results.**

Kids aren't usually aware of the goals of their misbehavior, but they are aware of the results. They usually know what to expect if they behave in a certain way. In the above example of Charlie, he knew, "You don't care about me," accompanied by tears would get him what he wanted. If the parents remain firm in their denial of Charlie's demands and refuse to feel hurt or give in, Charlie would eventually learn his behavior would not pay off.

How Can I Identify My Child's Goal?

There are two clues to determining the goal your child is seeking when she misbehaves:

1. How you feel. If you are merely *annoyed*, the chances are your child is seeking *attention*. But if you' re *angry*, the goal is most likely *power*. When kids seek *revenge*, parents feel *hurt*. If your child is *displaying inadequacy*, you'll feel *despair*—like giving up.

2. How they react. What you do about the misbehavior and how the child responds also give you a clue. With *attention-getting*, you're most likely to *remind* and *coax*. Your child will *stop* the misbehavior for a while, having gotten the attention. But his attention "fix" doesn't last very long, so he'll *resume* the same behavior or do something else to attract your attention.

With *power-seeking* kids, you either *fight*—to try to get her under control—*or give in*. If you *fight*, the child *fights back, intensifying* the misbehavior. Or, she may *do what you tell her to, but not to your satisfaction*. Her objective is to defeat you. If you *give in*, the child *stops*, because she has gotten what she wants.

Revenge provokes *retaliation*—you *punish* him to get even. He *responds* with *more revenge*—using the same weapon or choosing another.

Displaying inadequacy involves *giving up*—on the part of both kids and parents. If your child is displaying inadequacy, you become as discouraged as she is. You *take no action* because you agree with the child that nothing can be done to improve the situation. So the child *doesn't respond or improve*.

Examples of Misbehavior

- **Active attention-getting** could be interrupting, pestering, hitting (just to get your attention).

- **Passive attention-getting** could be forgetting, dawdling, waiting to be served.

- **Active power** could be temper tantrums, making demands, arguments, and violent behaviors designed to force compliance.

- **Passive power** could involve being stubborn, "foot-dragging," and some kinds of depression.

- **Active revenge** could be verbal insults, violence, and some forms of suicide and suicide attempts.

- **Passive revenge** is difficult to explain, but you know it when it happens. The child is passive in such a way that you feel hurt. Rudolf Dreikurs called this "violent passivity." For example, the child "forgets" to do something that's especially important to you.

- **Displaying inadequacy** can only be pursued passively because it involves giving up. The child gives up in areas where he or she feels the adult's standards can't be met.

Kids can use the same behavior for different goals in different situations. For example, Bill may act up to seek attention from his parents. At school he may use the same misbehavior to seek power. Why? Because at home he has a smaller audience and can get noticed more easily than in school. In school he may have to struggle to gain recognition.

Kids can also use different behavior for the same goal. Janice may seek power through being argumentative in one situation and using stubbornness in another.

Different kids can use a particular misbehavior to achieve different goals. One child may dawdle at bedtime in order to seek attention. Another may dawdle in order to show the parents they can't make the child go to bed—a power move.

Children are perceptive individuals; they do what works to belong. The way you can identify a child's goal is by checking the two clues: how you feel and what happens when you try to correct the misbehavior.

Sometimes kids will change goals in a single interaction. For example, if trying to attract your attention doesn't work, they may proceed to try to involve you in a power contest. This can be confusing when you're trying to identify the goal. The best thing to do, when you're thinking about the incident later, is to ask yourself, "How did I end up feeling?" You may have started out simply feeling annoyed, and as the incident progressed, you may have ended up feeling angry. Also, think about your actions and your child's response. "How did I end up responding and what did he finally do?" If these interactions happen frequently, you may be able to see them coming and have an appropriate response before the situation deteriorates.

> The way you can identify a child's goal is by checking the two clues: how you feel and what happens when you try to correct the misbehavior.

Young Children

Babies cry—it's their way of communicating. A baby's cry can mean he's hungry, tired, sick or injured, wet, frightened, angry, or just plain bored. Most parents have a tendency to attend to every cry—no matter what the reason. While certainly one wants to attend to cries of real need, what happens when parents attend to cries that say, "Get in here. I'm bored"? They teach their infants to demand attention and even power.

Terrible or Terrific?

A word of caution: Parents often encourage toddler misbehavior by accepting the myth of the "terrible twos." Because toddlers are naturally curious and trying to explore their world, they make mistakes and get frustrated. But to label this behavior as "terrible" just sets us up for more problems. Expectations are powerful—*what we expect is often what we get*. What would happen if we expected toddlers to cooperate—if we looked for the "terrific twos" instead?[4]

Realize that cooperation begins in the crib. Dr. Rudolf Dreikurs said that six-week-old babies can learn to control their parents through crying. Babies do not pursue revenge, and displaying inadequacy is rare and often a result of child abuse when it occurs.

Toddlers learn how to get attention or express power as they interact with their family. At times they may seek revenge if their demands are unmet. Displaying inadequacy may occur if the child is abused or feels very frustrated in not being able to do things.

As preschoolers explore their world, they continue to seek belonging. If they get discouraged and feel they can't belong in useful ways, they will misbehave to find a place. All four goals (attention, power, revenge, and displaying inadequacy) can come into play, depending upon how they view what it takes to belong. Most preschoolers are involved in seeking attention or power. But some can seek revenge if they feel things are unfair. A few may display inadequacy if they believe they just can't live up to adult standards.

Elementary School–Age Children

Kids six and older can pursue any of the four goals of misbehavior (attention, power, revenge, and displaying inadequacy). Preteens will also pursue the goals of excitement and peer acceptance, which are discussed in the following section.

What About Teenagers?

In addition to pursing the four goals of misbehavior, teens are often interested in excitement and peer acceptance. The goals of excitement and peer acceptance can be pursued positively or negatively. Kids can gain positive excitement through participating in sports, for example. They can seek peer acceptance in a group that promotes positive behavior and values. Serious misbehaviors such as violence, sex, and drugs can also be used for excitement or peer acceptance.

The goals of excitement and peer acceptance are often pursued in the peer group, which is outside the parent-child relationship. Still, these goals can be connected to the relationship between parent and teen. A boy who uses drugs to get a high—a form of excitement—can also be engaged in a power struggle with his parents over his use of drugs. He could also be using drugs to get even with his parents. But if he uses drugs to escape his responsibilities, he's also displaying inadequacy. Or, he may use drugs for peer recognition while at the same time engaging in power struggles with his parents over his choice of friends.

A girl who's violent can be gaining peer acceptance by running with a gang and living up to its standards of violent behavior. At the same time the violence is exciting. She could also be defeating her parents who try to get her to stop running with the gang.

A teen's negative pursuit of excitement or peer acceptance doesn't have to involve serious misbehaviors, but the misbehaviors annoy and frustrate parents just the same. For example, a boy may dress in a fashion that pleases his friends but displeases his parents. In addition to peer recognition, he could also be using the clothing to gain his parents' attention.

While it's important that you recognize when your teen is pursuing negative excitement or peer acceptance, it's especially important for you to recognize the four goals of misbehavior. Attention, power, revenge, and displaying inadequacy occur in your relationship with your teen. By changing your reactions to these goals, you are in a position to influence your teen.

The Limits of Peer Influence

Peer acceptance is important to preteens and teens, but parents have more influence on their teens than they think. In working with teenagers and their parents as counselors, therapists, and educators, one of the myths we hear is that peers are more important than parents to teenagers. This comes from parents more often than from teenagers. In their struggle to prove that they are no longer children, many teenagers give parents and adults the idea that they don't care what the adults think. This is often communicated directly in the teens' speech and through gestures or body language. It seems to be an assertion of their independence from adults. Adults often accept this message and give up trying to influence them. This seems to be one of the biggest mistakes adults can make.

Most teenagers care what their parents and teachers think, believe, and feel. Many teens complain that their parents and teachers don't care about them. This is especially true of teens who are engaged in power struggles with their parents and teachers, seeking revenge, or displaying inadequacy. Many teenagers go through power struggles with parents and teachers. Only the more discouraged progress to revenge or displaying inadequacy; teens who progress this far are deeply discouraged. The more frequent the power struggle, the more serious the revenge; the more frustrating the display of inadequacy, the more seriously discouraged the teenager feels.

Communication Between Parents and Teens

Dr. Newbauer points out:

> In talking with discouraged teenagers, I find that they often feel adults don't care because they don't talk to them. Teens find adults very busy with their own lives. One of the bad things about being a parent of a teenager is that it often comes during the parents' middle age when they are facing increased responsibility at work and in the community. It is easy to assume that the teenager is already mature and "should know better." Adolescence is the time when teenagers are struggling with their own identities and values. During this period it is very important that they are engaged in thought-provoking discussions with adults who take them seriously and who respectfully challenge their way of thinking.[5]

Teens who say things that challenge our beliefs and values are trying to come to their own conclusions about who they are, what other people are like, and what life is all about.

Open, honest, and straightforward discussions with teenagers help them evaluate their own beliefs and values. Teens who say things that challenge our beliefs and values are trying to come to their own conclusions about who they are, what other people are like, and what life is all about. Teens depend on adults for challenging their newly developed views and insights.

Take a quick look at who are the most popular teachers and adults with teenagers and you'll find they are the adults who are open to questions and have answers that are honest. Teens don't expect these adults to know everything, but they do expect straight answers. Adults who meet this challenge gain the trust and regard of teens.

Parents who continue to be involved with their teenagers are in for rewards. The rewards come from interesting discussions in figuring out the problems of life. There are only two requirements. One is that adults don't act as if they know all the answers (even if they think they do). The second requirement is that they keep the dialogue going by continually showing interest in their teenager. In chapter 4, you will learn communication skills that will help you talk effectively with your child.

Positive Goals

THERE ARE ALTERNATIVES to seeking the negative goals of attention, power, revenge, and displaying inadequacy. Through the positive approaches you will learn in this book, you can help your kids move from negative to positive goals.[6]

Kids who have positive goals are respectful kids. They see themselves as belonging to the family and the greater community. These kids accept responsibility for their behavior and their problems. We, in turn, are more respectful to our children and ourselves when we let our children accept the responsibilities they are capable of handling. We can encourage positive goals with the following parental strategies:

• **Moving from Attention to Involvement.** Kids who want attention want to be involved. They want to be part of things. You can help them move from demanding attention to getting involved by encouraging the kids to join in. Let them know you appreciate their help. Give them recognition when they are not asking for it.

• **Encouraging Independence.** Kids who want power also want to be independent. They want to make their own decisions. While we can't let them do whatever they want, we can give them opportunities to make decisions within limits and learn from the consequences or results of their decisions. We can encourage their independence—a goal we all want for our children when they become adults. We can let them do what they can do for themselves and others according to their age and abilities. By doing these things, we emphasize the positive side of power: being responsible for oneself and contributing.

> Kids who have positive goals are respectful kids. They see themselves as belonging to the family and the greater community.

• **Seeking Fairness.** Kids involved in revenge believe things are unfair, so they get even. While life is not always fair, as parents, we can make things as fair as possible. We can treat our children with consideration and expect the same in return. We can encourage them to act fairly toward others and recognize it when they do.

Sometimes your kids won't think you're being fair even if you're doing your best. When this happens, check out the interaction between your child and you. Are you feeling angry or hurt? In this case your child may be seeking power or revenge. Don't play into it. Just be as fair as you can.

- **Encouraging Competence.** Children who display inadequacy and give up in an area of their lives actually want to be competent. In fact, when a child decides he can do the very thing he felt he couldn't do, he attempts to do it perfectly. Many children who give up are failed perfectionists. While we don't want to encourage perfection—the impossible dream—we do want to encourage competence. You can encourage competence by recognizing your children's strengths and noticing when they make good decisions. While all kids need encouragement, kids who are displaying inadequacy need massive doses of it.

Children need to know that failure is okay and that one can learn from one's mistakes. Learning from one's mistakes is how the child grows and gains confidence and competence.

Who Owns the Problem?

SOMETIMES, AS PARENTS, we may take over responsibilities or problems that are best left to our kids to solve. When we do this, we deny them the opportunity to learn responsibility. The challenge comes in deciding which responsibilities belong to the kids, or "who owns the problem."[7]

Basically, if your rights are not involved, if no one's property or safety is threatened, or if the child's old enough to handle the situation, then your child owns the problem.

> Your 10-year-old's Cub Scout troop is going on a hike on Saturday. Your son wants to go, but he sleeps in. By the time you get him to the meeting place, the troop's already left. He's very disappointed.

This child is old enough to set an alarm clock and get himself up. It's not your problem that he decided to sleep in and miss the event. He owns the problem. You can acknowledge his disappointment, but resist the temptation to say, "Well, you should've set your alarm."

You have a visitor and your eight-year-old keeps interrupting. You tell her that you're trying to have a conversation and ask her not to interrupt. She keeps doing it anyway and you get angry and order her to her room.

You own this problem. Your rights are being interfered with. But you could have handled it more effectively. You could have said, "Mary and I are having a conversation. When we're finished, I'll be glad to talk with you." If she interrupted a second time, you could give her a choice. "You can wait quietly here until we're finished, or you can go to your room and wait." If she interrupts again, she has decided to go to her room.

Aaron, six, and his friend Brent are playing catch with a baseball in the backyard. They're throwing the ball toward the window.

You own this problem because potential property damage is involved. You express your feelings, "When the ball is thrown toward the window, I get scared because it might hit the window and break it." If the boys accept your feelings, fine. If not, you could give them a choice. "Either move away from the window, or stop playing catch—you decide."

Three-year-old Shelly runs toward the street. You panic, run and get her, and spank her on the bottom. "Don't you ever run in the street; you could get hurt."

You own this problem because Shelly's safety is involved. Also, she's not old enough to know better. But hitting her will only teach her to be afraid of *you*, not the street. A better way would be to give her a choice. "You can play in the yard or you can play in the house." Keep an eye on her, of course, and if she heads toward the street, she's decided to play in the house.

You have an agreement with your teenager that he will put gas in the family car after he uses it. He leaves you with a near-empty tank.

You own this problem. You can tell him that if he's not willing to stick to the agreement, he won't be driving the car for a while, until he's ready to keep the agreement.

Your 11-year-old is using the computer to do some homework. The computer crashes and she loses her file.

While you can be empathetic, this problem still belongs to your daughter. If she wants to, you could discuss with her how this problem could be avoided in the future.

Your 12-year-old tramples your neighbor's flower garden.

You own this problem because someone's property is involved. But, you can have your child take some responsibility, too—you can share the ownership of the problem. For example, he can pay for some new flowers out of his allowance and help the neighbor replant the flowers.

Your kids are fighting in the backyard and one of them picks up a rock to threaten the other one.

You own this problem, as one of the kids could get seriously hurt. You separate the kids, giving them time to cool off.

Your two-year-old makes a mess on the table at dinner.

You own this problem, as the child is too young to take responsibility for it. But, she can help clean up as much as she can. You hand her a rag. "Whoops, you had an accident. Let's clean it up." And the two of you clean up the mess.

To sum up, you own the problem when:[8]

1. The child's or teen's behavior interferes with your rights.

2. Destruction of someone's property is involved (unless the child destroys his or her own property).

3. Anyone's safety is involved.

4. The child is *not* old enough to handle the problem.

Your child or teen owns the problem when *none* of the above conditions exist. If *one* of the conditions exists, then you own the problem.

When your child or teen owns the problem, you may decide to listen, help the youngster figure out a solution (chapter 4 discusses reflective listening and exploring alternatives), or sometimes ignore the situation and let the child or teen handle it. When you own the problem, you may communicate your feelings (in chapter 4 we'll talk about I-messages) or give a choice and let the youngster experience the consequences (we'll discuss consequences in detail in chapter 6), but some problems may need to be negotiated (see chapter 4).

Deciding who owns the problem and letting kids handle those that belong to them shows consideration for your children. When you handle problems you own in respectful ways, you also give your kids a model of respectful behavior.

> Deciding who owns the problem and letting kids handle those that belong to them shows consideration for your childrem.

Throughout this book, you'll learn respectful ways to relate to your kids and help them develop positive goals and respectful ways to relate to others. You've taken the first step—learning what kids' behavior means. Once you understand your child's behavior, and who owns the problem, you're in a position to encourage positive goals and behaviors. (See table 2.)

Chapter 3 will focus on helping kids value themselves and others. You will learn how to help your kids develop positive

Table 2   Goals of Behavior

Negative Goals	How Parent Feels	What Parent Does	How Child Responds
Attention	Annoyed	Reminds and coaxes	Temporarily stops misbehavior. Later resumes misbehavior or attracts attention in different way.
Power	Angry, provoked	Fights or gives in	If parent fights, misbehavior is intensified or child submits but doesn't perform to parent's standards. If parent gives in, misbehavior stops.
Revenge	Hurt	Punishes; gets even	Retaliates by intensifying misbehavior or choosing another way to get even.
Displaying inadequacy	Despair; like giving up	Gives up	No response or improvement.

Source: Adapted from Rudolf Dreikurs and Vicki Soltz, *Children the Challenge* (New York: Dutton, 1987); Don Dinkmeyer Sr., Gary D. McKay, and Don Dinkmeyer Jr., *The Parent's Handbook* (STEP program) (Circle Pines, Minn.: American Guidance Service, 1997).

self-esteem and "people-esteem" through using encouragement skills. You will also learn how to encourage yourself.

Alternatives for Parent	Positive Goals	Encouraging Positive Goals
Ignore misbehavior when possible. Give attention for positive behavior. "Catch child being good."	*Involvement*	Let child help. Show appreciation for child's contributions.
Don't fight or give in. Withdraw from power contest. Let consequences of misbehavior do the teaching. Win child's cooperation.	*Independence*	Give opportunities to make decisions within limits. Let child do what the child is capable of. Help child exercise power in useful way by asking for help in other areas where the child is willing to help.
Refuse to feel hurt and angry. Don't punish or retaliate. Help the child feel loved by building the relationship.	*Fairness*	Make things as fair as you can. Emphasize mutual respect. Encourage the child to be fair with others and recognize the child's efforts to be fair.
Give plenty of encouragement. Recognize *any* effort and positive steps. Don't criticize or pity.	*Competence*	Recognize child's strengths. Notice when child makes good decisions.

3

Teaching Kids to
Value Themselves
and Others

*A child needs encouragement
like a plant needs water.*
—RUDOLF DREIKURS

ENCOURAGEMENT IS THE most important skill parents can use. When parents continually support kids' advancing development and work to strengthen their inner resources, kids' chances of a bright future are greatly increased. This chapter is filled with ideas about how to be a more encouraging parent. It is important for parents to see their job not as assuming responsibility for their children, but as preparing their children to assume responsibility for themselves.

What Kids Believe

WHAT KIDS BELIEVE about themselves and others influences their behavior and their future. The most significant impact we have on our children is the impact we have on their developing beliefs about themselves and others. These beliefs affect their "self-esteem" and "people-esteem" and determine how effective and happy they will be as well as how respectful and responsible they will become.

Parents may be tempted to try to force certain beliefs onto their children. Kids today will resist and rebel against all things forced on them. Any real influence parents have on kids comes when parents replace control with respect. In a respectful relationship, kids are more likely to listen to parents and consider what parents have to offer.

Beliefs and Disrespectful Behavior

The four goals of misbehavior presented in chapter 2 provide a framework for understanding the purpose behind all disrespectful behavior. Underlying the four goals of attention, power, revenge, and displaying inadequacy is a discouraged belief system. The origin of the belief system is the feeling of inferiority—a natural feeling we all possess in early childhood as the result of being so small and undeveloped. The four goals are mistaken ways children seek to overcome these feelings of inferiority and discouragement. A misbehaving, rude, and disrespectful child is a discouraged child. By directing behavior toward one or more of the goals of misbehavior, the child is essentially acting on the belief: "Unless I am the center of attention, or the most powerful, or can get even, or avoid looking bad or failing in the challenges of life—I am worthless!"

The key to effective parenting is to counteract these discouraging beliefs kids so commonly internalize in the course of their development. We can do this by helping our kids develop positive beliefs.

Developing Positive Beliefs

Positive beliefs are nurtured in families by emphasizing the positive, the possible, the potential. Life is filled with rudeness, loss, disappointment, and rejection. If in addition to the difficulty and cruelty that life offers, our children are operating on pessimistic and discouraging beliefs about themselves and others, they're very much at risk of being overwhelmed by life, or—at the very least—of being less resilient. Kids who believe in themselves and have basic positive regard for others possess an inner resource that can pull them through most any challenge that life has to offer. This inner resource creates resilience. While there are many influences in the lives of kids that play a role in their beliefs, the atmosphere created in the family—the parent-child relationship—is an important one and the one you as a parent can do the most about. The values you bring into the family and your behavior and beliefs have a most significant impact on this atmosphere and the beliefs your children develop.

> Kids who believe in themselves and have basic positive regard for others, possess an inner resource that can pull them through most any challenge that life has to offer.

Positive Family Values

Family values are those values shared by parents and lived day in and day out in the life of a family.[1] For example, family values can include the importance of education, religion, honesty, or financial responsibility. Family values have a strong influence on kids. When values are forced on children, they tend to rebel against them. When values are modeled consistently by parents and respectfully encouraged in children, they tend to be adopted. The most important family values that affect the most significant beliefs of kids are social values, the values concerning human worth and human relationships. Kids who are respectful are influenced by the following family values:

- All human beings are worthwhile and deserve respect.

- Cooperation helps everyone.

- The importance of "people-esteem"—caring about and contributing to others; understanding, accepting, and appreciating the differences among people from dissimilar backgrounds, circumstances, and cultures.

- Conflict is inevitable and can be settled respectfully and peacefully.

Kids who have a strong positive sense of self-esteem are more likely to pick up positive family values. They see the importance of cooperation, responsibility, and respect. But many parents misunderstand what self-esteem really is.

> Self-esteem is the positive belief in our own worth and our own ability to handle the challenges life brings our way.

What Is Self-Esteem?

Self-esteem is the positive valuing of ourselves as people. It is the positive belief in our own worth and our own ability to handle the challenges life brings our way. Self-esteem increases as each of us develops in our knowledge, skill, and courage. This process is much like a muscle that grows stronger from regular exercise. Whenever parents do things for kids that kids can do for themselves, we interfere in the development of what psychologist Frank Walton calls "psychological muscle"[2]—just as parents would inhibit children's physical muscle development and strength by insisting on lifting objects kids could lift themselves.

Kids and adults who are consistently disrespectful are suffering from continual feelings of worthlessness—from low self-esteem. In most cases, the family environment has been conducive to this feeling, to the mistaken belief that "I am worthless." Their rude behavior is often an attempt to conceal their perceived inferiority or to make others feel as worthless as they do.

It is important not to confuse self-esteem with what parenting expert Don Dinkmeyer Sr. calls "ego-esteem."[3] Ego-esteem reflects the belief that "I am better than others and therefore entitled to special treatment." Ego-esteem is in reality a compensation for feelings of extreme inferiority. We have all experienced being around certain people who brag about their knowledge or accomplishments, are self-righteous and condescending. This is an artificial form of self-esteem and *not* the goal of the respectful parent. A caution is called for here: Parents who use the parenting style of the servant (see chapter 1) tend to reinforce the child's notion that, "I am superior and entitled to be treated as a 'prince' or 'princess'." Parents with otherwise good intentions sometimes like to tell their kids they are "special." But treating kids as special tends to send another message: "You are better than everyone else." These approaches tend to bolster ego-esteem rather than self-esteem, and are therefore discouraging. What we need to realize is all people are special—just because they're human beings.

Positive self-esteem is fostered by parents who know how to be encouraging. The encouraging parent possesses certain beliefs and skills that help kids feel good about themselves and others.

On Being an Encouraging Parent

NOTHING PRESENTED IN this book will matter, will have any positive impact, unless the principle of encouragement is consistently applied in the family. Children truly do need continual encouragement just like a plant needs water.

What is *encouragement*? To understand the term it is important to recognize the root word—*courage*. Courage is the belief in oneself and one's own abilities. It is the willingness to make an effort even when anxious and when success is not a certainty. Encouragement is the process of stimulating positive self-esteem and helping kids develop "psychological muscle." Parents whose verbal and nonverbal messages convey a belief in the child and the child's ability and worth are operating on the principle of encouragement.

Encouragement Skills

Parents who want to be encouraging and influence their kids' positive self-esteem develop certain skills. The skills are: avoiding discouragement, valuing and accepting, having faith and confidence, focusing on the positive, and giving responsibility.

Avoiding Discouragement

The first thing we have to do if we're going to be encouraging parents is to avoid being discouraging. Between home, neighborhood, and school, many kids encounter discouraging messages or experiences. While we have only indirect influence on the neighborhood and school experience, we have direct impact on our relationship with our kids—we determine whether our relationship is encouraging or discouraging. Life is discouraging enough for our kids without our help. Children already feel inferior. From their vantage point, parents, adults, and older or more accomplished kids appear so much more capable. Criticism, negative expectations, unreasonably high standards, and comparisons to more successful siblings, peers, or parents are just some of the ways parents can discourage their kids unintentionally.

In order to get a better understanding of how we can discourage our kids, let's examine the parenting roles we described in chapter 1 and the message that's sent when parents play these roles.

Parents who play the role of the boss communicate to their kids, "It's obvious that you are not capable enough to do things well enough on your own, so I will make sure you do them." When coupled with high or perfectionist standards, the discouraging message becomes, "Unless you are the best, you are not worthwhile." Doormats send the discouraging message, "You are not significant enough for me to care about you or what you do." Servants communicate, "It's obvious that you are not capable enough to do things well on your own, so I will do them for you." Here's an example of a kid who's unfortunate enough to have a servant and a boss for parents.

> Rachel, age 10, is awakened on a school day for the third time by her mother. (discouraging message #1) At breakfast Mom states, "Rachel, I can't believe you chose the red blouse and the purple skirt; they look bad together." (discouraging message #2) Dad reads his paper, ignoring Rachel because he is so disappointed in her recent school performance. (#3) Mom says, "Let me get your schoolwork together while you change clothes and comb your hair. You look pretty bad this morning." (#4 and #5) Dad finally says, "Listen, Rachel, it is essential that you concentrate in school today and not clown around in class." (#6) Later, after school, Mom says, "I received a call from your teacher today. I can't believe you had another bad day. Your father's going to hear about this when he gets home from work."

(#7 and #8) Later, Dad states, "Young lady, you are not doing your best in school and are grounded until your report card comes out next month. When I was in fourth grade, I got straight A's." (#9 and #10)

If Mom and Dad are to avoid being discouraging to Rachel, they are going to have to give up the servant and boss roles. First, Mom can let Rachel be responsible for getting up, dressing, grooming, and collecting her own schoolwork. She can give her an alarm clock and expect her to be responsible. If Mom's concerned about the clothes Rachel wears, Mom can give her choices between outfits. Both parents can give Rachel the responsibility for her school performance and leave it between Rachel and her teachers. They can arrange for a tutor if she needs extra help. They can comment on effort and improvement rather than trying to force her to be a straight-A student. In other words, these parents need to back out of the power contest and concentrate on developing a good relationship with their daughter if they're going to have any positive influence on Rachel's behavior.

> When kids know their parents accept and value them just the way they are, despite imperfections, their confidence is bolstered tremendously.

Valuing and Accepting

Many parents mistakenly believe kids are motivated when they remind kids they are falling short of expectations. Quite the opposite is true. When kids know their parents accept and value them just the way they are, despite imperfections, their confidence is bolstered tremendously. This principle of encouragement includes the importance of supporting the interests your

Separate the Deed from the Doer

When a child does misbehave, it is important to separate the deed from the doer, addressing the problem without condemning the child. For example, suppose your kids are running and chasing each other in the house. You're afraid someone will get hurt or something will get broken so you give them a choice. "I'm sorry, but running in the house is not permitted. If you want to run, you may play outside." The running stops for a short time but the kids start chasing each other again. You can say, "I see you've decided to play outside. You can come back in when you're through running." You didn't lecture or condemn them for their behavior, you focused on the problem.

kids may have that are legal and healthy. Especially important is supporting those interests that may not be shared by you or other members of the family. Communication, as well as actions, that convey the ideas that, "I love you just as you are," "am glad you are in my life," and, "I am interested in what you are interested in," are very encouraging.

Create an atmosphere where mistakes are seen as opportunities to learn. The message is, "So you made a mistake; what did you learn?" Realize that all of us, parents and kids alike, are and always will be imperfect beings. When kids are accepted despite their mistakes, they have the opportunity to develop what Rudolf Dreikurs called "the courage to be imperfect."

You can model the courage to be imperfect for your kids. When you make a mistake, point it out to your kids in a positive way. "I made a mistake here. Next time I'll . . ."

Another aspect of valuing and accepting the child is showing sensitivity to a child's feelings. To be human means to have feelings that are at times confusing and painful. Making the effort to understand a child's feelings without judging them or trying to change them, helps your child feel accepted, valued, and better prepared to tackle life's challenges. Suppose your child had a bad day in school. You could say, "Are you feeling down? Want to talk about it?" In chapter 4 we talk about reflective listening, a skill for showing kids you understand their feelings.

> Making the effort to understand a child's feelings without judging them or trying to change them, helps your child feel accepted, valued, and better prepared to tackle life's challenges.

Demonstrating Faith and Confidence

Holding the basic belief that, in spite of past problems or difficulties, your children are capable of learning, growing, and developing is essential to encouragement. When kids reveal uncertainty, apprehension, or fear, listening to their feelings and showing faith in their ability is important. Being able to say, "I know it seems difficult but I believe you can handle it," is so encouraging. It is important to consider the challenge the child is facing and whether it's developmentally appropriate. You would not necessarily expect a three-year-old to successfully ride a two-wheel bicycle, but she could handle a tricycle.

Possessing positive and realistic expectations facilitates a self-fulfilling prophecy. Kids will see themselves through the mirror of your positive belief in them and grow to believe in themselves.

Focusing on the Positive

We live in a competitive world that is focused on two things simultaneously: exceptional accomplishment and falling short. People seem to be increasingly classified into two categories: winners and losers. Instead of waiting around for perfection or finding fault with whatever falls short of perfection, encouraging parents are like talent scouts searching for anything that is positive in their children and recognizing it. It is important to notice and recognize the developing qualities and strengths in our children, which, while not fully formed, show evidence of their presence.

Strengths such as honesty, integrity, responsibility, kindness, sensitivity, courage, determination, persistence, and patience are examples of those positive aspects of character that our children will show hints of as they develop. Notice them; comment on them; show appreciation for them. "Grandma was sad and you kept her company. I appreciate your caring."

Accentuate the Positive Side of Traits

Some strengths go unrecognized because we are focusing on the negative. For example, if we are faced with stubbornness, we fail to see the "flip side" of this trait. The child who is stubborn is also determined and persistent. The challenge becomes how to encourage the positive side of the coin. A determined child will persist in a task she wants accomplished until it's completed. Parents can utilize this ability by asking for help on tasks the child is capable of and interested in. Some other examples of "flip sides" are: the child who's picky is also selective; the child whose feelings are easily hurt is also sensitive; the child who argues can see alternatives. Think of negative traits your kids have and look for the flip side (see table 3). How can you encourage the flip side?[4]

Table 3   Accentuate the Positive

Trait	The Flip Side
Argumentative	Logical, creative, verbal, reasoning, persuasive, principled
Disorganized	Creative
Irresponsible	Spontaneous
Picky	Selective, discriminating
Rebellious	Independent, knows what he or she wants or doesn't want
Rigid	Principled
Sensitive	Aware, perceptive
Stubborn	Determined, persistent, sticks to it
Timid	Cautious, careful

Don't wait until your kids succeed to notice the positive—notice effort and improvement as well. When we notice and comment on effort and improvement our kids maintain their self-esteem as they develop. Also, not every child is talented in all areas. If kids participate only in areas where they are immediately successful, their lives will be very narrow and they will not experience the joy and satisfaction that comes from a well-rounded life. In addition, they will not allow themselves the opportunity to learn, stretch, grow, and overcome adversity—experiences that build "psychological muscle." The message parents give to kids when they notice only exceptional accomplishment is discouraging. "You count only when you are successful."

Suppose your child brings home a spelling test with 10 out of 20 words correct. Focus on the words the child spelled correctly, not the ones he missed. If there's been improvement from the last time, comment on that, too.

Parents can also encourage effort by breaking down complicated tasks into manageable bits and encouraging the child as he completes each step. Focus on what the child has accomplished rather than what's left to be done. "Look at what you've got done already. You're halfway finished!"

> If kids participate only in areas where they are immediately successful, their lives will be very narrow and they will not experience the joy and satisfaction that comes from a well-rounded life.

Giving Responsibility

Giving responsibility to kids encourages them because we demonstrate our confidence in them. If we are truly working to prepare our children for life on their own, it's essential we hand more and more responsibility over to them as they grow and develop. As Rudolf Dreikurs stated, "We can't teach anyone responsibility, we can only give it to them." Learning to handle responsibility comes from first having responsibility and then learning through experience what works and what doesn't. Children can't "have" responsibility unless parents are willing to "give" responsibility. It's important to think about the development of children in the following way: When a child is 9 years old she is $9/18$, or 50 percent, of the way toward adult status; when she is 15 years old she is $15/18$, or over 80 percent, of the way toward adult status. The question is, are your kids assuming the same percentage of responsibility that will prepare them for life as an adult?

If giving responsibility is to be an encouraging experience for a child, it's crucial that the child be prepared. It's important for parents to take the necessary time for training—going through the steps, answering questions, helping the child to organize and plan the task or responsibility. Here are some examples:

• **First-grader Jessica,** whose mother dressed her each morning for kindergarten, is enthusiastically told by Mother that she believes Jessica is now capable of picking out her clothes and dressing herself. Mom was present the first and second morning while Jessica proudly picked out her clothes and dressed herself. When Jessica struggled, Mom coached her, but resisted doing it for her.

> Learning to handle responsibility comes from first having responsibility and then learning through experience what works and what doesn't.

• **Ten-year-old Kirsti,** who has been wanting a dog her entire childhood, is given the opportunity to pick one out as long as she takes full responsibility for the dog's care. Kirsti and her parents write up a list of all the tasks involved in caring for a pet.

• **Eleven-year-old Marcus** has been informed by his parents at a family meeting that he is now old enough and capable enough to launder his own clothes. His parents walked him through all the steps and supervised him the first time, offering guidance and support. When a couple of weeks went by and Marcus complained that he didn't have any clean clothes (implying that Mother wasn't doing her job), Mom merely said, "It's your responsibility now, Marcus."

• **Fourteen-year-old Maria** raises the issue of bedtime at a family meeting. This has been a hotly contested family issue,

Learning Domestic Responsibilities

In today's world, where it is more common than not for both parents to work, it's important that we prepare our sons and daughters to take their place as equals in the family. It's also common for young adults to live on their own or in a roommate situation for an extended period after leaving home. Too often, parents operate on sex role stereotypes and continue to prepare their daughters more than their sons for domestic responsibilities. This is truly a "setup" for later difficulty and conflict. Women today, and even more so in the future, will expect their husbands to be an equal participant in domestic responsibilities. Roommates will certainly expect no less. Also, girls should be taught traditional "male" skills. For example, they can learn how to use tools and change the oil in a car.

with numerous disagreements and conflicts. The parents, after talking together about the issue, decide it is time to let Maria be responsible for her own bedtime. They worked out an agreement that the curfew (the time when Maria must be home in the evening) continues, but Maria decides when she actually goes to bed. It is understood that if Maria has trouble getting to school in the morning the issue will need to be revisited.

• **Seventeen-year-old Frank** has a new job and resents the fact that his parents have to drive him to work, since Frank has not yet saved up enough money to buy a used automobile. At a family meeting options are discussed. One option is for Frank to earn enough money to be added to the family's auto insurance policy, and if he continues to make regular and timely payments, he can drive himself to and from work. Another option is for Frank to learn the bus system, something the parents have been resistant to and fearful of in the past, but now think he's old enough to take care of himself.

Another way of giving responsibility is to take the opinions of your kids seriously. When solving problems together, either tackling an issue in a family meeting or during everyday conversation, it is so encouraging for kids to have their opinions taken seriously. One important aspect of this, especially in the teen years, is asking your kids for advice and then sincerely listening to what they have to say. This is a valuable way of demonstrating your belief in them. It's certain to help teens see themselves as developing, having something to offer, and preparing for life as an adult. You, of course, are free to do what you wish with the advice. It's the fact that you asked and listened that matters. It's so encouraging for a kid to hear, "Thanks Katy, you've given me a new perspective. I appreciate it." Don't be surprised if your kids are wiser than you expect—all they need is a chance to prove it.

Isn't Encouragement Another Word for Praise?

SINCE ENCOURAGEMENT FOCUSES on the positive, many people, including counselors, confuse it with praise. Praise is a type of reward; it has to be earned. Encouragement, on the other hand, is a gift freely given. Praise is given for accomplishment—no one praises you when you're down or fail. Encouragement can be given for accomplishment, but it also focuses on effort and improvement, and unlike praise, can be given when a child doesn't achieve.

Praise worked well in the past when autocratic parenting was the norm. But as you've learned, autocratic parenting doesn't work the way it used to. Today's kids can either become dependent on praise—they won't do anything unless someone tells them how great they are—or rebel against parental attempts to control their behavior. Both of these responses to praise indicate a discouraged kid.

> Encouragement can be given for accomplishment, but it also focuses on effort and improvement, and unlike praise, can be given when a child doesn't achieve.

Praise contains value-judging words such as "good," "great," "wonderful." By using value-judging words, a parent is communicating, "I decide your worth and your worth depends on you meeting my standards." In other words, if kids don't meet adult standards, they are not "good," "great," or "wonderful," and since they are not "good," they must be bad or worthless. Praise equates the deed with the doer. Praise sends the message, "Your worth as a human being depends strictly on your deeds."

Encouragement separates the deed from the doer. Kids are worthwhile just because they're people. Accomplishment and meeting standards do not define a person's worth. Kids who are discouraged and struggle in their efforts to achieve will feel even more discouraged with the praise system. They will see themselves as never being good enough, and may stop trying. Encouragement increases true self-esteem and the development of inner resources, while praise emphasizes pleasing and measuring up to the expectations of others. (See table 4.)

Another parenting practice that parents think is encouraging—"I'm so proud of you"—is actually discouraging. Why? Because the parents' pride is based on deeds. Can you be just as proud of your children because they are worthwhile even when they fail? Besides, the pride belongs to the child. When she accomplishes something, the parent can encourage by saying, "I'll bet you're proud of yourself." Kids who learn to judge their own achievements take responsibility for their accomplishments—and their failures.

Encouragement is given in many ways. Encouragement has a special language as you have

> **Kids are worthwhile just because they're people. Accomplishment and meeting standards do not define a person's worth as a human being.**

Table 4 Comparing Praise and Encouragement

Examples of Praise	Examples of Encouragement
"I'm so proud of that great report card."	"I hope you are proud of yourself for learning so much and doing so well in school this period."
"What a good boy you've been all day."	"I appreciate how cooperative you've been today."
"Mommy is so happy that you've cleaned your room."	"I bet it feels good to have your room back in order."
"I am so thrilled being your parent when you play as well as you did today."	"I am so glad you are in my life."

Kidspeak:
The Importance of Strong Character

By Ryan Mansager, age 17

Influence on teenagers is a common issue with Adlerians.[5] But being brought up by an Adlerian family, it occurred to me that there is a simple answer to the issue: self-confidence. Having the ability to look within oneself for support and answers, rather than to outside opinions, builds strong character—something others think is no longer a top priority. Personal decisions are what ultimately matter, leaving outside opinions to be just that: opinions. This strong character is not only a great characteristic to have, but it is also something that rubs off onto others.

Teenagers tend to look up to other people for direction. Today, many of these people tend to be movie or

seen and will learn in the next section, but verbal encouragement doesn't tell the full story. You can be encouraging by giving responsibility and letting kids tackle challenges they can handle and problems they own. In this way you demonstrate your faith in your kids. Other nonverbal encouraging actions are as simple as a nod, a wink, a smile, a hug, and listening without interrupting.

Encouraging Words

The language of encouragement is nonjudgmental and intended to show acceptance, support interests, recognize effort rock stars. But what is forgotten is that influences also include the people closest to them: friends and parents. A somewhat forgotten fact is how much teens are actually influenced, negatively and positively, by other teens. Teens look up to peers who exhibit self-confidence and leadership skills, which are directly influenced by self-confidence. Since teens look up to self-confident peers, it turns out that every teenager has just as much ability as any other to [be a person of] influence.

So this quality of self-confidence plays a very important role in the teenager's daily circle of influence. Because of this, it's important for self-confidence to be taught at an early age. This is both for the personal benefit of the teenager, and also to provide for the ability to influence others in a positive way.

and improvement as well as accomplishment, show appreciation, focus on strengths, communicate faith, and promote self-evaluation. Throughout this chapter we've given examples of encouraging words. Here are some more:

"I really enjoyed our time together today."

"You seem to enjoy (name the interest or activity)."

"You gave it your best, and that's all you can do."

"You really worked hard on that."

"You're improving (tell how)."

"Thanks for helping me. It made my job easier."

"You have a talent for . . . Would you help me with this?"

"I know you can do it."

"I know it's tough, but I've got faith in your ability."

"How do you feel about your effort?"

"It seems to me you're dissatisfied with your work. What do you think you can do so it's more acceptable to you?"

Some parents will give encouragement with one hand and take it away with the other. For example, a parent might say, "I know you can handle it." This is encouraging, but what if the parent added, "So you better get busy"? Would the child feel encouraged or pushed? Another example: Parents often say, "Keep up the good work," after a strong effort or accomplishment. This implies that in order to be worthwhile, one must always achieve.

So far, we've stressed the value of helping kids feel good about themselves. But positive self-esteem also includes how kids feel about and relate to others. The next section discusses "people-esteem," the "others" part of healthy self-esteem.

Develop People-Esteem

KIDS WHO HAVE developed a positive sense of community feeling are happier individuals. Those who care about and help others are less prone to depression than those who are wrapped up in themselves. Parents can help their children develop people-esteem by encouraging respect, involving kids in helping out, and teaching tolerance.[6]

Encouraging Respect

Four-year-old Tina was playing with her friend Joan. Tina grabbed a doll from Joan who immediately started crying.

While this problem is between Tina and Joan and they own it, the situation presents an opportunity to teach respect to Tina. Mom could call Tina aside and ask her to focus on Joan's feelings. "How do you think Joan feels when you take the doll? How would you feel if Joan took a doll from you?" Mom could discuss a respectful way to deal with the situation. "If you want to play with the doll, how could you ask Joan nicely?" Then Mom could suggest Tina give the doll back to Joan and say she was sorry.

Young children are egocentric; they are just learning to share. Finding "teachable moments" as this mom did helps them learn respect. Another way is to take time for training by using puppets and role-playing scenes that relate to showing respect for others.

> Seven-year-old Nathan frequently scattered his dirty clothes around his room. On wash day Mom would keep after him to pick up the clothes and put them in the hamper. The problem was becoming a power struggle.

Mom could teach Nathan respect by showing respect for herself. She could tell Nathan that she would wash only what she found in the hamper. If Nathan neglected to put his dirty clothes in the hamper, he'd have to wear them dirty. When he complained, Mom could just say, "I know you're upset. If you put them in the hamper, I'll be glad to wash your clothes next wash day."

> Kristin was a divorced mother of two children, Jed, aged ten, and Karla, aged seven. Weekend dad Carl complained that when he picked up the kids they were unruly. They wouldn't follow his rules and implied that Mom didn't make them do what Dad wanted them to do. Carl complained to Kristin and asked her to speak to the kids.

While Kristin might be tempted to get into an argument with Carl, she needs to recognize that this is Carl's problem.

She can show respect for herself, her ex, and her children by not interfering. She could say, "You have different rules at your house. That's okay. The kids will just have to learn to deal with them. If I interfere, I'm showing disrespect for you and the kids. They are perfectly capable of learning to respect your rules. If I were you, I'd just tell them that rules are different in different places."

> When 12-year-old Marsha didn't get her way, she would go into a rage. One night she deliberately broke a lamp on a living room end table.

Beginning at a very young age, children want to be helpful. It's important for parents to encourage this natural interest in contributing to others.

Marsha needs to learn to be responsible for her temper. Committing violent acts is not only disrespectful, it's intolerable. After Marsha has calmed down, her parents could discuss with her how the lamp will be paid for. It may take many deductions from Marsha's allowance, but she will learn she is responsible for her behavior.

Another aspect of respect is showing good manners. Parents can teach kids appropriate social behavior through a variety of methods. Manners are discussed in chapter 7.

Involving Kids in Helping Out

Providing opportunities for contribution, and noticing and recognizing such opportunities, are important aspects of encouragement. Fully functioning and respectful people consider the welfare of others, see their part in the whole, and realize that life requires both give and take. This human quality is absent from people who practice rudeness and violence. Beginning at a very young age, children want to be helpful. It's important for parents to encourage this natural interest in contributing to others.

It often takes more time and effort to provide opportunities for younger children to lend a hand and help with chores and errands, but it's worth the effort. For example, three-year-olds usually are not able to vacuum the carpets, but they can help dust the furniture. Kids who grow up with the expectation that they are capable helpers and are needed, develop the all-important "work-ethic" and that special kind of self-esteem rooted in the feeling of belonging that comes from contributing. It's encouraging for a child of any age to be able to hear his parent say, "Thanks John, I really appreciate your hard work, and your help in getting that project done."

Helping out needs to go beyond the family. Kids need to know they are an important part of the larger community. Many families give to charities and some collect food and clothing for the homeless; important contributions, but kids need regular opportunities for hands-on experiences in helping out in their more immediate lives.

> Mrs. O'Leary, 85, heard the doorbell ring. Recovering from a broken hip, she slowly wheeled herself to the door, opened it, and saw the smiling faces of Greg and Ken, preteen brothers from down the street. The boys were carrying a covered dish. "What's this?" she queried. "Mom helped us make dinner for you," the boys replied. "We thought with you just getting out of the hospital, it might be hard for you to cook." It was all Mrs. O'Leary could do to hold back the tears.

Unfortunately, in the hustle-bustle society we live in, neighbors are often strangers. But our neighbors can be valuable for relationships and support. Imagine how good it feels

Everyone Pitches In

When kids learn to do things for themselves they are making a contribution as well as building their own self-esteem. Learning to contribute begins at home. There are many things kids can do for their families in addition to taking care of their own responsibilities. Kids can be encouraged to do chores. Families function better when everyone pitches in. Many kids balk at doing chores because they are handed down to them— the parents decide who will do what and when. A better approach is to involve the kids in deciding who will do what chores. This can be accomplished through the family meeting, a forum where the family meets on a regular basis to discuss family business. In chapter 4 we will discuss how to set up family meetings and win children's cooperation.

to Greg and Ken to help out Mrs. O'Leary. Kids can become involved in the neighborhood in a variety of ways—taking care of pets or plants when neighbors are out of town, for example. When neighbors move, kids can help out with moving chores and plan ways to stay in touch.

If your family attends a place of worship, there are many opportunities for kids to get involved or for all of you to get involved as a family. Most congregations reach out to the community. Volunteer in these efforts.

Many schools have service clubs where kids get an opportunity to help out on a regular basis. Check with your kids' school; are there service clubs? If not, consider helping the school develop these activities.

Through making contributions, kids learn to value people. Kids who are involved in helping out are less prone to get into serious trouble with drugs and violence. They feel connected to the community, which, in turn, helps them feel good about themselves.

Teaching Tolerance

> *You've got to be carefully taught to hate,*
> *before you are six or seven or eight.*
> —FROM THE MUSICAL *SOUTH PACIFIC*

We are becoming an increasingly multicultural society, especially as more people join in at the level of global society. Various races, cultural practices, and traditions can create an atmosphere of misunderstanding, disrespect, and violence. The door can be opened for more understanding and respect if we teach our children all people are worthwhile. Tolerance is more than a nodding acknowledgment of another's presence. It also includes acceptance and appreciation for the uniqueness of others. We can give our children opportunities to get to know people of different races and cultures in a variety of ways.

Encourage Friendships

Look for opportunities to involve your kids with kids of different races and cultures. For example, you can encourage your kids to bring their friends home. Be observant. Most schools have students of various ethnic, racial, and cultural backgrounds. Speak with your children about students in their school from backgrounds other than their own. Encourage them to grow by getting to know and appreciate the differences and similarities they share with diverse students. Encourage their friendships with all kinds of kids. Help your kids recognize that relationships with people different from themselves can be challenging and take effort. Help them appreciate how their own life is enhanced in the process. Places of worship are good places to see a cross section of society and to get to know people you might not otherwise meet. Tolerance includes acceptance of races and cultures, genders and religions, physically and mentally challenged folks, gay and lesbian people, and anybody who seems other than what you expect or not like you.

> Help your kids recognize that relationships with people different from themselves can be challenging and take effort. Help them appreciate how their own life is enhanced in the process.

Don't accept negative comments from your kids regarding typing people. Challenge them and ask them, "Where did you get that idea?" Point out the positive role models of all kinds of people. For example, if your child makes fun of someone in a wheelchair, discuss people like Christopher Reeve, the famous actor who crusades from his wheelchair to find a cure for spinal injuries.

When you're watching TV, notice how people who are of a different race or culture are portrayed. What does this say about how our society views different groups of people and how people can be stereotyped? Encourage your kids to think of other examples. When racial or other prejudice incidents are reported on the news, discuss them with your kids.

Another way to get your kids to appreciate cultural differences is to help them learn about their own culture. Who are we? Where did we come from? What different heritages and cultures make up our family? What are our traditions? Along with appreciating your own culture, you can celebrate and learn about other cultures and attend cultural events in your community.[7]

Model Acceptance

You probably grew up with prejudices; most of us did. Most of us have realized prejudice is not only inaccurate, but also wrong and destructive. Become aware of any occasional slips into prejudice. What are you thinking about this person? Challenge your own thinking. Your kids will pick up what you really believe and often accept what you say and do.

You probably know all kinds of people. You've met them on the job or in your place of worship or at the hardware store. Make an effort to get to know them better. Let your children see that you have friends and acquaintances from all walks of life.

Parents Need Encouragement, Too!

We realize that a parent's ability to encourage kids is directly proportional to how encouraged the parent feels as a person. The importance of self-esteem and people-esteem is no less important for parents, since parents with healthy self-esteem are much better prepared to encourage their children. Take a few moments and reflect upon all of the principles described in this section, but this time apply them to you and your own life. Answer the following questions (you may want to write down your answers for future reference):

• What are you doing to discourage yourself? What do you say to yourself when things are not going well? Do you criticize or condemn yourself? Do you expect yourself to be a perfect parent? Have perfect kids?

Kidspeak: The Benefits of Respect

By Hannah Ebner, age 12

There are all kinds of different people. There are some very quiet, shy people. There are some very outgoing, funny people. And then there are some people who aren't what they seem to be, people who put on a show when they're with their friends. If you can look past their act, and deeper into who the person actually is, you might find someone very different from what you might have guessed. I'm going to give an example. Adrian (that isn't his real name) acts like a punk, says he made out with a girl for half an hour (he's thirteen), and says he hangs out with people who smoke marijuana. But he's never beaten anyone up, he's never come to school having been beaten up, he doesn't smoke the marijuana himself, and as far as I know, he's pretty nice. That leads me to believe that he's not a bad kid after

• Are you able to accept and value yourself just as you are? Are you able to accept the mistakes that you make without condemning yourself? Do you accept your own feelings? Do you have people in your life who are sensitive to your feelings?

• Do you have faith and confidence in yourself? Do you say to yourself, "I can do it?" Do you have people in your life who believe in you?

• Do you focus on your own qualities and strengths? Do you give yourself credit for effort and improvement or only all; he just pretends to be so people don't mess with him. I can tell he doesn't have a very good home life, but he doesn't have cruel intentions. All of my close friends think he's a jerk and that he's your average big bully. Looks can be deceiving.

Because of the respect my parents have given me, I have learned to try to respect other people as well. I think that maybe if you give respect, you are more likely to get it back. I try to look deeper than what's on the surface, so it's easier to respect people and their feelings. With someone like Adrian, you do need to look a lot deeper to see what he's really like, but it definitely can be done. Then, since you can respect him for who he really is, hopefully he will respect you in return. When you respect everyone, you'll feel more comfortable around them, and you'll be able to like them for who they really are, not who they pretend to be.

recognize results? Do you acknowledge the contributions you make to others—even when they go unrecognized?

• Do you feel that you are developing as a person in your career, marriage, family, hobbies, and interests? Do you courageously accept new responsibilities, opportunities, and risks? Do you make the time to nurture yourself? Are there interests or dreams you have always had, but because they were never encouraged or responsibilities got in the way, you never pursued them?

• Do you have an understanding of your own historical and cultural roots? Are you connected to an extended family? How involved are you with your neighborhood, your community? Are you contributing to your community? Do your activities involve you with people from multiple parts of society?

If, after reviewing these questions, you realize there is room for development, we want to encourage you to consider doing whatever it will take to support your growth and development as a person. Realize that your function in life is not simply to be a parent or a spouse. You are a person entitled to your own life with and independent from your family. You may be basing your worth on your parenting effectiveness. This is a mistake. Your children aren't puppets; you can't make them succeed or fail. While you may enjoy their accomplishments and be concerned about their failures, let them be the separate persons they are. If you're overly invested in the success or failure of your children, you may not be living your own life.

> Realize that your function in life is not simply to be a parent or a spouse. You are a person entitled to your own life with and independent from your family.

If at first it is difficult to take action for just yourself, then we suggest you to do so for the sake of your child or children. A discouraged parent is often a discouraging parent. What do you need to do to become more encouraged? Consider the following possibilities:

1. **Develop a self-improvement plan.** Brainstorm ideas (it is helpful to write them down) of what it will take for you to be a

The Ladder of Self-Improvement

Visualize a ladder. Your goal is to get to the top of the ladder, not to reach perfection, but just the highest level of achievement possible for you. Many fail in maintaining a self-improvement plan because they immediately and futilely try to jump to the top of the ladder. The steps on the way to the top are all-important and cannot be missed, otherwise there is no upward movement. Think of each self-improvement idea as a rung on the ladder. Each one deserves its own time. Begin with one step, one idea, and work at it until you feel firmly grounded on that rung before taking another step. In order for your self-improvement plan to gain momentum, we suggest the first step you take be an idea on your list that does not have the highest rating. Starting at the top can backfire because it's so important to you and failure can be very discouraging. With each step, confidence and energy increase, placing you in a stronger position to take on a higher rated issue.

more encouraged and therefore encouraging person. For example, you may want take time for rest and relaxation, pursue a hobby or interest, take classes to widen your knowledge or to enhance your career, or address a relationship that lacks mutual respect.

2. **Rate your self-improvement ideas according to their importance to you.** You can rate each one on a five-point scale. It is important to think of your self-improvement plan as a process much like climbing a ladder (see sidebar).

3. Apply what you've learned in this chapter on encouraging your kids to yourself. For example, what encouraging words can you give to yourself? Author Richard Bach says it this way: "You teach best what you most need to learn."[8] In teaching your children respect and encouragement, remember you as a parent are learning those skills for yourself. Give yourself a break and don't expect to learn it all at once. Take it a step at a time. Look for improvement in your relationship and focus on your efforts. "I resisted the temptation to remind her." "I remained calm." "I'm getting better at letting him do things for himself." Have faith in yourself. You can do it (even though you'll never do it perfectly). If you find things like anger, stress, and guilt getting in your way, you can learn to handle these, too. See chapter 5 for ideas about how to manage anger.

4. Develop your sense of humor. A good laugh at yourself is like a multivitamin. Psychologist Walter "Buzz" O'Connell says, "Life is too important to take seriously." When you're able to laugh at yourself, your kids can pick up the habit, too. Laugh with your kids, not at them. Appreciate their sense of humor, and your own.

5. Learn to appreciate and affirm yourself. Each day take a few minutes by yourself to appreciate your uniqueness. By affirming yourself you appreciate your strengths and build your self-esteem. List five positive attributes about yourself as a person and spend some quiet time affirming them. Don't make them comparative (no ego-esteem), just make them descriptive. For example, if you're a friendly person who enjoys people, affirm that asset by telling yourself, "I am friendly and enjoy people."

6. Reach out to others. This will help you become more grounded and connected as a person. Is it time to become more involved in your neighborhood, your place of worship, your community? Would volunteering in your community add to your self- and people-esteem? Are there ways you can step out of your "comfort zone" and become involved with people with perspectives and lifestyles new to you?

7. You could decide to get personal counseling. We have found that parents who receive counseling about their own lives and address the present and historical influences in their lives, not only increase their self-esteem, but are able to work through issues that have been barriers to being more effective as parents. You will also be a role model for your kids with respect to the importance of reaching out for help and wisdom when it is needed.

8. Maybe couple counseling is in order. It's close to impossible to feel encouraged as a person when your primary relationship is strained or in conflict. Kids misbehave far more in homes with couple or marital tension. Often their misbehavior is designed to gain attention in order to distract the parents from the conflicts in their relationship. Don't put this off. Our experience strongly suggests that when relationships get to a point when conflict or alienation has become a pattern, most cannot be improved without outside help. Single parents who are in a relationship can benefit from couple counseling as well. Remarried parents often face challenges of blending two families and can benefit from couple or family counseling. If your partner refuses to participate, focus on what you can do. Arrange for personal counseling and once you begin to develop, she or he will decide to participate, or be left behind!

9. Consider attending a parenting class. In the appendix, "References and Resources," we've included our suggestions of where to find parenting classes that are compatible with the ideas presented in this book. It is challenging to change our patterns of parenting. Parenting classes can provide additional information and support that parents need to put ideas into action.

In this chapter you've learned your role in encouraging self-esteem and people-esteem in your kids. You've also discovered ways to encourage yourself. The focus of chapter 4 is effective communication, problem-solving skills, and family meetings. You'll learn how to connect with your kids, listen to their feelings, respectfully express your own feelings, and work through problems.

Respectful Communication: Skills to Connect with Your Kids

We must see with the eyes of another,
hear with the ears of another,
and feel with the heart of another.
—ALFRED ADLER

IN THE PAST it mattered little how parents communicated with their children. Parents were accepted as being rulers in the family, and all that was required was parents making their expectations known and then using rewards and punishments to force children to comply. When parents were seen as superior, skills such as respectful communication, understanding, empathy, sharing, encouraging, and solving problems together were irrelevant. But in today's more democratic world, we need respectful communication, for *how* we communicate determines the success of *what* we communicate.

Vertical and Level Communication

VERTICAL COMMUNICATION REFERS to from above to below, as in a vertical line. Any communication that involves talking down to children or dismissing what they have to say consequently conveys the attitude that, "I am better than you," "I have more power than you," or, "You don't count." Vertical communication is rude and often leads to resistance and rebellion.

Level refers to side by side, as in a horizontal line. Level communication conveys the notion that while parents have different roles and responsibilities than children, parents and kids have equal value and are worthwhile human beings. So, whenever we communicate in ways that convey the attitude of mutual respect and mean, "I value you as a person," and, "What you have to say matters," this is level communication. Level communication implies both speaking and listening with respect. This type of communication often leads to influence and cooperation, closeness, and connection.

The Anatomy of Human Communication

Human communication is a complex thing. There's much going on when two people are in communication with each other. There's activity both *externally* (what we can see and hear) and *internally* (what we can't see or hear). The process of two or more people communicating involves all of the following steps (see figure 1):

1. Person A verbally or nonverbally *sends a message.*

2. Person B *receives* and *perceives* the message utilizing the primary senses of sight and hearing.

3. Person B *interprets* and *evaluates* the message, which is "filtered" through her conscious and unconscious belief system, which activates feelings and emotions.

4. Person B *decides* what message to send in response. This often occurs outside of conscious awareness.

5. Person B verbally or nonverbally *sends* a message back to Person A.

6. Person A *receives* and *perceives* the message and the process continues for both until the communication is complete.

7. Both Person A and Person B are influenced by the communication, which becomes part of their memory and thus revises or reinforces their respective belief systems and future relationship.

These internal processes usually occur within seconds and are often outside of our conscious awareness. When communicating, the less aware we are (or choose to be) about our own internal and external process, the more *reactive* we are likely to be, communicating automatically and emotionally like a reflex action. The more reactive we are, the more likely it is we'll *mis*communicate and cause trouble in the relationship.

Conversely, the more aware we are about our own process when communicating, the more *responsive* we can be, communicating thoughtfully and respectfully. The more responsive we are, the more likely it is we will truly connect to the other person. It's this connection that allows us to effectively influence our kids. To increase our responsiveness and effectiveness as communicators, it's essential for us to become more aware of the following:

• Am I truly understanding the message sent by my child, the meaning and feeling being sent? (*listening* on the level)

• What's going on with me internally? What am I thinking and feeling in response to the message? What are my motives in this situation?

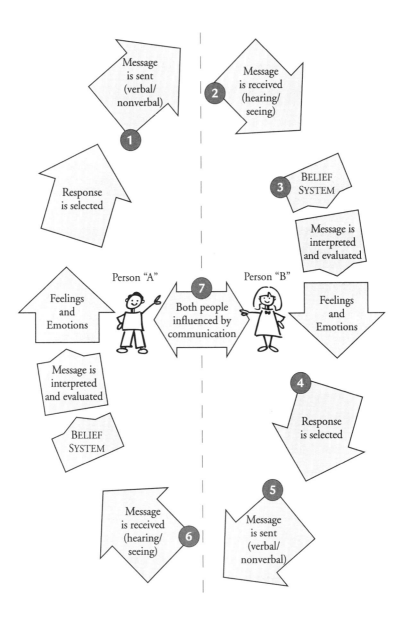

Figure 1.   The Anatomy of Human Communication.

Vertical and Level Motives

Examples of vertical motives include wanting to:

- Impress my child
- Assert my authority
- Prove I am right
- Hurt back
- Protect myself by avoiding the issue

Examples of level motives could be to:

- Understand my child's meanings and feelings
- Help solve the problem
- Encourage
- Stand firm on prior agreements
- Demonstrate self-respect

- How can I respond to the message in a way that will be sensitive and respectful to both my child and myself? (*speaking on the level*)

The Common Vertical Roadblocks to Communication

The typical vertical roadblocks to communication leading to misunderstanding, alienation, and conflict are identified through common parenting behaviors many of us revert to when we're under stress.[1] We learned these behaviors as kids by observing and interacting with our parents, extended family, teachers, coaches, other adults, and peers. Therefore, we may slip into ordering, commanding, threatening, controlling, preaching, lecturing, advising, evaluating, or judging. "You do what I say!" "I told you to go do your homework, now!" "I told you so!" "You know better than that!" "It's all your fault!"

Or we may engage in name-calling or ridicule. "You think you're so smart, don't you?" Some of us become sarcastic. "Your teacher can't be all that bad. If I had to deal with a bunch of clowns like you . . ." Sometimes we may decide to play psychiatrist and begin to diagnose and analyze. "You know what your problem is . . ." And some of us may feel sorry for our kids and try to comfort. "Don't worry about it; things always work out for the best."

Now, imagine you are a child and feeling strongly about some issue, and you get a response like those outlined in the above paragraphs. How do you feel? Does the response increase or decrease your desire to share further? Do you feel connected or disconnected from your parent? Does the response add or subtract from your desire to share a future concern with your parent? What have you learned as a result of the interaction?

> Too often communication is a competition to see who can send the most impressive or dominating message.

Keep thinking about being a kid and consider what you'd want from your parents if you shared some upset feelings with them. We'll bet you'd want them to listen and try to understand. Do you think your kids might want the same?

In its simplest form, communication involves a "sender" of a message and a "receiver" of the message. Real and effective communication occurs when these two functions connect, when there is shared understanding between parent and child.

Listening has become a lost art. One of the reasons our world is becoming more rude and violent is the growing inability to truly listen to one another. Connecting and problem solving are not possible unless we learn to listen effectively.

The most common deterrent to listening occurs internally. The next time you're in an important conversation with someone where emotions are involved, notice what happens as you internally process the conversation. Frequently, even before the other person completes her message, we are preparing our response. Too often the communication is a competition to see who can send the most impressive or dominating message. Refer back to figure 1, "The Anatomy of Human Communication," (page 92). What frequently happens is while step 1 is still in process with person A (for example, a child) sending a message, person B (the parent) has already internally traveled through steps 2, 3, and 4. The time required for the child's message to really be heard is not available, and yet the communication continues. No wonder there is so much miscommunication and the misunderstandings and conflicts that arise from it.

When a child shares a problem, issue, or uncomfortable feeling, a natural tendency for parents is to try to fix it. This is often what parents are thinking about in steps 3 and 4 of the communication process. While seemingly a logical thing to do, this effort is not helpful. Think of a time when you felt strongly about something and chose to share your feelings with a family member, friend, or coworker, and instead of empathizing with your feelings and situation, the listener offered advice on how the problem could be fixed. How did you feel? Did you feel accepted? Understood? Cared for? Connected? Or did you feel rejected, judged, and alienated?

Connecting with Listening Skills

LISTENING, LIKE MANY other human behaviors, requires certain skills. The skills of knocking (opening the door), clarifying (meaning), and reflecting (feeling) will help you connect with your kids.

Listening Skill #1—Knocking (Door Openers)

One of the obstacles that interferes in connecting with our kids is the pace of modern family life, which gives us limited opportunities for quality communication. When kids are upset, they won't always bring it directly to your attention. Sound familiar? To maximize connecting opportunities, it is important that we at times initiate communication. This listening skill is called a *door opener*.

> Knocking is respectful. It shows interest and concern and gives the person on the other side of the door the choice of a response.

Door openers send an invitation to our kids when we notice something is concerning them or when we as parents desire to make a connection. Symbolically, we are "knocking on their door." When something is bothering them, we don't want to just walk on by without connecting and we also don't want to barge in. So we knock and ask, "Can I come in?" Knocking is respectful. It shows interest and concern and gives the person on the other side of the door the choice of a response. He can request we go away, ask us to come back later, tell us he will come out and join us after a while, or invite us in. Here are some examples of door openers:

"Leslie, you look sad to me. Do you want to talk about it?"

"William, I've noticed how frustrated you've been lately. I'd like to hear about it."

"Tina, it seems like we haven't connected in so long. Can we spend a few minutes together and catch up?"

"Ken, you seem angry lately. Want to talk about it?"

Simply by sharing your interest and concern you will be making a connection. It's vital you accept the child's response to your desire to communicate. When you accept the child's decision to decline the offer, or talk at another time, or not to talk at all, you are demonstrating the ultimate in respect. In this way you are increasing trust and the likelihood your child will open up sometime in the future.

In addition to initiating communication, door openers are used throughout the dialogue. In order to continue and deepen the conversation, it is helpful to say, "I'm really interested; can you tell me more?" or, "How do you think the other person felt?" or, "Is there anything else you want to tell me about what happened?"

Whether the discussion is parent-initiated through "knocking," or your child is voluntarily sharing a concern, you are now in a position to further connect. The next step in the listening process is to make sure you have a clear and complete picture of what the child is sharing.

Listening Skill #2—Clarifying

When you find yourself unsure of what is being said about the content or meaning of the message, such as the timing, order of events, the people involved, the circumstances, or the outcome, it is a time to *clarify*. This can take the form of a direct question or a paraphrase.

Examples of direct questions:

"I'm confused—who was at Mary's house when all this happened?"

"Help me get this right. Did you lose your homework or did you forget to do it?"

"Which happened first, the trouble on the playground or the conflict in the classroom?"

Examples of clarifying paraphrases:

"Cindy, let me see if I have this right. You've been spending time with your friend Stacey lately. You seemed to have a lot in common. For the last few times you've been with her, she didn't seem to want to talk. You've tried to draw her out, but you don't get anywhere. Is that right?"

"Carlos, I want to see if I understand what's been happening. You've had a series of disappointments. You were late for practice and the coach suspended you for a game. You've been lost in math class lately, your face has been breaking out, and your best friend is moving away?"

> While the content of the message is important, the most humanly sensitive aspect of any message is the feeling associated with it.

The above efforts to clarify the story or message your child is sharing are critical to the connection process. We can't connect until we have the same picture the child has. While the content of the message is important, the most humanly sensitive aspect of any message is the feeling associated with it.

"I Understand"

A common mistake parents make is to share their understanding in a superficial way. The most typical example is a parent responding to a sensitive communication with words like, "I understand." Those words don't demonstrate anything and, in fact, tend to create a barrier. When kids hear this kind of response they may say to themselves, "How could she possibly understand? She has no idea what I'm going through."

Listening Skill #3—Reflecting

A third and powerful listening skill is a method called reflecting or *reflective listening*. Reflective listening is a way of connecting with kids at the feeling level, heart to heart. This skill involves an empathic response to the child's communication by reflecting back, in your own words, what you heard the child say, with an emphasis on how the child is feeling (sad, happy, angry, frustrated, confused, and so forth). Reflective listening is a way of demonstrating our understanding of what the child is experiencing.

Reflective listening is a skill that seeks to fully communicate, and thus demonstrate, an effort to truly understand. It's an appropriate listening skill when the child owns the problem (see chapter 2). The child owns the problem when the issue being shared by the child is one that primarily affects his life and is not interfering with your rights or responsibilities as a parent.

There are four important ways parents can prepare themselves to connect with their kids at the feeling level:

1. Develop trust and respect. It's difficult for human beings to reveal intimate, personal, and sometimes embarrassing feelings. It is nearly impossible to share these feelings when we lack trust in the other person.

> When engaging in reflective listening, it's essential to realize that your child is a separate and unique human being and, as such, will see and feel things differently than you will.

Imagine yourself being called upon to speak with your supervisor, a person you feel disrespected by and distant from. Your supervisor is concerned with a work-related issue and begins to ask you sensitive questions regarding how you feel about the situation. How comfortable are you opening up to your supervisor?

It is unlikely that your kids will be comfortable sharing feelings with you unless you have spent time strengthening the relationship in ways outlined in this book. Valuing kids as equals and employing respect in all aspects of the relationship—communication, problem solving, discipline, encouragement, and anger management—will add to the trust and, therefore, your ability to connect on the feeling level.

Specifically, when engaging in reflective listening, it's essential to realize that your child is a separate and unique human being and, as such, will see and feel things differently than you will. Accepting this reality is necessary to being able to truly listen to and connect with your child.

2. Develop your powers of observation. In order to sensitively connect with your child through reflection, it is important to develop your observation skills. Feelings are most often revealed nonverbally. Feelings can be revealed through:

- **Facial expressions**—the human face reveals much of what is felt. Examples are crying (sad, frustrated, angry, in pain), smiling (happy, nervous), degree of eye contact (connected, alienated, ashamed).

- **Body language**—the sense you get from the way in which your child is "carrying" himself (attentive, exhausted, guarded).

- **Tone of voice**—voice tone that accompanies the verbal message. The words often reveal what the child is expected to say; the tone reveals how the child really feels. For example, you ask your child how her day at school went and she replies in a flat monotone, "Fine." The words and voice tone don't match. Trust the voice tone as revealing how she actually feels, which may be frustrated, mad, or bored.

Remember, your child is an individual and her body language is unique as well. While for any one person, the meanings and feelings associated with nonverbal behavior tend to have a characteristic pattern, they vary from person to person and culture to culture. As you develop your powers of observation, these will become more evident.

3. Develop your ability to be fully present. Your child's willingness to connect with you on the feeling level will also be affected by how you are perceived both verbally and nonverbally. Children are keen observers. If you are not fully present and focused on this moment and this conversation, your child will pick it up. A common example is a kid coming home from school all upset about something, and while still reading the newspaper, Dad asks, "How was your day at school?" How much do you think this child is likely to share?

Make eye contact without staring, give your child the time and space to speak without interrupting, and demonstrate your presence verbally ("I see, uh-huh") and nonverbally (occasionally nodding, leaning toward the child). All of these ways of demonstrating that you're focused on the conversation send the message that, "I value what you say and I care how you feel."

4. Develop your feeling vocabulary. To effectively reflect your child's feelings, develop your feeling vocabulary. Most adults have limitations in this area. When we were children, parents were superior, so obedience is what counted, not feelings. How many times have we all heard the phrase, "You shouldn't feel . . ."? Feelings matter in a relationship where the members have equal value.

Table 5 includes a list of feeling words. You will find increasing your feeling vocabulary will allow you to more fully connect with your kids.

Forming a Reflective Listening Response

The intent of reflective listening is to connect heart to heart with our kids. The manner in which you reflect should be natural for you. As long as your motivation is to respectfully empathize and understand the child, you will make a positive connection and contribute to your child.

For a response to be a complete reflection, it's helpful to reflect both (1) the feeling, and (2) the situation that led to the feeling. In order to offer some direction to get you started, we offer the following "formulas" for constructing reflective listening responses.

• **Through a question.** One way to reflect is in the form of a question. When you guess what a child's feeling through a

Table 4 Feeling Words Vocabulary

Unpleasant or Painful Feelings		Pleasant or Positive Feelings	
abandoned	hopeless	accepted	included
afraid	hurt	appreciated	independent
aggravated	indifferent	balanced	interested
angry	insecure	beautiful	loved
annoyed	insignificant	brave	loving
anxious	irritated	calm	patient
ashamed	jealous	capable	peaceful
bad	lonely	comfortable	pleased
betrayed	mad	composed	prepared
blamed	nervous	confident	proud
bored	overwhelmed	connected	relaxed
cheated	picked on	cooperative	relieved
confused	put down	courageous	respected
criticized	rejected	creative	responsible
defeated	resentful	dependable	satisfied
depressed	sad	determined	secure
disappointed	self-conscious	effective	significant
discouraged	shocked	encouraged	stable
disgusted	shy	energized	strong
disrespected	tense	enthusiastic	surprised
dissatisfied	tired	excited	sympathetic
distrusted	uncertain	friendly	trusted
distrustful	uncomfortable	glad	trustworthy
embarrassed	unhappy	good	understood
exhausted	unloved	grateful	wanted
frustrated	upset	happy	warm
grumpy	violated	hopeful	whole
guilty	worried	important	wonderful

question, you avoid coming across as "the psychologist" and allow the child to respond to your guess. Some examples are:

"Are you feeling angry about what Mrs. Johnston said?"

"It sounds like you're feeling nervous about the recital, is that right?"

"Could it be that you feel hurt because Mary was gone when you arrived?"

• **Through a statement**. Another way to reflect is in the form of a sensitive and tentative statement. It's important that any reflective listening statement not be a judgment, but rather a genuine effort to connect by guessing what the child is feeling and what the feeling is related to. One formula is framed like this, "You feel _____ because _____."

This formula has many variations. Some examples are:

"You feel frustrated because your sister bothers you while you're doing your homework."

"You feel proud when you can do it all by yourself."

"It seems to me that you get nervous whenever you speak in front of the class."

Additional reflective listening variations can include questions such as, "I wonder if . . ."; "Is it possible that . . ."; "Do you feel . . ." Or statements such as, "You're feeling . . ."; "You sound . . ."; "It sounds to me like you're feeling . . ."; "I'm sensing that . . . " Reflective listening is a personal and heartfelt communication and it's helpful for parents to find a variety of ways that fit with their personal style. Like anything else, with practice you will develop your skills.

Because children appreciate the effort made to understand them in a nonjudgmental way, even when the reflective statement is off the mark kids usually respond positively. The child's response to the effort tends to further the understanding and connection, which is the point of reflective listening. Here's a typical example:

Reginald (age 11): I can't believe that David (his friend) ran off like that! We were planning to go the movie together!

Dad: Sounds like you're feeling hurt that David left because you were looking forward to his company.

Reginald: No, actually I'm feeling mad. This is the second time he's done that to me!

Dad: So you're feeling angry because David has violated your trust not once, but twice.

Reginald: Exactly.

The Benefits of Listening Skills for Parents

Forming a close connection increases your kids' overall sense of belonging and adds to your significance as a resource in their lives. Kids who are alienated from their parents are at much greater risk for the whole range of problems that plague our youth, from depression to violence, from substance abuse to gang involvement. In addition, kids who regularly have the opportunity to communicate their feelings and have them accepted and understood are much less likely to "act out" their feelings in negative and destructive ways.

> Through the parents' model of listening skills, kids begin to develop their own feeling vocabulary and are better able to express themselves in all areas of life.

Through the parents' model of listening skills, kids begin to develop their own feeling vocabulary and are better able to express themselves in all areas of life. Kids who experience this level of connection with their parents are in a better position to overcome their day-to-day problems. When parents really listen to their kids' feelings, they help reduce emotional reactivity and help kids move to a place of inner calm and stability. When we're emotionally reactive, most of us make poor choices and decisions. When we are emotionally calm, we're in the optimum position to make good choices and decisions.

When Not to Use Listening Skills

If kids are pursuing one of the goals of misbehavior—attention, power, revenge, or displaying inadequacy (see chapter 2)—using listening skills may reinforce their goal. It's common for your emotions to be involved when kids misbehave. Other parenting skills are called for here, such as disengaging from the goal, using I-messages or addressing the issue at a family meeting (later in this chapter), utilizing anger management techniques (chapter 5), or choices and consequences (chapter 6).

Connecting Through Talking and Sharing with Respect

PARENTS OFTEN FEEL their kids don't listen to them and when they do, don't respect or respond to what they have to say. Children and teens of today are hypersensitive to parents talking down to them in a vertical manner as described earlier in this chapter. Based on their sense of equality, kids will ignore this type of communication (parent deafness), defend themselves, or (openly or secretly) defy their parents.

In the previous section on listening skills, we discussed ways to communicate effectively when the child owns the problem. However, the moments when it's most common for parents to communicate vertically—to talk down to kids—are when they as parents own the problem, when their rights are being violated. Here are some typical vertical messages parents send to their kids:

> "You get off the computer right now. I don't want to have to tell you again!"
>
> "How many times do you have to be told to close the front door? Can't you remember anything?"
>
> "Don't you talk to me like that, young lady!"

During moments of frustration, most of us have sent these types of messages. Unfortunately, when we communicate with such disrespect, our children have little reason to respect us. Rudeness begets more rudeness, which, over time, can lead to a family climate of anger, conflict, and alienation.

There are communication skills parents can learn to address the same concerns as in the vertical examples given above, but in a way that makes kids more likely to listen. These level communication skills are tools to use to talk both directly and respectfully and add to an atmosphere of family cooperation.

You-Messages Versus I-Messages

Whenever we have a concern to address with a child there is a tendency to emphasize the word *you* in the message. Because the parent owns the problem, these "you-messages" often come across in a vertical, accusatory, and dictatorial manner, like "the boss." Messages such as, "You always . . ."; "You never . . ."; "You should . . ."; "You'd better . . ." are examples of "you-messages."

In contrast to vertical and ineffective you-messages are level and effective "I-messages."[2] When parents responsibly communicate their concerns and feelings emphasizing the word *I* or *me*, they are using a communication skill referred to as I-messages. When a parent states, "I can't sleep when the

Alternative Messages

Imagine you're a child, and in a threatening and commanding tone, your parent exclaims, "You get off the computer right now. I don't want to have to tell you again!" How would you feel at that moment? How cooperative are you likely to be? What if, instead, your parent stated in a friendly manner, "When you stay on the computer so long, I feel frustrated because we agreed to a time limit." How would you feel at this moment? Take a minute to reflect upon the differences you see between the two messages.

In the first message, your parent gave an order followed by an implied threat. The entire message was vertical in both tone and content. In the second example, a message was sent that simply included what the concern was and how your parent felt about it. There was no blame in the message, and the parent took responsibility for her own feelings.

television is on so loud," or, "I'm disappointed when you leave your toys out because it's important to me to keep the house looking nice," he is using an I-message.

I-messages are much more palatable for kids to hear. When parents communicate through you-messages, they are talking down to the child, which invites antagonism and resistance. When parents use I-messages, they still address the problem, but do so by sharing their own experience. I-messages are sent from a position of responsibility taking. In the message, the parent is assuming responsibility for her own perceptions and feelings. In turn, this manner of communication when received by the child places the child in a position of responsibility. When a parent sends a message that conveys the parent's concern and discomfort, the child is in a position to decide what he will do in response. The honesty and responsibility communicated in the parent's message encourages the child to respond with honesty and responsibility.

> I-messages are sent from a position of responsibility taking. In the message, the parent is assuming responsibility for her own perceptions and feelings.

There are many ways to formulate an I-message. Once again, it's important for the communication to be natural for you. As long as the communication is based on the desire to respectfully address an issue by sharing your own experience, you will be communicating more effectively. The following is a three-part model for creating a complete I-message:[3]

1. **Describe the situation or concern**—the behavior you find objectionable—in a respectful manner: "When I find my tools have been borrowed and not returned . . ."

2. **Describe your experience or feeling about the concern:** ". . . I feel frustrated . . ."

3. **Explain how the consequences of the behavior affect you as a person:** ". . . because I am unable to find the tools when I need them."

The simple formula for a complete "I-message" is:
"When _____, I feel _____, because _____."
When (state the concern), I feel (state your feeling), because (state the consequences the child's behavior has for you).

To effectively communicate through I-messages it's again helpful for a parent to develop a "feeling vocabulary." Table 4, on page 105, is a useful resource for increasing your ability to share feelings.

Since first names are such an important aspect of human identity, it is also helpful to personalize the message by using the child's first name. When we use first names in any communication, it increases the connection. Here are examples some typical situations and the use of I-messages.

> **Situation:** You have noticed when John uses a bathroom shared by several family members that it is left in less than ideal shape: towels on the floor, products left out on the sink, and so forth.
>
> **I-message:** "John, when the bathroom is left this way, I feel discouraged because I have to clean it up before I can use it."
>
> **Situation:** You have plans to go to a matinee with your daughter Karen. She gets up too late to go.
>
> **I-message:** "Karen, when we make plans and you oversleep, I feel disappointed because I look forward to spending time together."
>
> **Situation:** You are entertaining some friends and your kids are playing around the house in a loud and boisterous manner.
>
> **I-message:** "Kids, when you play so loud, I feel annoyed and embarrassed because I'm unable to enjoy my friends."

Situation: You discover the next morning that your son Greg, who borrowed the family car for an evening out, left the garage door open.

I-message: "Greg, when you leave the garage door open, I worry because we have so much valuable equipment stored there that could get stolen."

Sometimes, due to the nature of the situation you are addressing through an I-message, one of the three parts of an I-message will be left out. It's still an I-message and still effective. For example, "I'm not willing to cook in a kitchen when there are dishes in the sink," (I-message absent a feeling) or, "When you borrow my things without asking, I feel violated," (I-message minus a consequence) or, "I'm feeling hurt right now because I respect myself too much to be spoken to this way," (I-message minus identifying the specific concern).

Please note that while it's vital to avoid blame when using I-messages, and the word *you* can convey blame; using *you* to describe the situation, concern, or behavior is fine. The above situation with Greg is an example of using *you* in an appropriate way. "When you leave the garage door open . . ." is not placing blame, it merely states a fact.

When sending I-messages, be aware your child or teen will pick up not only the words you send, but also the tone of your voice and your body language. If your verbal and nonverbal messages are incongruent, your child will pay more attention to the nonverbal.

> When sending I-messages, be aware your child or teen will pick up not only the words you send, but also the tone of your voice and your body language.

Special Considerations for I-Messages

Talking too much during times of conflict or stress is a common mistake that parents make. Parents tend to talk the most when their children are misbehaving in some way. Whenever children are pursuing one of the goals of misbehavior discussed in chapter 2, it's time to keep communication to a minimum. Too much communication at these times reinforces the goals of misbehavior. A brief I-message, followed by action-oriented methods discussed elsewhere in this book, such as taking a time-out or offering choices or logical consequences are what's called for in these moments.

There are special considerations when we're feeling angry. An angry I-message is almost always perceived by the child as a vertical you-message. Why? Because, as you will learn in chapter 5, anger is often an emotion based on power we generate during times of threat. It's therefore very difficult to communicate effectively at the same time we are angry. Chapter 5 contains a number of effective options for responding to the challenges anger poses. One of them is to use I-messages. When doing so, it's important to monitor your tone of voice and body language.

Once you have sent an I-message, it's important to be prepared for a range of responses. Your child may acknowledge your statement and handle the problem. It also may be that your message creates a problem for your child who then communicates this concern. This is the time to utilize the listening skills such as reflective listening described earlier in the chapter:

Parent: When I noticed that you had been in my room, I was concerned because I value my privacy and thought we had an understanding about that.

Child: You and Mom have been in my room lately. I was just looking for a hairbrush in the bathroom.

Parent: Are you feeling like it's unfair for us to go into your room, but insist that you have to ask to enter ours?

Child: Right, and I don't think it's such a big deal when I'm just looking for something I need.

Parent: That's understandable. It's important for you to know that our agreement and my privacy matters to me. Now that I know it also matters to you, I can accept that we each have to ask before we go into each other's bedrooms.

Child: Okay, I'm sorry for going into your bedroom; I should have asked first.

Parent: Apology accepted, and thanks for talking with me about it.

To this point we have limited the use of I-messages to situations that present a problem for the parent. This same communication model can also be an encouraging way of expressing positive feelings. Remember that communication skills will be effective only to the extent that the whole relationship is characterized by encouragement and respect. Here are some examples of encouraging I-messages:

"When you come home on time, I feel so appreciative, because I'm glad to see you and it makes the whole evening go smoother for me."

"When you complete the chores for the week, I feel so proud about how nice the house looks."

"When you and your sister are treating each other so well, I feel grateful that there's peace and respect in our home."

A Natural Next Step to Connecting— Problem Solving

THE LISTENING SKILLS described earlier in this chapter, and the talking and sharing skills just described, are powerful tools to bring parents and kids closer together. These skills stand on their own merit because they increase the intimacy and respect between family members; they will add to the level of cooperation in the family and minimize the frequency of problems and conflict. Problems and conflicts will still arise, however, as they do in every family. At times, the communication skills just presented will naturally lead to a resolution of the problem. Other times, after connecting, an unresolved problem will remain.

A natural second step to reflective listening and I-messages is a mutual problem-solving process called exploring alternatives. While there will be many times when it's important to listen for the sake of listening and to send a respectful I-message, giving it time to sink in, there will be other times when a problem-solving discussion is necessary.

Exploring Alternatives: Mutual Problem-Solving Steps

The steps involved in problem solving are simple and logical. Parents, as leaders in the family, should have this important tool available and, by example, teach it to their kids. There will be plenty of opportunities for problem solving in regular day-to-day living, as well as during family meetings (described later in this chapter). The problem-solving steps of exploring alternatives are:[4]

1. **Clarify the problem.** What is the problem or concern? Who does it affect and how? What feelings are related to the problem?

2. **Explore alternative solutions.** What alternatives or options are there for responding to this challenge? This is a creative process. Too often we limit alternatives to the obvious and don't look "outside the box." It's therefore helpful to allow any and all alternatives to be identified no matter how relevant

or irrelevant. Use brainstorming—the free flow of ideas no matter how strange some may seem at the time. Just let the ideas come; hold your evaluation for the next step.

3. Evaluate the alternatives. Look at the consequences of each option. Weigh the advantages and disadvantages. Can more than one option be combined? Which alternative or combination of ideas is the best match to meet the challenge posed by the problem?

4. Agreement, commitment, and follow through. Is there sufficient agreement and motivation to commit to a course of action? If so, clarify the chosen option and confirm the commitment. Make plans to check back in with each other and evaluate how well things are working.

Exploring Alternatives When the Child Owns the Problem

When your child owns the problem and it is a pressing one, in addition to connecting through the use of listening skills, you can be an additional resource by offering an opportunity to address the child's problem or concern. Don't undermine this opportunity by trying to fix the problem for the child. It's far more encouraging and empowering to use your communication skills to help kids solve the problem for themselves. This is another way to help kids build their "psychological muscle." While keeping the exploring alternatives steps in

> It's far more encouraging and empowering to use your communication skills to help kids solve the problem for themselves.

mind, combined with listening skills and the use of relevant questions, parents can provide a rich opportunity to help kids seek answers to difficult challenges.

Avoid imposing this process on your kids. They may prefer to mull the problem over for a while or work on it on their own. After connecting with your child utilizing a listening skill such as reflective listening, you can determine her receptivity by using a door opener, an invitation to further address the issue. Here's an example of how a mom helped her 10-year-old solve a problem.

> R. J. was a whirlwind of activity—soccer, school clubs, church activities; you name it and R. J. was involved. One day she expressed her exasperation at trying to get everything done. Mom said, "It sounds like you're feeling overwhelmed with all of the responsibilities you're facing at once." "Right, and I can't seem to figure out how to do it all," replied R. J. Mom asked, "Would you like my help in trying to figure it out?"

If R. J. is agreeable, Mom can utilize the problem-solving steps, listening skills, and open-ended questions to help her work through the problem. Open-ended questions are questions that help the child to think through the situation; they are framed in an "open" versus "closed" manner. A closed question usually requires a limited yes or no answer and doesn't stimulate thinking. Questions such as, "Do you really think soccer is that important; you seldom get to play?" and, "Don't you think it's time to give up drama club?" are examples of closed questions. Open questions begin with words that stimulate the child's exploration ability: *who, what, when, where, how,* and *why.* (Be aware that *why* questions have the potential to come across as an accusation leading to defensiveness, so be careful with these). Open questions Mom could ask would be, "How many different activities are you involved in these days?" or, "Of your many activities, which do you consider to be the most satisfying?" or, "How do you feel about soccer?" Mom should also ask R. J. for her ideas on how to solve the problem. If necessary, Mom can make a suggestion.

As Mom continues to communicate through the exploring alternatives steps, and she and R. J. are getting closer to a solution, more focused closed questions are appropriate. An example would be, "It sounds to me like you've arrived at a decision to end at least one optional activity, is that right?"

The problem-solving process may or may not result in a conclusion. More time or more information may be necessary. Since this is the child's problem, it is important to accept the result—including an incomplete result or one that you don't happen to endorse. The child will experience the consequences of her decision, which is the best possible teacher.

Exploring Alternatives When the Parent Owns the Problem

Situations that create problems for parents can be handled in a number of ways as described throughout this book, such as disengaging from goals of misbehavior, utilizing anger management skills, and providing choices and consequences. One additional way is to invite your child into a problem-solving discussion employing the exploring alternatives steps. This is a very effective tool the older your children become and is especially useful with teens.

Once again, it is important not to impose this process on your child or teen. It may not be the right time to address the issue. After connecting with your child utilizing an I-message, followed by listening skills, you can open the door to further discuss the issue. For example, suppose your teen comes home late from a date.

Parent: When you come home late, I feel worried, because I don't know where you are and if you're safe.

Teen: I'm usually with Beth, and there's so much going on with her that we begin talking and I lose all track of time. I wish you could get that.

Parent: Are you feeling that I am not understanding or supportive of your friendship with Beth?

Teen: Kind of. It's not like I plan to be late.

Parent: I believe you. Can we try to work this out together?

Teen: Sure. I have an important call to make; can we talk after?

Parent: Okay, we'll talk just after your call. How long will you be on the phone?

Teen: Shouldn't be longer than 10 minutes. I'll come find you then.

The same communication and problem-solving skills used when the child owns the problem apply when you own the problem as well. The difference is, since you own the problem, you have a stake in the outcome—it must be acceptable to you as well as your child. In the above example, perhaps after you and your teen talk, the idea of his phoning when he's going to be late may be a decision you can both live with.

There may be times when it is not possible to arrive at a mutually agreeable solution. If this occurs, you may want to return to step 2 of the mutual problem-solving steps on pages 116 and 117. A respectful option when the situation, your tolerance level, and time permit, is to allow more time for both of you to think it over and discuss it again at a later time. An option when this is not feasible (in the absence of a mutual decision) is to make a decision yourself for now. You might say, "It seems as though we're not able to come to a mutual decision, so I'll make the decision for right now, and we can discuss it further at another time."

If either you or the child is in an emotionally reactive state prior to or during the mutual problem-solving discussion, it is best to postpone this process. When emotions are heated, the tendency is to see the discussion as a contest and try to win. This, of course, means the other person has to lose. So it's best to wait and discuss it later as this is a process designed to arrive at a mutually compatible solution.

Family Meetings: Building in Regular Time for Family Communication and Problem Solving

MANY FAMILIES FIND that holding a weekly meeting of all family members makes a positive difference in how well their families function. It is difficult for busy families to find quality time to connect, solve problems, plan activities, and encourage each other. Holding weekly family meetings provides "built in" assurance that quality time and positive connection happens.

Effective family meetings incorporate all of the skills outlined in this book: I-messages, reflective listening, exploring alternatives, encouragement, natural and logical consequences, civility skills, and anger management. The meetings give kids the sense they are participants in and co-shapers of their own family, their own world. It's empowering for them to have a part in the decisions that affect them.

In a manner similar to any business meeting, family meetings work best with some structure. The following steps are recommended, yet not intended to limit what will work best for your family:

1. **Identify the roles for this meeting.**

   Chair: The leader and facilitator of the meeting (in younger families this is usually a parent, as kids grow older they can be rotated in as chair along with the parents).

Minutes taker. A person designated to jot down the highlights of the meeting, such as decisions and plans.

Time keeper. Keeps an eye on the clock, announcing when the meeting is half over, when five minutes remain and when the maximum time period has been reached.

2. Check in. Make the rounds, having each person briefly share how his life is going and how he is feeling at the moment. For example, a child might tell you something like this: "I'm mostly doing well lately, and I'm really proud of how well the choir is doing. But I'm worried about the upcoming math test." During check-in, restrict any comments to asking for clarification and demonstrating empathy. Avoid evaluations or recommendations at this point.

It's important that everyone feels free to "pass" and not share or speak to a question or issue. Forcing participation reduces motivation and cooperation. Allowing for and accepting nonparticipation on any topic is the ultimate in respect and increases communication in the long run.

3. Old business. Read the minutes of the previous meeting. Discuss how solutions or plans agreed upon at the previous meeting are going. What worked well? Celebrate your success. What didn't work well? Identify the barriers. Does the family want to stick with their decisions or change them? Does the solution require more time for everyone to "get on board" and do their part? If change or modification is desired, follow the mutual problem-solving steps covered earlier to arrive at a new decision. Acknowledge and encourage any progress.

4. New business. Set the agenda for this week's meeting. You may want to ask an open-ended question. "How are things going around here?" Review agenda items members have suggested during the week and add them to the new business. Include not only concerns and problems, but also updates on who is doing what, individual and family accomplishments, and plans for future fun activities.

5. Problem solve. Discuss any new issues using the "exploring alternatives" steps outlined earlier in this chapter.

6. Summarize and evaluate the meeting. Call for a summary and evaluation. Make the rounds with the question: "How did today's meeting go?" Allow everyone to comment. Be open to ideas for improving future meetings. Every few meetings it is helpful to discuss how family meetings are going in general and what improvements are desired with respect to format, topics discussed, quality of communication, and so forth.

7. Share appreciations. Ask everyone to share appreciations about the family. This a way to keep the meeting from being too problem-focused. Again, it's important to accept nonparticipation. If someone is left out of the appreciations, be ready to share your appreciations to that member.

8. Set up the next meeting. Confirm when the next meeting is and who will occupy which roles.

Based on our experience the following additional recommendations will add the success of family meetings:

- Meet the same day and time each week, whenever possible, and meet for a designated period of time, such as thirty minutes to an hour. If you have young children, meet for fifteen or twenty minutes. We recommend that meetings not be held during mealtime.

- Maintain the principle of mutual respect throughout.

- Focus on "solving the problem" instead of "who is to blame."

- Work toward consensus whenever possible. The guiding principle is: "We can work it out."

- Maintain a creative and experimental environment: "What can we agree upon that we can do for just one week?" You can always change decisions at a future family meeting.

- Use the family meeting to distribute family chores in a respectful way.

- Maintain a positive atmosphere. Strike a balance between addressing issues and solving problems, and planning fun activities and encouraging one another.

Communication Skills in Action

Twelve-year-old Justin arrives home from school again in what appears to be a foul mood, looking and acting frustrated. He passes by his mom without acknowledging her presence, straight to his bedroom and slams the door. Mom, who realizes Justin has been acting rude and disrespectful lately and has "had enough," goes right in after him and without knocking barges into Justin's room. "What been bugging you lately? (without waiting for a reply) And who do you think you are acting so selfish, like you're the only one who matters in this world? I've about had it with you!"

Mom's communication certainly won't win Justin's cooperation. She's ignoring the clues that something's bothering her son and assuming he's just being rude. She doesn't bother to connect with Justin to see what's eating him. Imagine how the rest of the afternoon and evening might go for Justin and the rest of the family with this as the first interaction after school. Imagine how Justin's life and family might be affected day after day and year after year with this as the pattern of communication.

Suppose Mom took a different look and used different tactics to relate to her son. Let's rewrite the story with a brand new mom who's read this book.

Mom realizes that Justin has been discouraged lately and is concerned enough to want to connect with him about it. She knocks on Justin's door.

Mom: Justin, may I come in? (door opener; Justin says yes.) I've noticed that you have been down about something lately. (reflective listening) I'm worried about you. (I-message)

Justin: Not now, Mom. I just don't feel like talking.

Mom: That's okay. Can I check in with you later this evening? What about after dinner?(door opener)

Justin: That's fine with me. Mom, thanks for understanding.

Later that evening after dinner and cleanup:

Mom: Justin, can we talk now? (door opener).

Justin: I guess so.

Mom: Can you tell me what is going on with you lately? (door opener)

Justin: It's school; nothing seems to be going well.

Mom: Is it that everything isn't going well or is there something specific that's bothering you? (clarifying)

Justin: Well actually, it's Mrs. Gibbons and also math class.

Mom: Tell me about it. (door opener)

Justin: Mrs. Gibbons seems to have it in for me. I'm always in trouble with her. Today she sent me to detention for talking in class and all I was doing was helping the person next to me understand the assignment.

Mom: You're feeling picked on by Mrs. Gibbons? (reflective listening)

Justin: Right, and it doesn't seem like there's anything I can do to make it better.

Mom: Do you want to talk about it? (door opener—invitation to problem solving)

Justin: Sure.

Mom: What have you tried so far to work things out with her? (open-ended question)

Justin: What do you mean?

Mom: Well, in addition to trying to get along with her on a daily basis, what else have you done? (open-ended question)

Justin: Nothing really.

Mom: What alternatives are available to a student having this kind of problem? (open-ended question—exploring alternatives, step #2, through brainstorming by getting Justin's ideas)

Justin: Well, I could make an appointment with her and talk about it.

Mom: Anything else? (open-ended question)

Justin: I could talk to the principal about it.

Mom: Okay, those are two ideas. Anything else? (Justin shakes his head no.) Which do you think would work out best, taking both you and Mrs. Gibbons into account? (open-ended question—evaluating the alternatives, step #3)

Justin: If I were Mrs. Gibbons, I'd rather have a student come to me directly before going to the principal.

Mom: That's really perceptive of you. You could always consider talking to the principal if you're not able to work things out directly with Mrs. Gibbons. Just so you know, Dad and I would be glad to meet with you and Mrs. Gibbons if things don't get better. (encouragement—evaluating alternatives, step #3)

Justin: That's good to know.

Mom: Will you check in with me after you speak with Mrs. Gibbons and tell me how things are going? (open-ended question—agreement, commitment, and follow-through, step #4)

Justin: I will, and thanks, Mom.

Mom and Justin also discuss math for a few minutes and come to the conclusion that Justin needs some tutoring assistance. They make a plan to discover what tutoring resources are available at school and in the community. Dad comes in while they're talking, and Justin fills him in. Dad's very supportive of Justin's courage to talk with his teacher and says he knows about a math tutor because the daughter of a friend of his had needed help in math and was tutored by a capable person.

What a difference a change in communication can make! It's not how many problems families face that matters, since all have their share. What makes the difference is how problems are dealt with through the pattern of communication and family relationships. The difference between vertical communication and level communication is like night and day. With Justin's parents offering leadership in a respectful and level manner, can you recognize the difference in how life is likely to go for him? While Justin is still discouraged about his difficulties, he has allies in his parents and is not alone with his challenges. Through communication skills that connect with Justin in a

> It's not how many problems families face that matters, since all have their share. What makes the difference is how problems are dealt with through the pattern of communication and family relationships.

respectful and empowering way, he has the support and courage to improve his life.

Parents tend to overvalue their own ability to arrive at solutions to daily problems and undervalue their children's ability. If you take the time to seriously listen to your kids and consider what they have to offer, you may be surprised by the many good ideas they have. Sometimes they'll come up with ideas you haven't considered. When children are given the opportunity to participate in problem solving and thereby participate in shaping their own lives and the life of their family, they are being prepared to face their future with optimism, hope, and a belief in their own ability.

Younger kids can participate in negotiation of parent-owned problems when it's kept simple. Often this means giving a choice between options that are acceptable to you for solving the problem.

Communicating Through "Eye Messages"

I-MESSAGES ARE AN important communication skill. Yet, as we mentioned earlier, kids attend even more to what parents are communicating nonverbally, through tone of voice and body language. While the customs about eye contact vary from culture to culture, we all pick up what the eyes are communicating. When your child returns home or when you arrive home from work and you first make eye contact, what message are you sending through your eyes? Are they sending the message you are happy to see your child and you are on her side, or do you store up frustration and anger and send a different message?

Each day offers a new opportunity to improve and strengthen our family relationships. What we send through our "eye messages" is mostly a function of attitude and choice.

As challenging as it may be at times, we can choose our attitude toward every situation and every person. What our kids see when they look into our eyes is most significant, affecting the parent-child relationship and their self-concept.

One of the authors is reminded of a time when his son was going through some serious problems that affected the whole family. There was a period of tension and alienation as the family struggled through this time together. One day the son said to his dad, "I can't stand what I see when you look at me.

> What our kids see when they look into our eyes is most significant, affecting the parent-child relationship and their self-concept.

It's like you aren't even glad to have me around. I long for the day when you look at me as you used to, with love and with pride!" That's all it took for this dad to begin to work on his attitude and his "eye messages." While it may have been a coincidence, after much effort that resulted in Dad making a shift in his attitude, as well as the "eye messages" he began to send, his son began to make a positive shift in his life.

In this chapter we've discussed effective communication skills such as knocking, clarifying, reflective listening, I-messages, and exploring alternatives. These skills allow you to connect and effectively solve problems with your kids. We've also discussed using your communication skills to conduct family meetings. Chapter 5 presents specific techniques to help you deal with your anger, as well as suggestions for helping your kids with their anger.

5

Anger
Management for
You and Your Kids

We don't lose our tempers,
we throw them away.
—RUDOLF DREIKURS

A NGER IS EVERYWHERE. Our cities, roads, restaurants, and grocery stores are often overcrowded. We're
spending more time waiting in line. Manners and respect for
others are suffering; we're becoming more selfish, wanting
things our own way—rage is all the rage. "The media report incidents of road rage, airplane rage, biker rage, surfer rage, grocery store rage, rage at youth sports activities."[1] Some of this
rage erupts into violent incidents like physical altercations between drivers and among youth sports fans (parents), sometimes ending in death.

Everyone's in a hurry, there's too little time and too much to
do, tempers flare. Technology, which is supposed to save time,

often invades our space and takes time. You have a cell phone and you receive even more calls than before you had one. The number of e-mails you find when you get to work is staggering.

Numerous daily incidents like these, not to mention phone sales calls, red tape, people acting stupid, uncooperative kids—you name it—can incite our ire. But does getting angry help us or hurt us? And what example are we setting for our kids?

Think of times when someone is angry with you. How do you respond? You probably feel blamed or afraid. You may think you're a bad person or that the person who is angry with you is a bad person. Rarely do you think, "Oh, well, I goofed. The person just doesn't like this behavior. I'm okay as a human being." You may get angry back, leading to a conflict.

Kids feel the same way. Anger can discourage them. They may think they're bad kids even though you are simply angry at a particular behavior. When we occasionally get angry with our kids, they may do what we want. But frequent anger often fails to impress them. If we get any cooperation, it's usually short-lived.

Anger often provokes power and revenge contests with kids. This is because (as we said in chapter 1) kids today picture themselves as equals and often resist and rebel against any effort to dominate them. Also, our kids have learned they can get us angry about certain things. Even though we may punish them, they still feel in control because they provoked us to anger. So anger often reinforces the uncivil behavior you don't want.

> Anger often reinforces the uncivil behavior you don't want.

Your anger can give your children a model for handling problems. If they see you getting angry with them, your spouse, neighbors, and so forth, they may see this as the way to handle disturbing situations.

Anger is the energy to carry out violent acts. Parents or kids who frequently get angry often act on the anger. This can lead to an escalation of the conflict possibly leading to verbal or physical violent acts. Too much anger in relationships can teach kids to act only when someone is angry with them.

> A woman was standing on a street corner waiting for a bus. A little girl was playing nearby. Another woman leaned out the window of the apartment building above where the little girl was playing. "Jenny, time for lunch." The little girl continued playing. The woman leaned out the window and called again, "Jenny, time for lunch." The little girl continued playing. This happened another time; Mom calling out the window and the little girl continuing to play. Finally, the woman waiting for the bus asked the girl, "Pardon me, but is your name Jenny?" "Yes," replied the little girl. "Don't you hear your mother calling you for lunch?" "Yes, but I don't have to go yet," replied the girl. "Why not?" asked the woman. Jenny replied, "Because she hasn't yelled yet."

The Myths Surrounding Anger

PEOPLE GENERALLY MISUNDERSTAND emotions. They see them as magical and mystical. Anger, the most misunderstood emotion, is surrounded by myths.[2]

Myth 1: We Are Born Aggressive

People justify this belief by pointing to our warlike nature. They don't realize that wars usually occur because of economic, religious, or political conflicts. Those who believe humans are naturally aggressive fail to see that society has advanced more through cooperation than through war.

Myth 2: Holding Back Anger Hurts Our Health

Some people believe that if we hold anger in, we're doing damage to our health; therefore, we should express it. But the problem is not the *direction* of the anger; it's the anger itself. Chronic anger is hazardous to your health. It puts a strain on the heart, and can cause high blood pressure, stomach distress, and a host of other problems.

Myth 3: Expressing Anger Is Cathartic

Unless they are on the receiving end, some people think letting anger out is cathartic and therefore "good for the soul." But does it really feel good to express a negative emotion? Expressing negative emotions can lead to more negative emotions, such as guilt.

Myth 4: We Should Get Rid of Our Anger by Acting It Out

Does the angry feeling really "go out"? Angry behavior begets angry behavior. The more one is angry, the more one practices being angry and is therefore likely to continue responding in angry ways. Acting angry toward others, beating pillows, or screaming to "get the anger out," only reinforces being angry. It is good to find out if you are acting out of angry feelings, but the next step is managing your anger, not "outing" it.

Why Do We Get Angry?

MANY SEE THEMSELVES as victims of their own emotions or see their emotions as caused by others. It is so common to hear people say, "I can't help being angry," or, "You make me feel angry." This common view represents "emotional irresponsibility"—a major factor in rude behavior. We see emotions quite differently—we believe in the importance of emotional responsibility, which is a major component of mutual respect. Remember the "3 R's"? Respect for self, respect for others, and responsibility for all actions.

We're not victims of internal drives or our environment. We make decisions about what we think, do, and feel. Emotions are actually a form of energy; we use them to fuel our behavior. The emotions we generate are based on our beliefs. If we believe people are basically friendly and trustworthy, we'll create positive emotions such as warmth and compassion to invite people to be close to us. But if we believe people are unfriendly and can't be trusted, we'll generate hostile emotions such as anger to encourage people to keep their distance.[3]

> Emotions are actually a form of energy; we use them to fuel our behavior. The emotions we generate are based on our beliefs.

So anger, like all emotions, is within our control. We're in charge or our anger, just like we're in charge of our behavior. Consider this: You're in a shouting match with one of your kids and you get a phone call from your boss. Do you shout at your boss? Not likely; you probably become calm immediately.

Taking Responsibility for Your Anger

IF YOU ARE to manage your anger, you must first take responsibility for the emotion. Taking responsibility involves examining and reconsidering the purpose of your anger, identifying and changing your beliefs, recognizing your anger "triggers," and avoiding jumping to conclusions.

Examine and Reconsider the Purpose of Your Anger

Anger is a power move designed to get others to do what you want. We find anger serves four purposes or goals:

1. To win

2. To control

3. To get even

4. To protect your rights

Trying to win an argument or disagreement with your kids can create resentment and rebellion. But there don't have to be winners and losers in relationships. If you're in a conflict with your kids, look for ways to settle the conflict on a win-win basis. What changes are you willing to make? When you focus on what you will do rather than what your kids will do, you'll find your anger disappearing. You can then calmly negotiate a solution that is acceptable to all parties.

If you want to be in control, consider the price you pay. Trying to make kids do what you want just sets up power contests and encourages kids to defy you. Instead of getting angry and trying to force compliance, set limits and let the child choose within those limits. Concentrate your desire to control on controlling your anger.

> Concentrate your desire to control on controlling your anger.

When you feel hurt or put down, you may use anger to get even. But, if you get even with your child, you can be sure he will get even with you. Realize that if your child has done something that you find hurtful, it's likely that the child is also hurting, whether or not you've done anything hurtful to the child. Consider how you can improve the relationship so you won't feel the need to hurt each other. Find areas of nonconflict where you can enjoy being with your child.

If someone interferes with your rights, anger is one approach. But you have to weigh the consequences of your response. Will the other person respond the way you want her to? Or will your anger make things worse? You can protect your rights without becoming angry. Set your limits. State what you're willing to do or not willing to do. "I'll prepare dinner once the kitchen is cleaned up."

Sometimes protecting one's rights may also involve protecting one's self-esteem or person, as in instances of emotional and physical abuse. Anger can be used to get the attacker to back off. There may also be times when a parent has to protect his children from others. Anger can serve that purpose as well. But sometimes the anger in these situations can make things worse. Seeking professional help may be the best alternative in these instances, for example, an abusive relationship or kids using drugs.

The Beliefs Associated with Anger

Think of a time when others were angry, but you remained calm. Obviously you and the others were looking at the situation differently. We *feel* as we *believe,* so if we think angry or "hot" thoughts we're going to be angry. Likewise, if we think calm or "cool" thoughts, we're going to be calm. We can choose how we wish to view a situation.

"Hot" Thoughts

If a person is angry, she has created "hot" thoughts. We can say that the person has a case of the MADS. The MADS is a simple formula for understanding how we create hot thoughts and actually talk ourselves into anger.

M: Minimizing your personal power. An angry person believes: "I can't stand it." "I can't help being angry." "He made me." "I lost my temper." "Something came over me." "I'm not myself today." Or the person gives ethnic or cultural excuses such as, "I'm Irish," "I'm Italian," and so forth. Such beliefs render one powerless to manage his anger.

A: Awfulizing. Angry people tell themselves: "This is awful, terrible, horrible, catastrophic." They make "mountains out of molehills."

D: Demanding. The angry person makes demands on herself or others, or life itself: He, she, or it should, must, or needs to be different. Or the person declares things must "always" happen or "never" happen. She won't accept others or life as is. She demands it be "my way."

S: Shaming and blaming. An angry person shames and blames others, life, or himself for the problem: "You're worthless." "Life's worthless." "I'm worthless." "You're a rotten kid."

You can see that minimizing your power, awfulizing, demanding, shaming and blaming will certainly make you angry. Let's look at an example of how this hot thinking works in a parent-child conflict.

Dad constantly had battles with eight-year-old Keith about bedtime. Keith wanted to stay up late and Dad wanted him to go to bed so Keith would get enough rest for school the next day. Plus, Dad and Mom wanted some time alone. Each evening would start off with reminders about bedtime and end up with Dad being angry, ordering Keith to bed, physically taking him there if necessary and locking the door. Keith would scream through the whole process.

Let's examine what Dad might be thinking to make himself angry about Keith's refusal to go to bed. He might be thinking, "I can't stand this kid not going to bed when I tell him to." (Minimizing his personal power) "It's terrible that he won't do what I tell him." (Awfulizing) "He should go to bed when I tell him to." (Demanding) "He's a bratty kid for not going to bed on time." (Shaming and blaming)

Obviously, if Dad tells himself something like this, he's going to be pretty angry. Hostile or hot thoughts like Dad's create anger. You reinforce your anger by constantly repeating your hot thoughts. The more you think in hot ways, the angrier you get.

When we notice the MADS, we can say to ourselves things such as the following: "I can manage." "Things are okay." "We are all going to be okay." "I am going to hang on with good communication."

Creating "Cool" Thoughts

If you concentrate on changing your internal language, you can change your beliefs. It's not just changing the words, however; you really have to *believe* your new language in order to change your beliefs and create less anger.

In our example of Keith, Dad made himself angry by minimizing his personal power, demanding, awfulizing, shaming and blaming. If Dad changed his thinking to something like this, his feelings would change: "I don't like it that he won't go to bed when I tell him to, but I can stand it. It's unfortunate that he won't do what I tell him. I would really prefer him to go to bed when I tell him to. But he's not a bratty kid, he's just being stubborn about bedtime."

If Dad told himself this instead of his angry thinking, he'd have "cool" thoughts. Although his cool thoughts wouldn't produce happy feelings, he wouldn't be angry. He certainly would feel disappointed and perhaps annoyed and frustrated, but these are milder feelings than anger.

Our demands, our shoulds and musts, get us in all kinds of trouble. Whenever we make demands on how our kids should be, we set ourselves up for disappointment. And the disappointment associated with demands is more than disappointment; it's anger. We see the situation as unfair because we believe our kids should do what we want them to. If you believe this, then you're in for considerable disappointment and a heavy dose of anger.

Instead, we can change our self-talk. We can see our demands for what they really are: wishes. We *wish* or *prefer* our kids would do what we want them to, but this is very different from demanding they do so. Our wishes are not our commands; they are just the way we prefer things happen.

> Whenever we make demands on how our kids should be, we set ourselves up for disappointment.

Psychologist Albert Ellis tells us that instead of complaining that we can't stand something our kids do, we can tell ourselves, and honestly believe, that while we don't like it, and will probably never like it, we can stand it.[4] We do have the personal power to change our beliefs.

When our demands are not met, we often see the situation as intolerable—"It's awful, terrible, catastrophic" when the kids don't do what we demand they do. But that's not reality either. A kid's death would be catastrophic and horrible, but failing to do what we want hardly qualifies as a catastrophe; it's only *unfortunate* and *inconvenient*.

Finally, judging our kids as bad for failing to meet our demands defies logic. Does that mean they are good for doing what we want them to? Judging our kids as bad or good implies that they are always that way. Do you know any people who are always good or always bad? We all do both good and bad things. As you learned in chapter 3, it's vital to accept your children as they are, not just as they could be or as you want them to be. You separate the deed from the doer, judging the behavior, not the child. So instead of thinking that he is a bad kid, tell yourself that your child is *okay;* it's just the behavior that concerns you. As Keith's father would say, "He's not a bratty kid; he's just being stubborn."

> It's vital to accept your children as they are, not just as they could be or as you want them to be.

Reframing

Reframing is another way to change your beliefs and your angry feelings. To reframe something is to look at a situation in a different way. You put another "frame" on it. In the example of Keith refusing to go to bed, Dad could reframe the situation by seeing Keith as a determined little guy who knows what he wants, even if some things he wants aren't in his best interests. Still, being determined has some positive features. If Dad looks at it this way, there's no need for Dad to create hot, angry thoughts. Instead, Dad can consider how to teach Keith the benefits of going to bed at a reasonable time. Perhaps the best way is to let him stay up and experience the consequences of going to school tired. A few days of being tired may do the teaching for Dad.

In the meantime, Dad and Mom can get time for themselves by going to their room and leaving Keith up. Or the parents could stay up, but focus their attention elsewhere such as watch-

Watch Your Language!

Here are some examples of mad, "hot" internal language and calm, "cool" thoughts.

"Hot" Thoughts	"Cool" Thoughts
I can't stand it, can't take it, can't handle it; it's too much.	I don't like it but I can stand it, take it, handle it; it's tough but I'll survive it.
Awful, terrible, horrible, catastrophic.	Frustrating, disappointing, inconvenient, annoying.
Should, must, need, always, never.	Prefer, wish, it would be better if, sometimes.
The child is bad, rotten, bratty, worthless, lazy, stupid, or any other names we call kids.	The child is not bad, not (negative name you called the child); the child is okay in spite of the bad behavior.

ing TV, listening to music, working on a project, and so on. The point is that after a bedtime has been discussed with Keith, when that time comes, the parents say goodnight, and from that point on, they assume Keith is in bed. Spending some positive time with Keith before bedtime can help prevent bedtime hassles.

Reframing often involves seeing the positive potential in the negative. It can also involve seeing an opportunity in a distressing situation. In Keith's case, Dad could see an opportunity for Keith to learn the value of getting enough sleep. This approach could be applied in other areas of Keith's life, too. Let him experience the consequences of his choices.

When you encounter a problem with your child, think about reframing. Ask yourself "What's positive in this situation?" For example, if your child is argumentative, at least she won't be pushed around; she'll stand up for herself. Ask yourself, "What's the opportunity in the situation?" In other words, how can you help your child learn responsibility? Finally, if you become angry over a situation, after it's over you can reframe the situation by asking yourself, "What did I learn from this?" This is much better than blaming yourself for being angry.

> When you encounter a problem with your child, think about reframing. Ask yourself "What's positive in this situation?"

Let's look at an example of how you could change your hot thoughts to cool thoughts and reframe a situation. Suppose you and your six-year-old are shopping for a birthday present for Grandma. You've told your child that getting a gift for Grandma is the purpose of the trip. When you get in the store, your child begs you to go to the toy department. She wants a new toy she's seen advertised on TV. You remind your daughter of the purpose of the shopping trip. She whines and complains that all her friends' parents will buy them the toy and she'll be left out.

You're worried about other's opinions of your parenting skills; you're feeling embarrassed and angry. You may be telling yourself something like, "I can't stand this. All these people must think I'm a terrible parent. This is awful. She knew the purpose of the trip, and she should not be embarrassing me this way. Just wait till I get this little brat home!"

Of course, if you told yourself these things, you'd be pretty mad. But, what if you told yourself this instead: "I don't like this, but I can stand it, hard as it is in front of others. It's annoying she's behaving this way but it's not awful. I wish she'd stick to the purpose of this trip so we can get out of here. She's a good kid most of the time, but this behavior is unacceptable." If you told yourself this, you would probably be embarrassed and annoyed, but you wouldn't be angry.

Now, how could you reframe the situation? Parents are vulnerable in public. They worry about what others must think. Consider there are three possible scenarios: Some will be thinking, "Poor parent, I know how that is." Others will be thinking, "There but for the grace of God go I." And some will be thinking, "What a lousy parent. My child would never do that!"

The first two aren't a problem; you can accept their empathy. But the third one; what do you do about people who think that? Despite any embarrassment you might feel, first realize that it's none of your business what others think of you. Second, if a person has to look down on you, then he must be feeling one down. If this is the case, then you're doing this poor soul a favor—by looking down on you the person can feel good for a while! Also realize that worrying about what strangers are thinking is immaterial to your outing with your daughter. What you want to deal with is your daughter's immaturity, not that of strangers (or your own).

What could you do in this situation? After calmly reminding your daughter of the purpose of the trip, concentrate on the task, ignoring her whining about the toy. Or, if her behavior is obstructive, you could take her by the hand, lead her out of the store, and go home, leaving the shopping until later.

Become Aware of Your Triggers

We all have things that trigger our anger. Being tired, busy, in a hurry, feeling backed into a corner, getting interrupted, making mistakes, or seeing something as unfair can trigger one's anger. Triggers can be situations that remind you of similar incidents in the past when you've been angry. A trigger can be a look, a gesture, a tone of voice. Sometimes, your child may have mannerisms or do things that remind you of someone you don't like. Realize that your child is *not* that person.

> Triggers can be situations that remind you of similar incidents in the past when you've been angry.

Becoming aware of your triggers enables you to be on guard when those triggers happen. When you notice that look or stance and begin to feel your hackles rise, back off. Give yourself a mental or physical break by taking yourself out of the situation.

Avoid Jumping to Conclusions

Sometimes we may misjudge our child's or another person's comments or actions. We don't bother to check out our assumptions; we simply conclude the person meant what we think he meant. When we jump to conclusions, we may be prone to unjustified anger. Think of times when you've made invalid assumptions with your kids. How could you have avoided the misunderstanding?

How to Manage Your Anger

ANGER IS OFTEN a rude response to a situation that could be handled in a respectful way. But anger is not all bad; sometimes it's the best response. Occasional anger; expressed in an appropriate way, can be healthy for your body and for a relationship. The problem is not occasional anger; it's chronic anger. The challenge becomes when to be angry and when to make other choices.

Examine the Consequences of Your Anger

Consider whether your anger helps or hurts in a particular situation. Will being angry encourage cooperation and put a stop to damaging behavior, or will it make matters worse? Would it be better to decide not to be angry and seek another approach to gain cooperation? Only you know how your kids will take your anger and whether it's best to express it or to learn how to stop angry thoughts.

Expressing Anger with I-Messages

If you decide it's best to express your anger in certain situations, you can send an I-message. For example, you're with your four-year-old in the mall and she wanders off. When you find her you could say, "When you wander off, I get very angry because something might have happened to you." Or, you could identify the feeling behind your anger—probably fear—and express that instead. "When you wander off, I can't take care of you and I get very scared because something might happen to you." Your expression of the fear will probably get more cooperation than being angry with the child.

Anger is a secondary emotion. That is, it comes after another emotion you experience first. Some common feelings related to anger are:

afraid	frustrated	overwhelmed
blamed	guilty	pressured
challenged	hurried	put upon
cheated	hurt	threatened
embarrassed	mistreated	

The more you can identify the feeling behind the anger and express it, the better chance you have at cooperation because the child is less likely to feel attacked. For example, suppose your child is pestering you to make a decision on something he wants to do. You could say, "I'm feeling pressured right now to give you an answer, and I need to think about it. I'll let you know in an hour." Contrast this to, "Get off my back or the answer is no!"

But if you find that in certain situations expressing your anger is the best response, you can still use an I-message to express it (unless it's an emergency; then you say whatever you have to). Remember an I-message involves three parts: "When _____, I feel _____, because _____." For example, suppose in a family meeting everyone has agreed to clean up after snacking, and later you find your kids have left the family room in a mess. You could say, "When I find crumbs on the family room couch and floor, I feel angry because we agreed people would clean up after snacking." Sometimes, depending on how your kids take it, you may want to add an "I wish" or "I'd appreciate it" or "I'd prefer" statement to your I-message: ". . . and I wish you'd keep our agreement."

There are several techniques you can use to stop angry thinking. The techniques work best when you use them in combination.

Technique #1: Logging Your Anger

Keep a log of your angry incidents. After each angry incident, rate your anger on a scale from 1 to 10 with 1 being the lowest, such as being annoyed, and 10 the highest, such as experiencing rage. Make a brief description of each angry incident. That way, you can see which types of situations have high scores and low scores. Jot down your thinking at the time of the incident. You can then see the influence of your thoughts on your scores. If high-scoring incidents happen several times a day or week, you may find that as you make the log your score will start lowering because you naturally monitor yourself. If so, note what new thoughts helped you lower your score. If the score

Catch It, Check It, Change It

Psychiatrist Aaron T. Beck recommends a three C's process for dealing with negative beliefs:[5]

Catch it. Identify what you are telling yourself that makes you angry.

Check it. Evaluate your thinking. What evidence do you have that you can't stand this, that it's awful, that your child must do what you want, that she's a rotten kid? What's the evidence to the contrary? You've stood it before; it's unfortunate but hardly qualifies as "awful." You wish she would do what you want, but what's the reason why the child should? What makes the child a rotten kid? What are the good things you can list about her? How can you reframe the situation?

Change it. Now create new beliefs or "cool" thoughts, changing your demands to preferences: "I wish" or "I prefer"; seeing the situation as unfortunate rather than awful; deciding you can stand it; seeing your child as an okay kid even though you don't like the behavior.

remains about the same or goes higher, note how you're maintaining your anger.

Keep recording and rating incidents in your log. Write out how you made yourself angry in the situation. What did you say to yourself about the situations? How did you minimize your power, awfulize, make demands, shame and blame?

Anger Log

Here's a way you could log your anger-provoking incidents. Use a notebook. Set it up this way:

1. What happened? (What my child did, what I did, and how my child responded to my behavior.)

2. How angry was I? (Rate from 1 to 10.)

3. My "hot" angry thoughts—what I told myself about the situation. (*Catch it.*)

4. What evidence do I have to support my belief? What evidence do I have to the contrary? (*Check it.*)

5. Cool thoughts I could have had—what could I have told myself instead? (*Change it.*)

6. How would I feel if I told myself these cool thoughts?

7. How could I reframe the incident (another way to change your thoughts)?

8. How would I feel if I reframed it this way?

9. How could I behave in a nonangry way?

Record your hot thoughts. What could you tell yourself instead? What cool thoughts could you create? How would you feel then? Look for ways to reframe the incident. Decide what action you could take besides being angry.

Technique #2: Deep Breathing and Relaxation

When you find yourself feeling angry, stop and take a few deep breaths. If you're angry or feeling stressed, your breathing usu-

Relaxation Exercise

Lie down or sit in a comfortable chair with head support. Take several deep breaths until you're feeling calm. Then start to relax your muscles. Begin with your head, face, neck, and shoulders. Tense each area and then relax it. Then proceed with your upper and lower arms, hands, and fingers. Move on to your chest, stomach, and upper and lower back. Finally, tense and relax your buttocks, thighs, calves, ankles, feet, and toes. Tense each section for five seconds. Slowly release the tension and say to yourself, "Relax and let go." Build relaxation exercises or activities into your daily routine.[6]

ally comes in short bursts. By forcing yourself to take deep breaths, you can calm yourself down. It also helps to mentally count to 10 slowly. You can't concentrate on hot thoughts while you're concentrating on breathing and counting.

Relaxation takes many forms. Some people find a bath relaxing; others find physical activity like jogging relaxing. Do what works for you. You can also practice simple breathing and relaxation exercises.

Technique #3: Visualization and Self-Talk

Visualization helps you prepare for anger-provoking events. Visualization and self-talk work together, so it's important for you to think of some positive, relaxing self-talk before you visualize. For example, you could tell yourself, "Take it easy, calm down, be respectful, relax, stay cool, be specific, stick to the point, work for the win-win, maintain mutual respect, chill out."

Start by using a situation in which you feel annoyed or mildly irritated—one you scored low in your log. As you successfully deal with such a situation, you can gradually move up to high-scoring situations.

Begin your visualizations with deep breathing to relax. Create a recent scene or one that frequently occurs. See and hear yourself and the child. When you begin to feel angry, use your self-talk phrases. Repeat the scene until you feel calm.

If you have trouble inserting your self-talk, you can forcibly interrupt your angry thoughts by silently shouting, "Stop!" or, "Get out!" Do this until you've successfully gotten rid of your anger. Then insert your positive phrases. In effect you are getting angry at your anger—a positive use of anger.

> You can use visualization and self-talk to prepare for expected anger-provoking behavior.

You can use visualization and self-talk to prepare for expected anger-provoking behavior. Practice your visualizations for about ten minutes three times a day until you notice significant improvement.

Technique #4: Use Your Sense of Humor

Humor defuses anger. It's impossible to laugh and be angry at the same time (unless one is maliciously laughing at someone else, of course). As Bill Cosby says, "You can turn painful situations around through laughter. If you can find humor in anything, you can survive it."

Recall a past angry incident: What humor can you find in the incident? If this were a sitcom, how would you make the incident funny? Develop some humorous self-talk or humorous visualizations to keep in your toolbox for when your kids' behavior invites your anger. Write them in your log. When future anger-provoking incidents occur, ask yourself, "What can I find that's funny about this?"

Technique #5: Develop Empathy

Put your focus on the child instead of yourself. "What might be the purpose of this behavior?" If you're angry, remember the child's goal is usually power and sometimes revenge. You can also ask yourself, "Does my child think I'm being unfair?" "Is there something in our past relationship that is influencing this behavior?" "What does my child expect me to do?" "If I get mad and punish my child, what will be the most likely outcome?"

Maybe your child is going through something outside your relationship that's contributing to the misbehavior. Perhaps he's having a problem getting along with a peer or a teacher. If you suspect there's an outside influence, ask, "You seem pretty upset, want to tell me about it?" Then listen. Use the listening skills you learned in chapter 4. Explore alternatives with him if necessary.

Technique #6: Recall Past Successes

Were there times in the past when you were tempted to be angry with your kids but you kept your cool? Note these in your log. Figure out how you did it. What were you telling yourself? Write the answers in your log.

The more exceptions you can find to your usual angry way of responding, the better. These exceptions show you that you are capable of avoiding anger. Analyzing your thought processes helps you see how you did it and how this knowledge can apply to future provocations.

Technique #7: Develop a "To Do" List for Angry Situations

In your log, write down what you can do the next time you start feeling angry—things like breathing deeply, positive self-talk, taking a walk, counting to ten, and any other things you've learned in this chapter or from your own experience. Create some new ideas of your own as well.

Handling Anger in the Heat of the Moment

Many of the things listed above can be used when you're alone with your thoughts. You can also keep these in reserve for when your kids catch you off guard. Positive self-talk and humor can be kept on hand. You can develop some brief visualizations to have in reserve as well. A picture of a calm lake or of yourself by the seashore—whatever you find relaxing—will help you diffuse your anger.

Become aware of your body language. With practice, you can learn how to quickly tune into your body language and learn what your body is trying to tell you as well as what it's communicating to others. For example, when you're becoming angry does your face get red; do you raise your eyebrows; squint or widen your eyes; cross your arms over your chest; raise your posture as if you're trying to make yourself taller; point at the child; clench your fists or your teeth; pace; raise your voice; or speak harshly? Your spouse, friend, or your children may be able to give you information on your body language and your anger.

Using empathy and considering your child's point of view can be helpful in unexpected anger-provoking moments. Ask yourself, "What's her goal?" "What does she expect me to do?" "What can I do instead?"

If you find your ire starting to rise, take a time-out. We'll discuss time-out in the next section.

Helping Your Kids with Their Anger

REMEMBER, ANGER IS a power move. Kids want to win, to control, to get even at times, and to protect their rights. How you handle your anger and their anger gives them a model of anger management.

When Your Child's Anger Is Directed at You

If your child says, "I hate you," this is enough to provoke hurt, anger, or guilt in most of us. You could respond by reflecting her feelings. "You're very angry with me now." She might respond with, "Yeah." You could respond, "Okay, let's talk about it." You could continue the conversation in a sensitive way, helping her resolve her anger. At a later time, you could talk to her about how to respectfully express her anger. You could even give her the words and practice—"I'm angry at you now because . . ."

Time-Out

There will be times when it's better to take action than to respond to anger verbally. Temper tantrums, for example, usually escalate if you try to reflect the child's feelings. As psychiatrist Rudolf Dreikurs said, "Temper tantrums need an audience." So, if you take the child or yourself out of the situation, the child has no one to complain to. Time-outs can help kids gain control of themselves, but they can also fuel the power contest if not handled properly.

Realize that by having the child take a time-out, or if you take time-out, this does not mean that you're trying to make the child or yourself feel bad. In *Positive Time-Out*, Dr. Jane Nelsen points out that "children do better when they feel better."[7] The same can be said for adults. Berating yourself when you take a time-out for your anger will not help you. Both you and your child need to feel better so you can do better and behave civilly toward each other.

It's best to talk with your kids about the concepts of a time-out before using it. Explain that sometimes we all get angry and feel bad and need to cool off or calm down. When this happens we can each go to our cool-off or calm-down place. With young kids, explain that the calm-down place for the child will be in his room. If your child wants to, he can decide to set up a corner of the room for time-out. The area could have special toys or books or whatever the child decides will help him feel better. Finally, you say, "If you get really mad, I'll know you need to calm down and you can go to your calm-down place. I'll set the timer and when you hear the buzzer you can come out if you're feeling better. I'll be in the (name your calm-down place) so that I can feel better, too."

> Time-outs can help kids gain control of themselves, but they can also fuel the power contest if not handled properly.

You may find the child comes out still angry. Then you say, "I see you're not feeling better yet, so I'll set the timer again," and escort him into his room. Leave him there for two or three minutes, and if he's still upset, increase the time. Don't go over five minutes. That's a long time for a young child.[8]

With older kids and teens, tell them in advance that when you're both too angry with each other to talk it over at the moment, you'll take some time out either by ignoring their anger or removing yourself until you feel better. You can suggest that they may want to go somewhere such as their room and stay there until they feel better. Offer to help them design their own cool-off or calm-down place with things that will help them feel better. Explain that after everyone feels better, they can talk about it if it seems that will help.

While you're in your time-out, analyze your anger: What's the purpose, what am I telling myself, and so forth? What might my child be going through or what's his purpose? What action can I take—send an I-message, explore alternatives, apologize for anything I've done?

At a nonconflict time, you can discuss the behavior with the child. Share you're feelings and explore alternatives to tirades. "When you get so angry, I feel disrespected and don't want to be with you. What are some other ways you could respectfully express your anger so we can talk about it?" Be sure to reflect his feelings, too. With some children and teens, it may be better not to discuss the issue as it may get worse. You know your child; only you can decide.

Be careful with time-out. Some parents put kids in time-out for almost every misbehavior, no matter how slight. This can lead to power contests and revenge. Take some time out from time-out; use the procedure for serious, anger-provoking incidents only.

Take Time for Training: Teach Kids Appropriate Anger Expression

You can talk with your child about how to express anger at a nonconflict time. You can also teach young children through puppets and role-playing. Set up conflict situations and demonstrate how to share anger and how to respond.

With older kids, you can discuss incidents later and explore alternatives as suggested above. Television can also be a good tool. When you're watching a TV program involving anger, discuss the incidents. "What did you think about how the person handled her anger in that scene?" "What happened as a result of her actions?" "If this were real life, is there another way she could have responded?" "What might be the results if she did that?"

Let your kids know that anger management is a life skill we all have to learn.

Educator Amy Horton suggests the "Stop, Think, and Act" technique in working with kids' anger.[9] You could also use it to work on your own anger.

Stop: Stop your body.

Think: Count to 10 to give yourself time to think. Think of a good action.

Act: Carry out your action.

You can have a discussion with your kids on how to use the Stop, Think, and Act technique. First, help them recognize how their body feels when they are starting to get angry. Does their breathing get rapid? Do they feel tense? Are their fists or teeth clenched? Do they tighten the muscles in their face? Do they feel a knot in their stomach? Do they pace the floor?

> Let your kids know that anger management is a life skill we all have to learn.

Next, teach them to tell themselves to "stop." Discuss slowing down their breathing and counting to 10, giving themselves time to think of a good choice in the situation. Finally, talk about how to act on their choice.

Help kids practice the technique. First, have them become aware of their bodies by breathing rapidly and tensing their body. Have them tell themselves to stop, first out loud until they get the idea, then silently. Next, have them count to 10 again, first out loud and then silently. Have them practice this a few times until they're used to it.

Set up role-play situations such as: "Your brother takes your baseball glove out of your room without asking you." "Your friend teases you." Or you can use other situations you know anger your kids. Have the kids stop their bodies, count to 10 and think of actions, and then act on their choices. Discuss the results of each role-play. "How did your action work?" "What might be some other ways to respond?" You could also share some of your own anger examples and how you used the technique.

> Each person chooses how she will feel about something, just like she chooses how she will behave.

You can also help your kids manage their anger by teaching them breathing and relaxation exercises. You could share other ways you've learned to manage your anger. If they're old enough, you could suggest they read this chapter.

When discussing anger with your kids or in thinking about your own anger, avoid phrases such as, "What makes you angry?" or, "That makes me angry." This minimizes one's personal power because nobody "makes" anybody feel anything. As we've said, each person *chooses* how she will feel about something, just as she chooses how she will behave. Phrases that show one's taking responsibility when angry could be: "I (you) get angry when . . ." "When you . . . , I feel angry because . . ." "I got angry because (you, he, or she) . . ." "You got angry because . . ."

When Your Kids Are Angry with Someone Else

Kids don't come by problem-solving skills naturally, and they see arguing (and sometimes physical fighting) on TV and between parents, older siblings, peers, and so on. So when kids get angry, they are likely to strike out verbally or physically.

When Siblings Fight

Most siblings argue and fight, and these conflicts are often hard for parents to take. Here are some ideas on handling children's fights:

- **Use the incident to teach appropriate anger expression.** When you find them fighting, you can step in and redirect their anger.

   Six-year-old Misha and her four-year-old sister Sedona are coloring at the kitchen table. All of a sudden both kids are crying. Mom comes in from another room to see what's going on. "Misha tore up my picture," sniffs Sedona. "Sedona hit me," cries Misha. Mom uses the conflict as a teaching moment. "Sedona," Mom says, "instead of hitting Misha, say, 'I'm mad at you, Misha, for tearing my picture.'" Sedona complies. Misha replies, "I'm sorry. You can have my picture if you want."

   With young kids, moments like this are great opportunities. This usually doesn't work with older ones. It's better to talk it over later with them. "How could you have expressed your anger at your brother without hitting?"

- **Change the arena.** When kids fight, offer them a choice. "If you want to fight, take it outside." This interrupts the fight without your trying to referee, and kids often stop fighting once given permission to fight but not in the place they're fighting. It works extremely well if the weather is unpleasant.

- **Table the argument.** Interrupt the fight, tell each participant to go and cool off, then say they can bring up the disagreement at the family meeting.

- **Stay out of it.** When kids fight, parents have a tendency to step in and place blame or settle the contest. When they do this, kids discover they can get attention, power, or revenge. Arguing and fighting is a good way for kids to get attention—start a fight and parents come running. It's also an excellent way to express power, "We'll fight if we want to, and you can't stop us." Starting a fight and getting the parent to take your side can also be a good way to get even with your brother or sister. But this often backfires, as the blamed sibling often gets even in return.

If you discover your methods of handling fights and arguments aren't increasing the peace, it may be time to stay out of it and let the kids take full responsibility for the problem between them. If it's just a verbal battle, this isn't so difficult for parents to do. But when the fight turns physical, many parents have a hard time letting the kids settle it. Although we're against violence, sometimes kids learn not to be violent by experiencing the consequences of violent behavior. If you feel your kids won't be seriously hurt, you may want to consider letting them learn the hard way. If it becomes dangerous, of course you'll need to step in and separate them. But most sibling fights aren't dangerous.

> If you discover your methods of handling fights and arguments aren't increasing the peace, it may be time to stay out of it.

If you decide to let the kids settle their fights, realize it may get worse before it gets better, especially if you've been stepping in. The best way to take yourself out of a fight is to remove yourself physically—go to the bathroom or your bedroom and close the door. When you do this, you may find the fight ending up outside the door as the kids are trying to get you involved. Stick to your resolve.

If one of your kids comes tattling to you about what a sibling did, reply, "That's between you and your brother, and I'm sure you can handle it." This keeps you out of the fight and shows your confidence in your child's ability.

Parents usually can let kids handle their fights if the kids are close in age. But what about older and younger kids? Realize that younger kids often taunt the older ones to get them in a fight and then use you to take their side. If there's a considerable difference in age and physical size, the best strategy is to remove the younger one. This stops the fight, the older one doesn't feel punished, and the younger one doesn't get you to fight his battles. Just distract the younger one, "Come on, let's do something else."

Brothers and sisters fighting is another hard event for parents to take. But this situation is similar to older and younger kids of the same sex. Girls know most parents won't permit boys to hit girls and may use this to their advantage. But if a girl gets herself into a physical altercation with a brother, she can also learn from the consequences, again, as long as you feel she won't get seriously hurt.

Peer Conflicts

Some of the same ideas listed for sibling arguments and fights also apply to peers. You do have some other choices when a child has a friend over and they start to fight. You can give them a choice of stopping the fighting or sending the friend home. (Some peer conflicts involve bullies and victims. We discuss this situation in detail in chapter 9.)

> Chris, 14, comes home with an angry look, ignores his father who's sitting in the living room, goes to his room and slams the door. In a few minutes, Dad knocks on Chris's door and says, "You looked really angry when you came in. Want to

talk about it?" Chris opens the door, inviting his dad to come in. They sit on the bed and Chris tells his dad what happened.

Chris: Brent the Brat embarrassed me in front of the guys!

Dad: That's really tough. What happened?

Chris: He called me teacher's pet just because I volunteered for a project Mr. Jameson wanted to do. I only did it because I need the extra credit!

Dad: Yeah, I can see where that's embarrassing. What did you do?

Chris: I just stood there. I didn't know what to do I was so mad.

Dad: Did you tell Brent how you felt?

Chris: No, I just walked off.

Dad: Do you want to let him know how you feel?

Chris: Yeah, just wait. I'll get him!

Dad: I can understand your wanting to get back at him. What do you think will happen if you do?

Chris: I don't know.

Dad: Is it possible he'll just get even with you?

Chris: Yeah, I suppose so.

Dad: What would happen if you just told him that you need the extra credit and ask him if he wants to join you on the project?

Chris: I don't know what he'd do.

Dad: He wouldn't expect that. Want to give it a shot?

Chris: Why not, it wouldn't hurt.

Dad and Chris discussed how Chris could respectfully approach Brent. Chris decided he would use Dad's suggestion. They discussed what to do if Brent got defensive. Chris would just walk away.

Sometimes kids won't want to talk. Respect their decision and keep the door open. You could say, "If you change your mind, let me know and I'll be glad to listen."

Anger and Stress

STRESS IS ALL around us. When we feel pressured, over-whelmed, or pushed, many of us also feel angry. Feeling stressed, however, is not *caused* by stress, it's a response to stress. Some people take stress in their stride; they thrive on it. Most don't like stress and can react to it in discourteous and sometimes angry ways.

Manage Your Time

We live in a time when, in many families, both parents work outside the home or kids live in single-parent homes. You can manage your stress by changing your daily routine so things don't pile up. Make lists of your responsibilities and prioritize. Pay bills as they come in. You can double a recipe and prepare two meals at once. Involve the kids in the chores. Establish a network with others through a church or synagogue or community organization. In this way, you can help each other out with the babysitting, shopping, carpooling, and so forth. Don't try to be the perfect housekeeper; you don't have time for it. Remember that Martha Stewart has a staff, you don't! Of course you want your house clean, but it doesn't have to be a showplace. Get your kids to help out.[10]

On your lists of things to do, make sure you've scheduled some time for yourself and your spouse if you're married. Make time for friends too.

Practice Stress-Relieving Activities

We've discussed many things you can do to relieve your stress as well as your anger, such as monitoring your self-talk—what are you telling yourself that's making you so stressed? Are you demanding, awfulizing, and so on? Take some time for relaxation. Use visualization to practice handling an upcoming event that may prove to be stressful. Exercise—this helps to drain stress away. Finally, remember your sense of humor.

Anger and Guilt

THERE ARE TIMES when parents feel guilty after getting angry with their kids. Rudolf Dreikurs said: "Guilt expresses good intentions we really don't have." By feeling guilty, we get ourselves off the hook for behavior we consider bad. While guilt may serve as a signal that it would be better if you made a change, if you just wallow in the guilt feelings instead of creating a plan of action with resolve to carry it out, the possibility of change is minimal. As Dr. Dreikurs also said: "Either do wrong or feel guilty, but don't do both; it's too much work."

> By feeling guilty, we get ourselves off the hook for behavior we consider bad.

In this chapter we've given you several techniques to manage your anger and to help your kids when they get angry. These techniques help with stress, too. Practice the techniques over time and decide which ones work best for you. Chapter 6 focuses on the relationship of respectful discipline to developing important life skills. You will learn about natural and logical consequences—a major respectful discipline intervention.

PART II

Respectful Kids Learning to Operate in the World

6

Respectful
Discipline and
Life Skills

DISCIPLINE IS THE number one concern of most parents. While many parents rely on the old techniques of reward and punishment, it doesn't take much imagination to see that things like bribing, yelling, threatening, and hitting are disrespectful ways to deal with another human being. Since kids usually learn by example, if you model these rude behaviors, your kids will probably pick them up as well.

In this chapter we'll discuss the reasons for giving up reward and punishment and present effective, respectful alternatives. You'll learn about choices and consequences and other skills you can use to encourage respect and cooperation.

Reward and Punishment Don't Work

MANY OF TODAY'S kids see reward as their right and punishment as a violation of their rights. When we use rewards to get kids to do chores, schoolwork, and so on, we are, in effect, bribing them. We're giving them the message that they should expect payment for cooperative behavior.

While it's true there are rewards in society—people get paid for their work—there are many acts of cooperation that don't have rewards connected to them. Who pays parents to fix the meals, clean the house, get the car repaired, look out for the welfare of their kids, and so on?

> Reward and punishment make the parents responsible for kids' behavior. Choices within limits help kids take responsibility.

Another problem with rewards—they tend to escalate. A candy bar may motivate the five-year-old, but the reward could become a car when the child is old enough to drive. Have you checked the price of cars lately?

Finally, rewards don't always motivate. Kids who are rebelling will see rewards as an attempt to manipulate (which they are). With these kids, rewards often backfire.

Now let's look at punishment. Dr. Oscar Christensen—renowned family educator—tells us that kids, in their sense of equality, believe "if you have a right to punish me, I have a right to punish you, 'I'll fix your wagon'—and their skills at wagon fixing are unlimited!" Remember the example of Brenda in chapter 2—the girl who "cooked" her dad's record collection after he grounded her? She got even.

Many parents think punishment works if the kids stop the misbehavior. But what does "it works" really mean? True, sometimes punishment stops the behavior for the moment, but is the effect long lasting? For many kids it isn't. Punishment can lead to worse behavior (revenge) and strained relationships later (distrust, less involvement).

Most parents want their kids to grow up to be responsible, courageous, cooperative, successful, respectful, and self-reliant. All of these qualities require kids to learn to be self-disciplined. Reward and punishment make the parents responsible for kids' behavior. Choices within limits help kids take responsibility. When kids take responsibility for their behavior they are showing respect to others and themselves.

Yelling, Threatening, Lecturing, and Reminding

When parents yell, threaten, lecture, or remind, they not only show disrespect, they teach kids to tune them out. In chapter 5 we talked about the little girl who was called to lunch three times but didn't think she had to go in because Mom hadn't yelled yet. If you're a yeller, you're training your kids to listen only when you yell—if then.

"If you do that one more time . . ." Parents make threats hoping the threat will be enough to stop the misbehavior. But most parents don't carry out threats, and the kids know it.

> Reminding takes the responsibility for remembering away from kids. It's as if they need a personal secretary to follow them around and act as their memory.

Lectures go in one ear and out the other: "How many times have I told you . . . ?" or, "You should (or shouldn't) do . . ." Kids can finish these sentences—they know what you're going to say, but do they pay attention?

Reminding takes the responsibility for remembering away from kids. It's as if they need a personal secretary to follow them around and act as their memory. If you're going to play that role, why should they bother to remember? Forgetting can be a great attention-getting behavior. It's true that we all forget things from time to time; we're not perfect. But parents who remind frequently have kids who forget frequently. And, some kids "forget" in order to defeat their parents—a power move. They remember what they are supposed to do, but they don't want to do it, so they "forget." The parents get frustrated and a power contest follows.

"You're Grounded"

Grounding and withdrawing privileges are overused and often bear no relationship to the misbehavior. Therefore, they don't make sense to the kids and the kids resent it. For example, suppose a child makes a smart remark when a parent asks him to do something. The parent grounds him or takes away his TV or computer privileges until he learns to have more respect. This is pure revenge on the parent's part and will probably have no lasting effect on changing the child's behavior. Grounding is like a jail sentence—you're confined for a certain period of time. If withdrawal of privileges is used, the privilege withdrawn must relate to the misbehavior. For example, if a child gets mad and hits the computer because it freezes up, he loses his computer privileges for a while.

Physical Punishment and Disrespect

Ninety percent of parents admit they sometimes use physical punishment.[1] They don't realize spanking and other forms of physical punishment, such as slapping, are not only rude, but teach kids that the way to solve problems is to hit someone. Then we complain about the violence in our society.

Why do parents hit kids? Parents who rely on physical punishment do so for a variety of reasons. Do any of these reasons ring a bell with you?

- **You don't know what else to do.** Many parents hit out of frustration. They don't want to hit their kids—they may not even believe in it—but they've reached the end of their rope.

- **You think you should.** Who says you should? Your friends? Your parents? If your child tells you she has to do something because everyone else is doing it, what do you say? Likewise, why should you hit just because you think everyone else is doing it? And when it comes to your parents, did you always listen to them? Do you always listen to them now?

- **You think the child deserves it.** Why? No matter how badly your child behaves, what makes you think he deserves to be physically abused?

- **You think it makes you feel better.** For how long? Some parents feel better after they've given a bratty kid a good swat, but a few minutes later they feel guilty. As we said in chapter 5, "guilt feelings are good intentions we really don't have." So, if you find yourself feeling guilty, realize you have no intention of changing.

- **You think it works.** For how long? Kids who are hit may stop the misbehavior for a while, but many act that way again or do other things that violate your rules—sometimes things worse than the misbehavior that got them a spanking.

- **Your parents did it.** Your parents spanked you and you turned out all right, so what's wrong with it? You weren't raised in the same social climate that your kids are raised in today. Remember, earlier we said, "Equality is in the air and your kids breathe the same air."

- **"Because the Bible tells me so."** Many quote the phrase: "Spare the rod, spoil the child." But these parents don't understand what the Bible meant by the rod. The shepherd carried a stick called the rod and staff. As the shepherd was traveling with his sheep, some would get out of formation. He would use the rod—the straight part of the stick—to nudge the sheep back into formation. He didn't hit the sheep; he just nudged or guided them. So, the phrase actually means: "Spare the guidance, spoil the child." The stick that the Jewish scrolls were wrapped on was called the rod. Therefore, "spare the rod . . ." could also be translated as: "Spare the Torah, spoil the child."

Make a commitment—remove hitting from your parenting toolbox. Would you hit your best friend? Why should you treat your children any differently? As you read on, you'll learn effective discipline methods. You won't need any form of reward or punishment.

What Do Discipline and Cooperation Really Mean?

DISCIPLINE IS EDUCATION: A person who pursues a field of study such as medicine or law is following a discipline. She is learning a set of principles, facts, and skills. *Disciple* is part of the word discipline. A disciple is a student. In the case of parent-child relationships, the child is the student of the parent—learning the "discipline" of human relationships and responsibility. Discipline is also guidance—guiding kids in a direction that will benefit them and others, aiming towards mutual respect and cooperation.

"He won't cooperate," "She's uncooperative,"—statements like these often mean the child won't do what the parent or teacher wants. Cooperation doesn't mean do what I say, it means to operate together; in other words, to do what's good for all concerned. For example, kids do chores to learn responsibility, to learn life skills, and to contribute to the family.

Parents can effectively teach discipline and cooperation through democratic methods that promote responsibility and mutual respect. You can handle many discipline problems by giving kids choices within limits and allowing them to be accountable for their decisions.

> The child is the student of the parent—learning the "discipline" of human relationships and responsibility.

An Ounce of Prevention . . .

THE MORE CHOICES you can give your kids, the more they will learn about decision making. Giving choices can help prevent problems, and the more problems you prevent, the less you'll have to correct. There are many things kids can decide or help decide. Here are some examples:

- **Selecting clothing.** You can give kids choices between outfits you consider appropriate for attending school or your place of worship. They can help shop for their own clothes within price ranges that are comfortable for you.

- **Meal planning.** In a family meeting, you and your kids can make a list together of possible meals. Then the family can make agreements on what foods will be served and who will be involved in preparing the meals.

- **Allowances.** Kids can choose how to spend their allowance. They need to understand that once the allowance is spent, there's no more money until allowance "payday." Beginning in the preteen years, parents can give their kids allowances that cover more of their expenses, such as school lunches. Teens can have an allowance that will cover even more, such as their clothing purchases.

- **School lunches.** Beginning at about age six, kids can make their own lunches.

- **Homework.** Beginning at about age nine or ten, kids can plan their own homework times, such as before or after dinner.

- **Chores.** In family meetings, kids can help plan what chores are to be done and who will do each chore. The family can discuss when chores will be done and what happens if someone forgets a chore.

Choices for Young Children

YOUNG CHILDREN CAN do more than we think. Toddlers and preschoolers can dress themselves with some help and clothing that is manageable for them, such as pull-on pants and shoes with Velcro tabs. They can help clean up when they spill. They can choose between breakfast cereals.

Some other things young kids can do include: choosing between helping set the table and clearing it (use plastic plates for safety's sake and your own peace of mind); deciding what to wear to play in, such as jeans or sweat pants; putting away their toys; helping carry in groceries; hanging coats up on a low hook; putting things away on a low shelf; and placing dirty clothes in a hamper or basket.

As kids mature and show they can handle responsibility, their arena of choices increases. For example, teens can decide on curfews with their parents, use the family car when they obtain their licenses, have a checking account, and take on more chores around the house.

The keys to helping kids learn choices and responsibility are your expectations. Expectations are very powerful; kids often live up—or down—to them. The more you believe in your kids, the more likely they are to validate your faith. One principle that helps you build your faith in your children was proposed by Dr. Dreikurs: "Never do something for your children that they can do for themselves." For example, if you're letting your young child dress himself, realize that at first the child may put the shirt on backwards or shoes on the wrong feet. The color selection may not match. (If this really bothers you, give him a choice of matching outfits.) But, by being able to do it himself, the child is learning confidence and building psychological muscle—even if he makes errors. You can take some time for training at a relaxed time. With young kids it's best to make a game out of it. "Let's put the shirt on backwards—isn't that funny? Now let's put it on this way (show him the correct way)—how do you think it looks now?"

> The more you believe in your kids, the more likely they are to validate your faith.

Choices within limits can be used to correct problems as well as prevent them. Now we'll discuss how to be respectful in handling discipline problems.

Natural and Logical Consequences

NATURAL AND LOGICAL consequences replace reward and punishment. A natural consequence represents the result of

When the Kids Don't Follow Their Agreements on Chores

In order to increase responsibility for completing chores, it's useful to develop strategies and consequences when chores aren't completed in a timely manner. Some examples from families we have worked with are:

- **Redistribution.** It just may be that chores need to be redistributed for things to go more smoothly. The assignment may not be optimal, family members may be tiring of certain chore assignments. Continuing to fine-tune chore assignments at the family meeting is often required.

- **"Grandma's Rule."** Work before play. For example, kids can't watch TV, talk on the phone, or use the computer, or can't leave the house on a weekend day, until the work is done. Of course this rule applies to parents as well as kids. So, if you've agreed to take out the trash right after dinner and your son or daughter finds you watching TV or reading the paper and the chore's not done, don't be surprised if your child says, "I'm sorry, but you agreed to take out the trash right after dinner."

- **"Farmer's Rule."** No work, no grub! Family members may not sit down for the family meal until the work is done.

- **"One Word."** Parent uses a single word as a reminder about a chore (to avoid lectures, nagging, and power struggles). An example is when a parent notices the garage has not yet been cleaned as agreed to, looks at her son and respectfully, yet firmly, says only one word, "garage." Don't overdo this though; you don't want to get into a habit of reminding.[2]

- **Logical consequences.** These can also be used to increase responsibility for chore completion. Parents can, for example, choose not to cook in a kitchen where dishes haven't been cleaned up when it's time to make dinner. (Logical consequences are discussed later in this chapter.)

- **Going on strike.** This is a specific and extreme logical consequence to use only when all other efforts have failed. This strategy is based on the principle that when parents continue to do their part when it comes to household work and other forms of support routinely provided to the children, yet the kids are consistently not doing their part, a learning experience about give and take is called for. The parent announces at a family meeting that it seems that the kids are determined to not do their part in helping out, meaning the parent has to take the responsibility. "So for now (or a specified time period), I will no longer (drive people to basketball practice, cook meals, and so on.) If you would like to discuss this at a family meeting later on, I am willing to consider what you have to say."

going against the laws of nature. For example, a child who skips breakfast will probably get hungry before lunch; a child who doesn't go to bed on time will probably be tired in the morning if she has to get up for school; a child who neglects to wear a coat on a cold day will be cold. When using natural consequences, the parent doesn't have to do anything but let nature take its course—nature does the teaching.

> When using natural consequences, the parent doesn't have to do anything but let nature take its course—nature does the teaching.

Dustin, age nine, repeatedly forgot to take his lunch money to school. When this occurred, the school nurse called Dustin's parents, who would leave work to bring Dustin his lunch money. The parents grew weary of this pattern and decided to use a natural consequence. The next time the school nurse called, Dustin's dad explained why he would not bring the money. Dustin went without lunch that day. For the remainder of the school year Dustin forgot his lunch money only one more time, whereupon the parents responded again with a natural consequence.

Unfortunately, there are many areas of cooperation that aren't governed by natural consequences. In these cases, logical consequences can be set up. Also, some natural consequences are dangerous. In chapter 2 we gave the example of the child who ran into the street. Mom arranged a logical consequence for her daughter running in the street—she could play in the yard or play in the house. Once she headed for the street, she'd chosen to play in the house.

How Consequences Differ from Punishment

Logical consequences are designed to cover the many social situations where it's important for children to learn appropriate behavior. Logical consequences differ from punishment in some very important ways. If logical consequences *don't* fit the following criteria, they are punishments.

Logical Consequences Are Related to the Misbehavior

Punishment is arbitrary and seldom related to the misbehavior. Logical consequences "fit" the child's action.

> Tucker, 10, borrowed a screwdriver from Mom's toolkit. Mom asked him to please put it back in the box when he was finished with it. A couple of days later Mom was looking for the screwdriver for a job she needed to do in the kitchen. She asked Tucker what had happened to the tool. Tucker said, "Oh, I must've left it at Jimmy's." He called Jimmy but the screwdriver was nowhere to be found. Mom said, "I guess you'll need to buy me a new one out of your allowance."

Mom's action was logically related to the misbehavior— Tucker was responsible for an item he borrowed from Mom. Mom didn't lecture him on how careless he was; she just let him experience the consequences of his carelessness.

Logical Consequences Are Based on Mutual Respect

As we said in chapter 1, being a doormat and letting the kids walk all over you shows disrespect for you and your kids because (1) your rights are being violated, and (2) your kids are learning to take advantage of people. Playing the role of the boss and punishing kids violates respect for them, as does being a servant and doing things they could do for themselves. But as a leader and encourager, you show respect for both yourself and your kids by giving choices and letting the kids be accountable for the consequences.

> Eight-year-old Sydney keeps leaving her bike in the driveway and Dad has to move it before driving in or out of the garage. Dad gives Sydney a choice: "When you leave your bike in the driveway, it's an inconvenience for me to have to get out of the car and move it. You have a choice: You can park your bike somewhere else or I'll put it away for the remainder of the day. You can have it back the next day to see if you're ready to be responsible for the bike."

This action is based on mutual respect—if Sydney is to use her bike, she has to take the responsibility for putting it away so she doesn't inconvenience others. Dad approached her in a respectful way, refraining from lecturing, threatening, or taking away her bike for a long period of time. Giving her another opportunity to demonstrate her willingness to accept the responsibility shows Dad's faith in Sydney's ability to be cooperative and gives her a chance to change her behavior. If she still leaves it in the driveway, she's obviously not ready to take the responsibility and will lose the use of the bike for two days, and so on, if the misbehavior continues.

Logical Consequences Separate the Deed from the Doer

We all make mistakes, so a bad deed doesn't make the total person a bad person—just like a good deed doesn't make the total person a good person. Your disciplinary action must make it clear that you are rejecting the behavior, not the child. Your tone of voice, your body language, the words you choose, and your intention all convey messages to the child. Making sure you maintain mutual respect when applying consequences separates the deed from the doer.

> The Larsons had a West Highland Terrier named MacDuff. At a family meeting, Stuart, 13, agreed to feed MacDuff. At

the meeting, Mom said, "We all forget sometimes. What should happen if Stuart forgets to feed MacDuff?" The family agreed that the dog would eat before Stuart did. The second night of the agreement, Stuart forgot to feed MacDuff. When Stuart came to the table, he found no place setting at his usual place. He looked at the empty place for a moment and then said, "Oh, yeah, I forgot to feed MacDuff," and went into the kitchen to prepare the dog's food.

> Making sure you maintain mutual respect when applying consequences separates the deed from the doer.

Instead of lecturing Stuart on how inconsiderate he was in letting the poor dog starve—which would only imply to Stuart that he's a bad person—Mom simply acted on the agreement.

Logical Consequences Are Concerned with the Present, Not the Past

Parents who punish are usually focusing on past misbehavior.

Mandy, nine, wanted to ask her friend Samantha for a sleepover. Mom said no because the last time Samantha was over the girls refused to go to bed on time and created a disturbance.

This same situation could be handled more respectfully if Mom focused on the present. While she may be concerned about a repeat of the misbehavior if Samantha stays over, Mom could deal with what will happen now.

Mandy asks Mom if Samantha can stay over. "Yes," Mom says, "as long as you and Samantha are ready for bed on time and are quiet after bedtime. If you decide not to go to bed on time or make noise after bedtime, I'll call Samantha's mom and ask her to pick Samantha up. You'll need to make this clear to Samantha."

In this situation Mom has stated the limits and the consequence should those limits be violated—it's the girls' choice. If the misbehavior occurs, it would be best for Mom to refrain from reminders and simply call Samantha's mother. Mom could call Samantha's mother in advance and explain the situation to her so she's not surprised should Mom call her that night.

Logical Consequences Are Applied in a Firm and Kind Manner

Consequences can quickly be turned into punishments if you become annoyed or angry. Such emotions are interpreted by kids as punitive. You may give the most logical choice in a situation, but if there's hostility involved, the consequence is spoiled.

Being firm doesn't mean strict or harsh. It simply means sticking to the limits you set. You can be firm in a friendly and respectful way.

It was a rainy day and 11-year-old Allan neglected to take off his shoes and tracked mud into the house. Instead of yelling at Allan for being so inconsiderate or cleaning up after him, Dad simply said, "Allan, there's mud on the floor; you'll need to clean it up." Allan did a half-baked job of cleaning up the mud, went into the family room, and flopped down in front of the TV. Dad said, "I'm sorry, Allan, but there's still mud on the floor." Allan grumbled (Dad ignored the grumbling) and cleaned up the floor. "That's much better, Allan. Thanks for taking care of it."

Dad was firm in expecting Allan to take care of the mess he created. Allan could have chosen to take off his shoes and not track mud on the floor, but he didn't, so it was his job to take care of the problem. When the job was not fully completed, Dad held firm in his expectations. At the same time, he was kind and respectful by not attending to Allan's grumbling and by thanking him for his cooperation.

Your word choice and tone of voice can convey calmness or annoyance, respect or disrespect. Your body language must also reflect calmness and respect. Threatening looks, gestures and stances all convey hostility. Hostile body language coupled with a hostile attitude creates a condition Dreikurs called "shouting with your mouth shut."

Chapter 5 gave you ideas on how to handle your anger. Keeping anger out of consequences is vital to their effectiveness. One way to make sure you're using consequences in a calm, respectful way is to rehearse. For frequently occurring misbehaviors, practice what you will say or do in front of a mirror. Notice your body language and listen to your tone of voice. If necessary, use a tape recorder to hear yourself. Examine your attitude: What is your purpose—to gain control of the child or to let the child learn by experience?

Little Things Mean a Lot

The more kids get used to making choices and experiencing the consequences of their choices—either positive or negative—the more they become accustomed to accepting responsibility for their behavior. It's a good idea to practice when you can on smaller issues so that you know what you are doing when larger issues come up and it really is necessary to address them.

When you have a cooperation issue with your kids—no matter how minor it may be—think of ways you can give choices rather than saying, "Do this," or, "Don't do that." Suppose your three-year-old is playing roughly with a new puppy. You could say: "Pulling the puppy's ears hurts him. You can pet the puppy gently (demonstrating how), or we'll put him in his pen and you can try again later." Or, your eight-year-old likes a certain snack. You give her the responsibility of writing the item on the shopping list you have on the refrigerator before you go to the grocery store. She forgets and consequently you don't purchase more of the snack. She complains that she's run out of the snack. You simply say, "Put it on the list before I go next time." She complains that she wants it now and she just forgot, "Can't you go back and get it?" You go about your business, refusing to become engaged in a power struggle.

> The more kids get used to making choices and experiencing the consequences of their choices—either positive or negative—the more they become accustomed to accepting responsibility for their behavior.

Choices and Consequences for Teens

Choices and consequences work with teenagers, too. Here's an example of using logical consequences with teenagers:

Fourteen-year-old Mark asks his mom for a ride to the mall to meet his friends. Mom says she can drop him off on the way to her doctor's appointment. "I'll need to leave here at 10:00 and will be glad to drop you off if you're ready at that time." "Okay, I'll be ready," Mark replies. When Mom's ready to leave, Mark's walking around the house, still in his pajamas, listening to music on his Walkman, so Mom heads for the garage. He notices her leaving and shouts, "Hold on, I'll be right there," and heads to his bedroom to get dressed. He discovers Mom's gone when he finally throws on his clothes.

Consequences and Serious Issues

Consequences can apply to serious issues as well. By serious issues we mean not only the obvious such as lying and stealing, but also things that just drive you up the wall—they're serious to you. As with any consequence, you have to be careful not to become involved in a power contest or a war of revenge. You can take yourself out of the power contest by addressing the *issue* and keeping personalities out of it.

> You can take yourself out of the power contest by addressing the *issue* and keeping personalities out of it.

Suppose your four-year-old dawdles in the morning, making you late for work. Before bedtime you tell your daughter that if she's not dressed on time tomorrow, you'll place her clothes in a bag and she can go to preschool in her pajamas and dress at school. Earlier in the day you've told her teacher what you're going to do tomorrow so you can shift the responsibility to the child and get out of the power contest. The next day your daughter is dawdling. You remain silent, place her clothes in a bag, take her by the hand, and say, "Time to go." If your four-year-old has trouble telling time, set a timer and tell her, "When the timer goes off, we'll be leaving for preschool."

Lying is a difficult challenge for parents—you want to be able to trust your kids. Lying is often a power move to put one over on someone or avoid punishment. Kids may think if they tell the truth, the parent won't let them do what they want to do or will punish them for doing it.

Nine-year-old Adam tells his dad he's going down the street to a friend's house. When it's almost dinnertime and Adam's not home, Dad calls the friend's house and finds out Adam is not there and hasn't been there all day. Adam comes in while Dad's on the phone with the friend's mother. Dad decides not to comment at that time and sits down to dinner. All through dinner Adam's got a guilty look on his face, but Dad resists the temptation to comment.

The next day Adam tells Dad he's going to his friend's house. Dad says, "I'm sorry, but yesterday you told me you'd be at Ron's house and you weren't there. So you may not go out today. Tomorrow you can have an opportunity to show you'll be where you say you're going."

Dad would naturally be concerned about where his son was going when Adam said he'd be at Ron's. Dad can think of places he might have told Adam in the past that he shouldn't go; perhaps this will give him a clue. While he wouldn't want to follow Adam around, checking up on his every move, in a few days if Adam tells Dad he's going to Ron's, Dad could find an excuse to give Ron's mom a call to see if Adam's really there. If the lying continues, Dad can investigate further. For kids who lie a lot, family counseling may be in order.

Stealing is another difficult challenge, but in some stealing situations, logical consequences can help.

When Mom was at the store and went to pay for her grocery items, she noticed that money was missing from her wallet. She recalled that her 15-year-old daughter Rebecca had asked for an advance on her allowance so she could get some new CDs. Mom had said no.

When Mom got home she found Rebecca listening to her Walkman. In a friendly way, Mom asked, "Who's playing?" Rebecca got a guilty look on her face and replied, "Oh, just listening to an old CD." Mom said, "Can I listen?" Rebecca said, "You wouldn't like it." Mom said. "Let me listen anyway, okay?" Rebecca turned red and handed over the earphones. "Sounds like the Dirty Gravel, the group whose CD you wanted to buy." "Yeah, I found the money." Keeping her cool, Mom said, "And we both know where you found it. What should we do about this, Rebecca?" "I don't know," replied Rebecca. "What would you do if you were me?" asked Mom. "I guess I'd be pretty mad," Rebecca said. "Getting angry isn't going to solve this problem. Any other ideas?" asked Mom. "I could pay you back," Rebecca said. "Okay, but how do we keep this from happening in the future?" "I don't know," Rebecca replied. "Tell you what, for now, let's say that you borrowed the money. And when you borrow money, you pay interest on the loan. I'll charge you the current bank rate. You can pay me back out of your allowance. Would you like to discuss how you could earn extra money for things you want?"

Mom was smart; she avoided a power contest and possibly revenge seeking by avoiding calling Rebecca a thief. Since Rebecca knows she stole the money, what good would it do to start a fight over it? The consequence of charging interest and the offer to discuss how Rebecca can earn money may deter such behavior. If it doesn't, Mom may have to lock up her purse. If Rebecca exhibits stealing behavior in other ways, some professional help may be needed.

In chapter 9 we'll discuss other serious issues, such as drugs. For now, let's continue our discussion of how to use logical consequences effectively.

Making Consequences Work

Here are some things to consider when using logical consequences. Logical consequences are very effective when the rules listed above are followed. The consequences are related to the misbehavior, are respectful, separate the deed from the doer, deal with the present not the past, and are applied in a firm and kind manner. Here are some additional points to remember when applying consequences:

Understand the Goal of Misbehavior

Natural consequences are effective with any of the goals of misbehavior because you simply let nature do the teaching. Logical consequences work best with attention-getting behavior. With the goal of attention, there's no power struggle or revenge—unless the parents mishandle the situation; then those goals could come into play.

But logical consequences can work with power-seeking kids if the parents are careful and deal with the situation in a matter-of-fact, nonpunitive way. They work best with kids interested in power if the logical consequences are stated or negotiated in advance or the parent states what he will do, *not* what the kids will do: "I'll wash what I find in the hamper." "I'll fix dinner if the dishes are cleaned up." "I'll give you a ride if you're ready by seven." "I'm willing to . . ." or, "I'm not willing to . . ." When you focus on what you will do, you're withdrawing from the power contest because, just as you can't really make your kids do anything, your kids can't make you do anything either.

When kids are seeking revenge, logical consequences will be seen as a weapon. With revenge-seeking behavior, it's best to back off and concentrate on building the relationship. Consequences are also not appropriate for kids who are displaying inadequacy because they are deeply discouraged and their behavior—in the area of the "inadequacy"—is usually not disruptive. These kids require massive doses of encouragement.

Recognize Who Owns the Problem

Natural consequences apply when kids own the problem. For example, if a child decides not to take a raincoat on a day that looks like rain and she gets wet, this is her problem. Logical consequences may also apply to when kids own problems. If a child has an argument with a friend and the friend doesn't want to see her anymore, that's her problem. You can listen and help the child explore alternatives to her problem, but she owns the problem and the consequences.

Logical consequences often apply when you own the problem. For example, the child doesn't come home on time, destroys property, or does something unsafe.

Control the Situation, Not the Child

Few people, including kids, like to be controlled by others. You can give kids some control by letting them choose within limits. In other words, you control the situation—you set the limits; the kids control their choices within those limits.

Accept the Child's Decision

When you give a choice, there is no wrong choice. Kids may not make the decision you want, but that doesn't mean it's a wrong choice. For example, if you are trying to watch TV and your kids are in the room with you making noise, you could give them the choice of remaining quiet and watching the program or leaving the room. If they keep making noise, they've decided to leave the room. You may have wanted them to be quiet and remain in the room—especially if the program was something you'd like them to see—but you gave them a choice and they made it.

Talk Less, Act More

The first thing most parents do when their child misbehaves is talk. This is exactly what kids expect us to do, and talking reinforces their goals of misbehavior. Too much talking makes consequences ineffective—talking is not teaching, action is teaching. Kids tune us out when we constantly lecture and talk too much—they become "parent deaf." Save most of your talking for friendly conversations.

Keep talking to a minimum when you're applying consequences—use just enough words to state the choice and the consequences. Focus on the behavior, not the child as a person.

Eight-year-old Stan had to go to the doctor. He told his mom he didn't want to go because the last time the doctor gave him a shot. Mom listened to Stan's fears and explained this trip to the doctor was for a checkup and the doctor wasn't going to hurt him. Stan was still very nervous and upset.

When it came time to go to the doctor, Stan cried and said he wasn't going. Mom simply said, "I know you're scared, but it's just a checkup and we have to go. Do you want to get in the car on your own or shall I help you?" Stan still said he wasn't going. Mom took him by the hand and led him crying to the car.

Mom used as few words as possible in giving Stan the choice and she acted on his decision—his behavior indicated he had chosen to be helped to the car. More sympathy, pleading, or calling him a baby, wouldn't gain Stan's cooperation—action was the only way.

> The first thing most parents do when their child misbehaves is talk. This is exactly what kids expect us to do, and talking reinforces their goals of misbehavior.

Sometimes no words are necessary at all, particularly if a situation has been discussed in advance.

Dad and 12-year-old Fay had an agreement about her room. If the room was not cleaned up by a certain time, Dad would

Provide a Choice

When words are called for, choose them carefully and make sure a choice is stated or implied. Throughout this book we've given examples of how to word choices and consequences. Here are some more examples:

"You have a choice. You may _____ or you may _____."

"You may _____ or you may _____; you decide."

"You may _____ or you may _____. I'll know by your behavior what you've decided."

"I will (stating your limits such as 'cook if the kitchen is cleaned up')."

"If you plan to (go to the movies, have friends over), you'll need to (get your chores done first, help get the house ready)."

do it, but if he had to do it, he expected to be paid for "maid service." They negotiated what a clean room meant and a price that would be paid from Fay's allowance if Dad had to clean it. Two days after the agreement was made, Fay neglected to clean her room. Dan said nothing and went about cleaning the room. The next day Fay cleaned her room. Dad presented his "bill" on allowance day.

Follow Through

When kids choose the consequence, remain firm and let them experience the consequence. In the example of leaving the bike in the driveway, Dad would follow through if he found the bike still in the driveway after he'd set the limits—he'd put it away and his daughter couldn't use it until the next day.

Assure kids they will have another opportunity to demonstrate they are ready to be responsible. If the misbehavior continues, more time may need to be added before they have another opportunity.

Avoid Turning Consequences into Punishments

When parents first learn about natural and logical consequences they may misuse them in a punitive way. Consequences *are not* new ways to punish—they are designed to help kids learn appropriate behaviors through experience. Your attitude toward your child and his learning experience is crucial. If you apply consequences with an attitude of "This will show him," you are bound to fail. If your attitude is, "He needs to learn appropriate behavior and I'll let him experience the results of his misbehavior so that he can learn," you are going to be much more effective.

> Consequences *are not* new ways to punish—they are designed to help kids learn appropriate behaviors through experience.

Notice we said "experience" the consequences rather than "suffer" or "take" the consequences. This distinction is important because to suffer or take the consequences implies a punitive situation. Think of consequences as simply the result of an action (or inaction) and an opportunity to learn. Remember we said above that *discipline is education*—kids are learning the skills of respectful and cooperative living.

Consider this. If you had a friend who made a bad financial decision and lost money, would you be mad at your friend or would you be empathetic? Most likely you would feel bad for your friend rather than thinking your friend got what she deserved. Approach your children as you would your friend; be empathic. It's unfortunate your child made the choice to experience the consequences—no matter what the misbehavior is—but she is learning.

Set Up Consequences in Advance

When kids know what to expect, you can use less or no talk when applying consequences. For example, earlier in the chapter we talked about Mark, who wanted a ride to the mall. Mom had stated when she would leave, and if Mark was ready she could drop him off. He wasn't ready so Mom simply left—action not words.

In some cases, consequences can be negotiated in advance. Kids have more commitment to what they help set up.

Mom and Dad discussed curfews with 15-year-old Jessie.

Mom: What time to you think you should be home after the movie?

Jessie: How about midnight?

Dad: Okay, let's write that down as a possibility.

Mom: How about 10?

Jessie: Ah, Mom, that's too early; I'm not a baby!

Mom: I can hear that you're angry at that suggestion. I don't think you're a baby, but I really get worried that something might happen to you if you are out too late.

Jessie: (Calming down) Well, it just seems like you don't trust me.

Dad: I can hear you feel that way, but that's not it. I'm with your mom; I really worry. Suppose we just write down ideas for now—you know, get all the ideas we can and then decide, okay?

Jessie: Okay.

Mom: We have two ideas, midnight and 10—any other ideas?

The family had no other times to suggest so they agreed on a compromise—11 o'clock.

Dad: What should happen if you're late?

Jessie: Well, what if I can't help it—I mean, suppose Derrick and I get tied up in traffic?

Mom: If you start for home soon enough, that won't be a problem. So, what do you think should happen?

Jessie: I'm grounded?

Dad writes down "grounded."

Dad: How about this. If you come home late, instead of grounding you for a long time, we just say that you won't be able to go out the next night and then you can have another opportunity next weekend to demonstrate that you're ready to keep the agreement?

Jessie agreed to the consequence. She kept her agreement the next Friday and Saturday nights but violated it on the following Friday. As she announced her plans for Saturday night, Mom and Dad reminded her of the agreement and that she'd have another opportunity the next Friday.

This consequence is different from grounding. By grounding, the parent makes the decision and it's usually for a length of time beyond what's needed to do the teaching—the kids resent it. With a logical consequence, again, the child has a choice and a part in the decision.

Not all consequences can be set up in advance, nor should all of them be negotiated. Sometimes things happen requiring intervention on the spot, or they are too trivial for negotiation, which will just magnify the importance of the problem. For example, suppose you gave your daughter a choice of doing her homework before or after dinner. She doesn't do it before dinner, so you assume she's decided to do it afterwards. When the meal is concluded, you find her in front of the TV. You say, "I'm sorry, but this is homework time." "Dad, I just want to watch this program, then I'll do it." You don't buy in to further negotiation; instead you say, "Do you want to turn off the TV or shall I?" Then you act on her decision.

> Sometimes things happen requiring intervention on the spot, or they are too trivial for negotiation.

Then there are situations that are too serious to be negotiated—you just have to act.

> Six-year-old Kenny and his friend Paul are in the front yard throwing gravel at passing cars. Mom says, "Throwing gravel at cars can damage them. You can play in the front yard as long as you don't throw gravel, or you can come in the house to play; you decide." She watches from the window and Kenny picks up some more gravel as a car approaches. Mom comes out of the house and says, "I see by your behavior that you've decided to come in."

While some situations are not appropriate for advance notice or negotiation, many are. Whenever appropriate, talk with your kids in advance so they know what to expect.

Become More Consistent

While no one's totally consistent, the more consistent you are in your approach to your kids, the more effective you will be. If you hold firm one time and accept their complaints or excuses another, they'll know you don't really mean what you say. Kids who know what to expect are more likely to make cooperative choices.

Refuse to Fight or Give In

Consequences are not intended as weapons of war with your kids; instead, they are articles of peace. Since you're not in a battle, you don't have to win. You just set the limits and let the child decide. If the child chooses the consequence, just act on his decision in the ways we've outlined in this chapter.

Kids may try to get out of the consequence with comments like, "That's not fair" or "I'll behave if you'll just give me one more chance—please" or "Other kids' parents don't do that" or "Dad (Mom) wouldn't do this." Don't give in—once the child has made the decision, turn a deaf ear to pleading and excuses—resist the temptation to explain or argue—and simply follow through with the agreement.

Don't Allow Kids to Play "Divide and Conquer"

Kids may try to get their own way by pitting Mom against Dad in both married and divorced families. While a united front is best, it's not always possible—parents don't always agree. Don't let kids play divide and conquer by letting yourself get into arguments with their other parent about discipline. If you and your spouse or ex-spouse disagree, you handle the problems that occur between you and your kids your way, and let the other parent handle them his way. The kids will adapt to different methods; they'll know how to deal with each parent. Your approach of using the discipline methods you're learning in this book will have a positive influence, and your spouse or ex may learn from your example. An exception to different discipline methods would be child abuse, of course. If you believe the other parent is abusing the kids, you'll have to step in. Check with child abuse agencies in your community for help.

Using Consequences with Other Forms of Effective Discipline

SOMETIMES CONSEQUENCES CAN be combined with other approaches such as I-messages, exploring alternatives, ignoring, distraction, and structuring the environment.

I-Messages

As you learned in chapter 4, an I-message is intended to communicate your feelings about things kids do that disrespect your rights. When your feelings are ignored, it may be time for a logical consequence. Suppose you're ready to fix dinner and your kids have left their coloring projects on the kitchen table. You say, "When I find art materials on the table, I feel disrespected because I have to clean them up in order to set the table for dinner and I'd appreciate it if you'd clean them up when you're finished." If the kids ignore your message and repeat the misbehavior, you follow through with a logical consequence: They can't use the table today; they can try again the next day.

Some kids respond well to I-messages and consequences aren't needed as frequently as with other kids. Don't overdo I-messages, though—too much use of I-messages can trap you into giving undue attention. Kids need to learn to make good decisions and consequences are effective for developing decision-making skills along with family meetings (see chapter 4) and exploring alternatives.

Exploring Alternatives

Exploring alternatives (see chapter 4) not only helps kids sort out problems they own, but is also useful in negotiating parent-child conflicts. When you engage in mutual problem solving by exploring alternatives to negotiate solutions to conflicts, you employ the skills of reflective listening—to communicate understanding of your child's feelings on the issue; I-messages—to communicate your feelings; and brainstorming alternatives to resolve the conflict. Solutions to the conflict are often based on choices and consequences. The prior example of Jessie shows negotiation on a conflict over curfew. Mom and Dad listened to Jessie's feelings, stated their own feelings, and brainstormed solutions. The agreed-upon solution involved a consequence if Jessie was late.

> Ignoring is actually a form of a logical consequence—when you choose to ignore a behavior, kids must make another choice, which often means stopping the annoying or aggravating behavior.

Ignoring

Ignoring certain misbehaviors is often effective. Ignoring is actually a form of a logical consequence—when you choose to ignore a behavior, kids must make another choice, which often means stopping the annoying or aggravating behavior. Kids are smart; they don't do what doesn't work.

Ignoring can be effective for behaviors like pestering, begging, sulking, whining, interrupting, showing off, insults, power plays, and some temper tantrums.[3] Remember, when you ignore misbehavior, be sure to replace the attention that you are taking away: Spend friendly time with them, "catch them being good."

Also realize that when you decide to ignore something, kids may intensify their misbehavior to try to get you to respond. This is especially true if the misbehavior has worked in the past. But if you stick to your resolve to not respond, they'll get the message.

People think that ignoring simply means not saying anything. Ignoring actually means you don't pay attention to kids when they are misbehaving—any form of attention, including what you're thinking and feeling. Kids have radar; they know when they're getting through. The idea is to be unimpressed by the misbehavior.

Actually, ignoring doesn't mean you have to avoid talking. You can talk, just don't talk about what the child is doing. For example, plan your grocery or "to do" list out loud—anything that keeps your focus off the child.

Distracting

Another form of a logical consequence is distraction. Distraction works well with infants. For example, if a crawler is heading toward your favorite lamp—something too large to put out of her reach—and you're afraid she'll knock it over, head her in another direction. This is a form of a choice; it communicates, "you can move about the room as long as you don't go for the lamp." If the child still goes for the lamp, pick her up and put her in another room or her playpen. Give her another opportunity to roam the room where the lamp is a few minutes later.

Structuring the Environment

Putting away things you don't want the little guys to get into helps prevent conflicts. For example, don't put tempting snacks in reach of your two-year-old. Childproof your house. The use of gates to block off areas, or removing objects that are dangerous to the child, is one way to structure. Make sure you have areas of your house where your crawler or toddler is free to roam. You want the child to have more "hands-on" than "hands-off" experiences. As kids begin to respect your property, they will learn to keep away from your favorite things.

> Routines and rituals are important means of discipline and teach and ensure many life skills.

Setting routines also helps structure. Kids do better when they know what the routine is—breakfast follows getting dressed, bath time is right before bedtime, and so on. Routines and rituals are important means of discipline and teach and ensure many life skills.[4]

Frequently Asked Questions About Discipline

WHEN PARENTS FIRST learn our approach to discipline, they often have questions. Perhaps, as you've read this chapter, you've wondered about the following questions.

Q Aren't there times when kids don't have choices?

A Human beings are decision-making animals—we always have a choice. At the lowest level, kids decide whether or not to go along with us or rebel.

Look for ways to give choices. Take the example of an elementary school nurse who had two doors to her office. When a malingerer came in, instead of ordering him out, she just said, "You seem okay to me. Do you want to go back to class through this door or that door?" This nurse found a way to defuse conflict by giving choices. She gave a limited choice, one that fit the needs of the situation. There was no choice of staying in her office "sick" or going home "sick," but there was a choice of how the student went back to the classroom.

While kids always have a choice, you can't always give them a choice. There are some issues so serious that you just have to take a firm stand. For example, your teenager wanting to hang out in his room and smoke marijuana is not appropriate for choices—you have to intervene and prohibit this kind of behavior. Counseling may be in order in this type of situation. The point is simply that the more you give choices in the areas where it's appropriate for choices and let the kids experience the consequences, the more you gain in cooperation and the child's self-discipline.

Q : **Shouldn't kids learn to follow orders? Won't they have a boss someday?**

A : Kids who are raised with choices often do better on the job because they understand the reasons for the policies of the workplace and, if they disagree with the policies, they may set out to create better ones or find other employment with policies they find more acceptable. Kids who know how to make good decisions are more creative and can contribute more to their employer than kids who just know how to follow—or rebel against—orders.

Another downside of kids who are raised to follow orders is that pleasing can get them into trouble in their preteen and teen years when peer influence becomes stronger. For example, pleasers can be easy targets for drug use if they hang with a group into drugs. Kids who know how to make good decisions are in a better position with their choice of friends and activities.

Q : **What if I give my child choices and she wants something else?**

A   Throughout this book we've talked about choices within limits and that life doesn't present unlimited choices. If you give a choice and your child wants something else, the simple reply, "That's not one of the choices," tells her to choose among the alternatives presented. For example, if you think your young child eats too much junk food but wants a snack, you can say, "Would you like an apple or an orange?" If the child replies, "I want a cookie," you say, "That's not one of the choices."

Q   Couldn't getting a spanking be one of the choices?

A   This is a choice, yes, but it's not a logical consequence. As stated above, in order to be effective, a consequence must be related to the misbehavior. Spanking is not related to any misbehavior. It's a violent, rude approach to child-rearing.

Q   Shouldn't there be times when kids are rewarded?

A   Rewards teach kids they should be paid to cooperate. Do you want your kids to base their cooperation on this principle? Many parents pay kids to do chores or to get good grades, but there's a basic flaw in their thinking. Chores are part of kids' contribution to the running of the household, just like the unpaid chores you perform. Kids should be expected to do their share. Kids should also receive an allowance as their share in the family finances. But the allowance should not be connected to their contribution to the family.

If there are extra chores involved, that's different. If a child wants to make extra money, you could pay her to do extra work.

Parents who try to make their kids get good grades by paying them are sending the wrong message—kids are getting the grades for the parents, not for themselves. The real reward for doing schoolwork is learning, not money. School is their everyday work. They are expected to do it as well as they can.

There may be times when you want to express your appreciation to your child or celebrate an accomplishment by doing something special together or by surprising your child with a gift. It's important to distinguish these occasional ways of showing your support from utilizing a reward system to motivate responsible behavior.

Encouragement— The Bottom Line

ANY OF THE discipline approaches we've mentioned— I-messages, natural and logical consequences, exploring alternatives, and so forth—must be used with the spirit of encouragement or they will fail. When you base your approaches to your kids on mutual respect and belief in their

> Parents who try to make their kids get good grades by paying them are sending the wrong message—kids are getting the grades for the parents, not for themselves.

ability to handle life's challenges, you communicate that you care and have their best interests at heart.

In this chapter you've learned effective discipline skills for helping your children accept responsibility and show respect to others. Chapter 7 explores the specific issue of respect as manifested through "civility skills" such as basic manners, courtesy, and politeness. Such basic interpersonal considerations are enjoying a resurgence of interest in both home and school.

7

Civility Skills: Manners, Courtesy, and Politeness

CIVILITY IS THE practice of engaging in polite behavior. It is an outward manifestation of mutual respect and provides the blueprint for getting along with others. Civility skills help build a child's self-esteem and people-esteem. Synonyms for civility include: courtesy, politeness, mannerliness, respect, consideration, tact, and diplomacy. They are the behaviors we teach our children to enable them to become successful, fully functioning adults. In other words, we teach them the civility skills they will need to move with grace through life. And, on a practical note, manners are basic job-seeking and career-enhancement skills—whether the job is family, school, work, or community involvement.

Manners are not conformity. They are the individual's way of implementing the Golden Rule by treating others the way you would like others to treat you. This belief very clearly implies that no one is superior or inferior to another person. It provides both direction and a framework for practicing true equality. When seen in this way, what is considered appropriate manners will vary from culture to culture. In our multicultural society, it becomes important for each of us to learn about differences that exist among cultures and how these differences translate into culturally specific traditions, values, and standards of respect.

How Did We Lose Civility?

AS WE SAID in chapter 1, many people misunderstand equality and, unfortunately, manners and civility have been seriously eroded in our attempt to define and practice equality. Many of today's kids and adults perceive equality as a license to be rude.

Assertiveness is seen as an important asset. In a mistaken effort to be assertive without factoring in consideration for the other person, many people become aggressive. Aggression has thus become glorified and thought of as an example of effective and healthy conduct.

There is a central paradox about America's view of its own bad behavior. We do not like to see people being rude or disrespectful to each other, but at the same time, we tend to applaud rebels who speak and behave honestly but improperly. Sally Jessy Raphael believes that's "because a certain kind of incivility is key to being American . . . it is difficult for Americans to make up their minds about what actually constitutes bad behavior."[1]

Regardless of the causes, Americans have decided it's time to find our lost civility. Recent dramatic increases in the number of magazine articles, newspaper columns, etiquette books, Web sites, school programs, and TV shows dealing with this issue indicate our level of concern. Today's young people are also worried about whether they have the requisite etiquette skills to be viewed as employable and worthy of promotion. "But even good manners can only go so far. Many believe the real issue is to develop a more profound sense of respect to undergird those manners."[2]

How Do We Recapture Civility?

TO UNDERSTAND HOW to recapture civility we will look at several areas of manners and how they can be taught. Keep in mind, the best way to teach any skill is to model it. The chance of a skill being adopted by our children is greatly enhanced when we do it as opposed to simply talking about it. There will be times when verbal instruction is the only practical option. These might include behaviors kids engage in when you aren't there, such as sleepovers, bus trips, and so forth. In these instances, you would provide instruction and create an opportunity to discuss their reactions and entertain questions and comments. The time you take to model behaviors, provide instruction, and discuss ideas will show your children this is an important family value. Finally, use every opportunity to reinforce the behaviors you want to see repeated. Catch them using the appropriate behavior and comment on it.

As we discuss ways to encourage your kids to develop manners, or respectful habits, it is important to keep the following in mind:

- What is considered respectful conduct among people, including what is positive in the way of manners, differs from culture to culture. As you read our suggestions, realize they are being presented from the standpoint of mainstream American traditions and values. If you are of a different culture, you may have different standards and perspectives you consider important to pass along to your kids. We trust, as you read the following suggestions, you will value and incorporate these differences. At the same time, it is important to realize that helping kids develop their people-esteem (see chapter 3) includes supporting them in more fully understanding and valuing people with different backgrounds. In this regard, parents can be role models in learning and in teaching their kids about what people from different cultures in the community consider to be respectful, considerate, and mannerly.

> What is considered respectful conduct among people, including what is positive in the way of manners, differs from culture to culture.

- The way in which positive manners are taught and discussed is significant. Chapters 3 and 4 emphasized the importance of encouragement and effective communication. These skills apply to how we teach and discuss manners. If you try to teach manners by lecturing and using a lot of "shoulds," kids will perceive this as talking down. They will likely tune out or rebel. Practicing encouragement and the communication skills of I-messages and reflective listening will increase your positive influence.

- Parents often justify the importance of manners to their kids as being "right," "correct," or "appropriate." This approach not only invites resistance, but actually shortchanges their value. Demonstrating consideration through manners has a tangible, life-enhancing benefit for kids. It is most helpful for kids to understand that it is to their benefit to develop positive manners both because they are a way of expressing consideration to others and because they will be directly beneficial to kids themselves. Let kids know positive manners will create bridges between themselves and other people and create opportunity in their lives. Other adults, including parents, teachers, coaches, employers, and leaders, tend to go out of their way for kids who employ manners as a consistent way of demonstrating their respect. People will feel good about being in their company. They will be more liked and respected.

> It is most helpful for kids to understand that it is to their benefit to develop positive manners both because they are a way of expressing consideration to others and because they will be directly beneficial to kids themselves.

Meeting and Greeting

THE FIRST MANNERS are "hellos" and "goodbyes." Even very young children can be taught to look someone in the eye, put out their hand, and say hello. You will want to practice with them and show them what to expect. The good feedback and positive attention tots receive from adults for this behavior encourages them to do it again. However, some children are very shy and uncomfortable around adults when meeting them for the first time. If this is the case with your youngster, don't force him. Just talk to the other adult over his head. Eventually he may become curious, and you can suggest he say hello.

Some children don't understand why this behavior is important. Simply tell them people like to be recognized and a simple hello lets others know you are glad to see them. Goodbyes are handled the same way. It is another way of saying, "It's nice to see you." Children should be able to initiate hellos and goodbyes by the end of kindergarten with no prompting.

In her book *Elbows Off the Table*,[3] Carol McD. Wallace suggests by age six, children will have learned the basics, and you can expect them to initiate many polite behaviors without prompting. The new challenge is that they are away from you much of the time and you have to trust the training will be implemented in other settings. Kids (like adults) are often alarmed by new situations. So you'll want to role-play new behaviors and new experiences they may encounter, such as how to behave in line, on field trips, in car pools, and in sports activities.

> By age six, children will have learned the basics, and you can expect them to initiate many polite behaviors without prompting.

At this age (six years), your child can introduce you to her friends and her friends to you. For example, she could say, "Mom, I'd like you to meet my friend Sandy. Sandy this is my mother, Mrs. Norton."

Encourage your children to introduce adults by their last name. It's up to the adults to indicate if they wish your child to use their first name. Also, help your kids be sensitive to use of titles like aunt, uncle, grandmother, and grandfather. Suggest Susie may want to ask Aunt Marie if it's okay to drop "aunt" and just call her Marie. Some adults are offended and hurt if they are simply called by their first name and are quite proud to be someone's aunt, uncle, or grandparent. You would also want to share this with the offended relative, inviting him to tell your child how much the title means to him.

Preteens and teens are capable of introducing their friends to each other, explaining how they know each friend. "Sam, I'd like you to meet Karl. We met last summer at basketball camp. Karl, this is my friend Sam. We are on the school basketball team." This youngster knows both Sam and Karl and has identified for them a common interest. Teens also need to know it's okay to introduce themselves to a new group if no one else does. This is a skill they will need as adults in the workplace.

> Since children watch what we do and copy our behavior, you will know your instruction is being heeded when your child corrects you for an infraction of the manners code you taught her.

Most kids are curious about anyone who is different from them. This could include ethnicity, accents, religion, and physical conditions or disabilities. Point out it is not nice to stare, comment on, ask questions, or make fun of someone's differences. To do so is hurtful to that person. You can point that out with a "remember when." "Remember when you broke your ankle last summer and your friend Ito made fun of your cast. What was that like for you?" Or you can ask your child, "What would it be like for you if someone teased you about . . . ?" The important thing for kids to know is it is hurtful to make fun of, question, or comment about differences. When they want answers to these questions, the person to ask is you.

One final note: Since children watch what we do and copy our behavior, you will know your instruction is being heeded when your child corrects you for an infraction of the manners code you taught her. And, you will really drive home the point if you accept the correction gracefully with a simple "thank you."

Whatever Happened to Please and Thank You?

"PLEASE" AND "THANK you" disappeared from children's vocabularies about the same time the microwave, TV trays, and take-out dinners replaced the family dining table. Today's families tend to use that piece of furniture almost exclusively for holidays and other family celebrations. The niceties went out the window when we no longer had the built-in training opportunity to practice these phrases every day.

These two phrases are the easiest to recapture because children operate from a basic stance of self-interest. Let your children know that any request not preceded by please and followed by thank you will not be fulfilled. Then simply follow through. It will not take your children long to learn you mean business.

Older children need to know you expect them to follow this rule in other settings and when you are not with them. So an overnight at a friend's house begins with greeting the host and the host's parents. Then you expect them to say please, thank you, and may I when making any request. You also expect them to clean up after themselves in the bathroom, offer to help in the kitchen, ask before turning on the TV or changing channels, ask before using the computer (and know the rules and schedule for use), and observe bedtime curfew without grumbling. Let them know this is what you expect even if the host's house rules are more lax. Be sure to debrief them

Modeling Please and Thank You

Dot and Jim taught their three-year-old son to say please and thank you. Whenever they asked Billy something, they would model the behavior they expected. "Billy, would you please turn the TV down. Thank you." "Billy, would you please help Mommy in the kitchen? Please pick up Chipper's bowl so I can wash it. Thank you."

Billy learned to say please and thank you, but once in a while he'd forget. When he did forget to say please, Dot or Jim would simply refrain from fulfilling his request. It didn't take Billy too long to catch on and rephrase his request with "please." If Billy forgot to say thank you, his mother or father would simply say, "You're welcome." Most of the time Billy would respond, "Oh, I forgot. Thank you."

when they come home and discuss any problems that occurred. If things went reasonably well, provide encouragement by giving a verbal pat on the back. "Sounds like you're the kind of guest they will invite again."

Some additional skills pertain to celebrations such as birthday parties, holidays, weddings, graduations, and religious commemorations. Many of these activities require response to invitations and the giving or receiving of presents. Most responses to invitations can be verbal unless a written RSVP is requested by the host. In the case of presents, a simple thank you is all that is required when the giver is present. The giver's response need only be a short phrase such as, "Glad you like it."

There are special circumstances when thank-you notes are more appropriate, such as when the giver isn't present, the giver is a grownup who is special to your child, or someone plans a special treat for your child. Very young children can help you construct a thank-you note. Young elementary school children (ages six to nine) are old enough to write their own with you addressing the envelope. Older children are able to handle the whole process, including specific comments about how they will use the gift or why it is special to them. This is particularly important when thanking someone for a gift of money. Sarah writes to Aunt Jean: "I really appreciated the check you sent me for my birthday. It's been deposited in my summer camp account. Thanks for helping me be able to go."

> As they mature, encourage children to look outward at what they can do for others. This will facilitate the development of mutual respect—a balance between self and other interests.

Another kind of thank-you note is an "I appreciate . . ." When someone does something nice that makes life better, he really enjoys hearing about it. In fact, when children balk at writing a thank-you note, remember you have a built-in encourager—the child's self-interest. Explain that children who take the time to thank are more likely to continue to receive. This is not intended to promote self-centered materialism but to utilize an intrinsic behavior to get them to develop a new habit. As they mature, encourage them to look outward at what they can do for others. This will facilitate the development of mutual respect—a balance between self and other interests. But, if your children still balk, you can tell them they will need to complete the note prior to going out to play, eating dinner, watching TV, and so forth.

The Trough Versus the Table

PEGGY POST, ETIQUETTE editor for *Good Housekeeping*, states, "A child who's learned how to behave at the table gains an ease and confidence from knowing what to do, and shows his consideration for others."[4] On the other hand, sloppy table manners create problems for everyone. On a scale of "least" to "most," least might be a mess that someone has to clean up, while most could be manners so revolting no one wants to eat with that person. Where does your child fall on this scale?

Children are not born knowing what to do. Very few toddlers use correct table manners just because you do. You will need to teach them and reinforce your instruction using choices and consequences. The most important thing to remember is bad habits will persist unless corrected. "Nip it in the bud" needs to be the phrase you keep in mind. And also be aware, the issue of table manners will require you to add age-appropriate behaviors with additional instruction and practice. It is the one set of behaviors that will need practice and prompting no matter what the age.

Manners authority Letitia Baldridge says, "The essential point to be made in any discussion of children's table manners is that before any real training and the formation of good habits takes place, adults must sit down at a table and eat with the children."[5] As we have said before, children learn best from your example. Ms. Baldridge also contends they deserve to know when they are behaving correctly.

Carol McD. Wallace believes the most basic skill is to stay seated until the meal is finished, including dessert.[6] If your child leaves the table, it is understood she has finished eating and may not return. Sitting means sitting, not standing or kneeling. And, should she become hungry later in the evening, you can empathize with her but remark it was her decision to leave the table and breakfast will be the next meal. If she is allowed to snack, she has no motivation to learn this rule.

> **The most basic skill is to stay seated until the meal is finished, including dessert.**

No Scrub, No Grub

Cleanliness is another basic issue. Numerous studies show that washing hands frequently is the single best way to prevent spreading germs. This pertains even more when food is involved. Just visualize where your child's hands have been prior to any meal. Young children will need to be washed or helped in the process. Older children can learn through consequences. The bottom line is, no one eats with dirty hands.

> Mom discussed the importance of washing hands before meals to nine-year-old Troy. She told him that if he wanted to eat he would have to wash his hands at the kitchen sink before meals. At the next meal, Troy sat down at the table without washing his hands. Mom said nothing, but simply removed his plate and silverware. Troy looked at the empty space, then went to wash his hands. Mom returned the place setting.

"Yuck!"

Family educator Dr. Oscar Christensen says that *yuck* (and its alternate form *yucky*) is a word used by children around the world regardless of cultural or language differences. Work on eliminating this word from your child's vocabulary. Explain to your child the word itself is objectionable and it fails to describe what it is he doesn't like about a particular food. There are two ways to approach this problem. You can simply ignore it and talk about something else. If it continues, you can let him know that you will assume *yuck* means he is not hungry and remove his plate.

Like any behaviors you don't want to see in public, the eradication of yuck needs to be taught at home. Imagine your family at the boss's annual employee picnic and his wife puts her award-winning potato salad on the buffet. Your child's immediate response is a loud "yuck." You're probably embarrassed and the hostess is hurt.

This is obviously not the time or place to employ the procedure that works at home. A better approach is to sit down with your youngster at a nonconflict time prior to the event and explain why we don't use this word to describe food offered at another person's house. Let him know this kind of comment will hurt the hostess's feelings. Tell him it's okay to take a tiny spoonful and either taste it or leave it on his plate. No one will notice and feelings will not be hurt. What's important here is to remember children have the ability to be kind and usually will avoid hurting someone if they see an acceptable compromise.

Fickle is the word best used to describe children's food likes and dislikes. The macaroni and cheese they loved last week is poison this week. Any parent who has tried to find out why this sudden change knows it's a waste of breath. There is a very simple explanation—children don't know why. Like everything else in their environment, food is simply one more thing to be explored. Sometimes children will refuse a new food just because they've never tasted it. Most parents use the "try one bite" strategy and don't make an issue of it. If you offer a variety of foods and refuse to cater to the picky eater, your child is more likely to cooperate.

Realize that sometimes kids will eat the same food called by another name if they don't know what it actually is. For example some kids eat canned sandwich spread which contains liver but say "yuck" if liver is offered by itself.

"Food fights"—what kids will and won't eat—can be some of the biggest power contests in families. You can't force kids to eat. The best approach is to involve them in deciding menus in the family meeting (see chapter 4). If kids refuse to eat what's served, they can have another opportunity to eat at the next meal. The natural consequence of being hungry will do the teaching.

What Table Manners Should We Teach Our Kids?

Carol McD. Wallace created the following table manners training checklist:[7]

- Don't eat until everyone else is served.

- Chew with your mouth closed.

- Don't talk with food in your mouth.

- Don't eat with your fingers.

- Use the correct utensil.

- Don't wave utensils around.

- No playing with food.

- No shoveling food.

- Eat off your own plate.

- No "yucky" comments.

- Use your napkin.

- Elbows off the table.

- Keep your free hand in your lap.

- No singing at the table.

- Ask to be excused.

- Clear your place.

She suggests you may want to introduce and practice the skills one at a time. When your child has mastered one, move on to the next until all skills are addressed. As a general guideline, a six-year-old should be able to accomplish the list at home with prompting. You can expect your nine-year-old to use these behaviors in public with a minimum of reminding. And, the introduction of any new skills would need to be age appropriate.

"Do I Have to Wear That?"

Kids and parents have different opinions on what is appropriate to wear in different settings. Very young children have no choice; they are dressed by others. When they become toddlers they begin to express an interest in wearing their favorite outfits. As they mature, their peers will have a significant impact on their choices. In many communities, acceptance by the peer group will be determined by adherence to the fad of the day, and children believe rejection will occur if they don't comply. If this is the case with your child, you may want to consider some ways to negotiate and compromise.

Let's begin with toddlers. Small children tend to have favorite pieces of clothing they wish to wear all the time. Colors and patterns may clash, and the necessity to wash your son's favorite shirt may engender wails of protest. Actually, this is the opportune age to start the process of choices. Offer him several choices of outfits from which to select. He will begin to get the idea of what goes together and still have the final word.

This works with casual clothes worn for school, play, or informal outings. What about your cousin's wedding? When it comes to clothing, small children place comfort first. They want to wear their favorite play clothes that are totally inappropriate and often very worn-out. Take time to explain about special occasions and why we dress up for them. You can tell the kids this is one way we let the bride know we care about her and want to look nice on her special day. Young children like to please and often are willing to endure a little discomfort if they know the reason. Be understanding but firm about the fact this is not open to negotiation because it's not about them—it's the bride's special day.

Older children (middle elementary school age and up) often believe they will be rejected by their peers if they dress differently. By differently, they mean the kinds of choices adults would make. Just take a trip to the mall to learn the latest mode of dress in your community. Most parents find it's nonproductive to fight with youngsters about casual dress. It helps to put your child on a clothing allowance so she gets experience in how to budget. If the latest fad is designer labels, she will have some very difficult choices to make, both on clothes and budget. Your child may view one of your friends as a fashion guru and be willing to shop with her. Meanwhile, take comfort in the fact "they will grow out of it"—both literally and figuratively—and every parent of a same-age child is in the same boat.

> In many communities, acceptance by the peer group will be determined by adherence to the fad of the day, and children believe rejection will occur if they don't comply.

Dress clothes are another issue because special places and occasions call for appropriate attire. "Aleta, your school clothes aren't appropriate for Jana's wedding. We'll need to shop for a new dress this weekend." Since preteens and teens believe you haven't a clue when it comes to clothes, Aleta will probably answer, "But you never like anything I pick out and I don't want a new dress." Assure Aleta you are willing to explore alternatives and negotiate a compromise in order to find something acceptable to both of you. This is definitely the time to enlist the aid of your fashion guru friend. Aleta may test you by selecting a dress more appropriate for the role of streetwalker. You offer something much more conservative and then work together to reach a middle ground—a dress you probably don't love but can live with.

Here's another example of helping kids choose appropriate clothes:

> Carlos liked to wear sports clothing. He often dressed in jeans and a T-shirt with the logo of his favorite team. Mom and Dad told him such attire was not appropriate for church and gave him a choice between outfits they found acceptable.

Instead of forcing Carlos to wear a particular outfit, Mom and Dad gave a limited choice—one that fit the requirements of the situation. As Carlos learns what is acceptable, there may be no need to keep offering him choices between outfits—he'll know and make appropriate choices, though he may test his parents a few times to make sure they mean what they say.

With older kids, you can take them shopping for clothes. Give choices between outfits you find acceptable for activities like school and church.

One final note about grooming: No matter what the setting or occasion, cleanliness is not optional. It is a very basic expectation both for ourselves and others.

School Uniforms

Many schools around the country are advocating the wearing of uniforms. Like parents, schools are gravely concerned about the rise in school violence and gang activity. Both the kind of dress and the specific colors play a part in group identification for gang members. Unfortunately, this is supported by the child's belief that, "I only belong when I look like my friends."

A group of school administrators in Tucson, Arizona, found a way to use this belief to reduce gang membership on campus. The students voted to select one mode of clothing, a logo, and a color from a variety of options. Their final selection became the school uniform and the colors were depicted on the logo and other items such as pennants, caps, and jackets. The kids love it and the parent's pocketbooks love it. Parents report an added benefit—no more morning arguments or agonizing decisions about what to wear to school.

Technology Tips

MANY OF TODAY'S homes are so loaded with technology they resemble a set from a James Bond movie. In fact, the proliferation of technological equipment and the need to know how it works is a major stress factor for many people, often creating occasions for angry responses. Therefore, it's even more important to practice courtesy because the temptations to lose it are many. The training we give our children can be a refresher course for ourselves.

Telephone Tactics

The first technological interaction your child will probably have is with the telephone. Even very small children are able to answer the phone. The phrase they will need is, "Who may I say is calling please?" Then they need to carefully lay the phone down and get you. Explain that a dropped phone makes a very loud noise in the caller's ear and that yelling loudly for you to come is equally hurtful. Most kids don't like to hurt others and with some prompting will remember this bit of telephone etiquette. At the same time, you will need to instruct them to speak up so the caller can hear them. Some young children become so quiet the caller can't hear or understand them. Practice these skills with calls from friends or relatives. You can also use play telephones to teach phone etiquette.

Also give kids an opportunity to make calls. Until your children are old enough to dial, you will have to take care of that. Instruct them to say, "This is Michelle. May I please speak to Rachel?" Stress the importance of please, may I, and thank you by telling them the use of these phrases is more likely to produce the desired result. If the person isn't there, children will need to know how to leave a message or request a call back. Be sure they understand the rules for phone usage in your home. These might include: length of calls, no hanging up, no picking up extensions when the phone is in use, and no interrupting. Like any skill, polite phone usage is acquired only through practice.

Safety is always an issue today. Children need to know what they can and can't say to a stranger, what is okay to say to a family friend, and what to do if you aren't there. The answering machine can be a wonderful safety device when you are away from the house. Simply instruct your child not to answer the phone until she hears and recognizes that the caller is on your list of "safe" people to talk to when Mom and Dad aren't home. Be sure this list is always next to the phone and answering machine. This might be the same list of people who are appropriate for them to call if you can't be reached when they encounter a problem.

Netiquette

In his teen guide to manners, Alex Packer suggests, "computers are not only changing parent-child relationships, they're changing the world."[8] The way we handle correspondence, gather information, and converse with others has been affected. We use e-mail to correspond, search engines to do research, chat rooms to have conversations. Our children may be even more tuned in to this new technology than we are. Therefore, we need some guidelines to address the issues of safety, privacy, and courtesy.

Because online communication seems anonymous, kids may be tempted to share personal information. They need to be warned against becoming too intimate with PC pals. Chapter 8 provides further discussion of how to handle potential dangers on the Internet.

Computer technology has invaded our right to privacy. Institutions can use our social security number to gain access to almost every aspect of our life, such as finances, buying profile, medical history, marital status, size of family, and so on. Kids are even more curious than institutions, and they usually think adults have some great secrets. Discuss with them the idea that privacy is a right we all need to respect and expect. Therefore, anyone's personal, private files are off limits both to you and to them. However, don't overlook natural curiosity. Some kids are more adept at breaking passwords than the CIA. If you don't want your most private thoughts to be read, write them on removable media.

Privacy is also a safety issue. So caution your child not to share any private family information that may be requested by someone they encounter on the Internet, regardless of how innocuous that request may seem.

> Caution your child not to share any private family information that may be requested by someone they encounter on the Internet, regardless of how innocuous that request may seem.

Further evidence of the impact computers have on our lives is provided by a quick scan of the current bestsellers on etiquette. Many of these books contain a section on computer etiquette. Magazine articles and columns are also following this trend. Some suggested rules for kids and computer use are: don't have food or drink at the computer, have clean hands, put things back, don't snoop, back up files, use anti-virus software, ask before installing or playing games. Some additional suggestions with regard to e-mail include: use the correct address; restrict forwards; don't shout—CAPITAL LETTERS FOR EMPHASIS equal shouting; be discreet—e-mail isn't private; don't assume your message has been received; give people time to respond; avoid chain letters; don't post or forward e-mail without permission; and don't tie up the phone.[9]

Cell Yell

Many children carry cell phones or pagers. How they use this equipment will be determined by your instruction and their observation of your behavior. If you engage in conversations while driving or shopping, at a restaurant, or during a movie, kids will understand this to be acceptable behavior. So once again, do as you wish them to do. Stop the car, move out of the grocery aisle, and go to the lobby of a restaurant or theater when making or receiving a call. This demonstrates respect for others and models your beliefs about physical safety.

Model the appropriate behavior, instruct your child in proper usage, and negotiate a consequence for misuse. If misuse occurs, simply take the phone away and let her know there will be another opportunity to demonstrate correct usage.

Cell phones and pagers have become such disruptive items that in some schools students are required to check them at the office or leave them at home. Some schools have banned them altogether. Let your school know what you have done in instructing correct usage (your rules) and that you appreciate their efforts to construct a positive learning environment without interruptions.

> Many children carry cell phones or pagers. How they use this equipment will be determined by your instruction and their observation of your behavior.

Sports and Fair Play

PARENTS NEED TO set good examples and behave themselves at sports events. If parents yell insults at the officials and the other team, kids are likely to do the same. So you will want to model appropriate behavior, but you will also need to instruct your child in some specific do's and don'ts of good sportsmanship. Kids should congratulate the other team on their effort regardless of who wins. Team members should also thank the coaches and officials for their efforts in making the game possible. What they shouldn't do is boast, shout, boo, argue a call, make rude gestures, fight with other players, or put down opponents. In other words, engage in fair play.

Some parents become very antagonistic when a coach enforces the rules of good sportsmanship. So, it would be helpful if you let him know you have instructed your child in the rules and you will support the coach's decision about handling infractions.

> Kids should congratulate the other team on their effort regardless of who wins.

The same holds true with behavior expected during play dates at your home or elsewhere. Your kids need to know expectations for fair play behavior include any games they play with friends. In this instance you would also want to include a discussion on taking turns and sharing toys.

"School Days, School Days, Good Old Golden Rule Days"

IN A *National Association of Secondary Schools Principals Bulletin*, Ronald D. Williamson and J. Howard Johnson[10] state, "The vast majority of parents (90 percent) . . . believe schools tolerate too much rudeness and incivility. Many parents feel appropriate standards of behavior are neither modeled nor monitored." However, in the wake of the school tragedies in the 1990s this is changing. Many schools are placing an emphasis on civility and have instituted programs designed to address the issues.

There are several ways you can help:

- Tell your kids, "Don't check your manners at the school door; remember what we've been learning at home. Your teacher will really appreciate your kindness."

- Check with the school to see what they are doing about civility and let them know what you are doing at home.

- Offer to help at school. PTA member, parent aide, room monitor, guest lecturer, and field trip chaperone are just a few of the areas where parent assistance is welcomed.

Schools need to know your feelings and beliefs regarding incivility. They also need to know what kinds of specific changes you will support. In the past, some parents have sued schools when they implemented an unpopular student behavior program. So if we expect them to help us reduce incivility, we have to let then know what we will accept and support.

Say What You Want to Hear

MOST PARENTS WANT their children to be both honest and tactful. For young children, these are mutually exclusive constructs. So if you criticize someone and your child overhears the conversation, he will probably repeat it in public. The operant idea in this situation is if you don't want to hear it, don't say it.

Four-year-old Tony has accompanied you to Gram's house for Thanksgiving dinner. Great Aunt Ruth is also there, wearing her favorite ruffled pink dress. Now, Aunt Ruth is seriously overweight and Tony has heard you say (on more than one occasion) this dress makes her look really fat and you fail to understand why she wears it. At dinner you comment, "Aunt Ruth, you look so pretty. I know that's your favorite dress." Tony's immediate response is, "But Mommy, you always say she looks like a fat pink marshmallow in that dress."

Young children lack the ability to discriminate, but as they grow older, you can teach them we don't repeat such statements because of the potential for hurt feelings. You can say, "What would it be like for you if your friend told you something critical someone else had said?"

> Most parents want their children to be both honest and tactful. For young children, these are mutually exclusive constructs.

It's also helpful to share the importance of giving and receiving compliments. A compliment is a simple statement indicating you've noticed something about a person you think she will want to hear. Children are seldom aware how good this feels for the recipient. So, you can help your child learn by using the "what would it be like for you if . . ." formula. Receipt of a compliment requires only a simple "thank you."

An apology is often difficult because the child assumes it is an admission of wrongdoing. Start with a basic behavior like bumping into a stranger. "Sorry" is all that's required. As they mature, children are able to understand that apologies—like compliments—simply help the other person feel better. They will soon realize it's a two-way street. When the other person feels better your child will, too. And, when your child discusses it with you, you can comment, "I'll bet you both feel better."

Don't Interrupt, and Turn Down the Volume

A few other rules of polite conversation: Don't interrupt, and keep the noise level down. We are all guilty of interrupting, and children often believe what they have to say just can't wait. Give them a few pointers about when it's okay to interrupt and how to say "excuse me" before stating their problem. Noise tends to escalate and children usually can't hear themselves. Therefore, you'll probably have to alert them when the decibels get too high.

Back Talk

Back talk is disrespectful. It usually occurs when mutual respect and equality are being violated. When your child engages in this behavior, you may want to look at how you might have set him up. Did you perhaps say something demeaning or disrespectful like, "Joel, why do you always act so stupid? If I've told you once, I've told you a million times, don't . . ." Analyze the communication. First you demeaned him by calling him stupid. Then you disrespected him by reminding him. In a similar situation, you would probably talk back.

If you have cleaned up your act and you are still getting back talk, ignore it and talk about something else. Should it continue, remove yourself either physically or mentally. In other words, go to another room or plan your grocery list out loud. At a later time you can have a friendly discussion about how people insult each other and better ways to comment on what you don't like, such as using I-messages.

Toilet Talk

Young children go through a stage when the words used to describe bodily functions are totally fascinating. We call this bathroom language or toilet talk. Acknowledge you understand their fascination, but these are words we do not use at any time in public since others may feel embarrassed and the child is being vulgar. Then ignore the talk and it will go away when it no longer gets a shocked response.

Saying No

One final word about language—the word "no." We want and expect our children to say no to strangers, drugs, and other potentially harmful situations, but we give them little practice. In fact, we sometimes train them to say "yes." Often we are so intent on rearing polite children, we rob them of the ability to protect themselves in dangerous situations. Teach your child to discriminate between an impolite no and the appropriate use of the word in the interest of safety. Give them the opportunity to practice safe, firm ways to say no in dangerous or inappropriate situations, such as say, "No," and walk away; say nothing and walk away; or say, "No, my Mom doesn't let me do . . ." Of course, a polite no in the appropriate situation is a simple: "No, thank you." The important thing to remember is *no* is not a bad word. It's the context in which it is used that needs to be addressed.

> We want and expect our children to say no to strangers, drugs, and other potentially harmful situations, but we give them little practice.

Public Behavior

APPROPRIATE PUBLIC BEHAVIOR is best taught and rehearsed at home. If you put no limits on disruptive behavior at home, don't be surprised to see it in public. It's important for kids to know what is expected in terms of appropriate behavior. The best way to teach this is through modeling, which means, if you want the kids to keep their elbows off the table and stop shouting, you'll need to monitor your own behavior.

When you're tempted to think, "Where did he learn that?", remember the clichés "like father like son" or "the apple doesn't fall far from the tree." Both are excellent reminders of how children learn behavior. So, if you don't want to see it, don't do it. Modeling and taking time for training are the best ways to instill appropriate behavior.

> It's more effective to talk about expectations, choices, and consequences during a relaxed time before the event is to occur.

Once you have determined the behavior you wish to reinforce, children will need to know your expectations. It is also important for them to know there will be choices, and these choices will have consequences. As we have said in preceding chapters, it's more effective to talk about expectations, choices, and consequences during a relaxed time before the event is to occur. Then if they choose to violate the agreement, they will know what to expect. Let kids know that disruptive behavior in public is disrespectful to others and not acceptable.

Past experience has taught you that lecturing, scolding, threatening, and coaxing don't work, especially in the heat of the moment. You've modeled the appropriate behavior, taken time for training, and discussed choices and consequences. When the misbehavior occurs, you simply act on the kids' choice by implementing the consequence with a minimum of talking. Later, let them know there will be an opportunity to try again.

> The family is out to dinner with their three children, ages twelve, nine, and seven. The kids start to fight at the table. Mom says, "Either settle down or we'll have to leave." The kids settle for a while and then resume fighting. The parents

signal for the check, take the kids by the hand, and leave with the meal unfinished.

You may balk at leaving an unfinished meal you're paying for, but consider what the kids are learning from this consequence, and we're sure you'll see it's worth the price. They are learning to respect the rights of others and that they are responsible for their behavior. Of course, there are no snacks when the kids get home. They will have the opportunity to eat at breakfast. There's no reason why the parents should not have a snack after the kids go to bed because they did not create the problem.

There is, of course, an endless list of disturbing public behaviors. A few examples: shouting, talking during a movie, breaking in line, pushing, shoving, interrupting a conversation, insulting, making faces, and so forth. You probably can add others. The important thing to remember is the behavior is inappropriate if it violates mutual respect and interferes with the rights of others. Therefore, the remedy for all these behaviors is the same. You provide instruction, give choices, and apply appropriate consequences—which means the choices and consequences must fit the behavior and be logical to the child. (See chapter 6 for a discussion of logical consequences.)

Kids know we don't like to look bad in public. They also bank on us not being consistent. So, if you want some behaviors to change, improve your consistency and be prepared to ignore a little embarrassment.

Civility skills help kids get along positively in the world. When you model and teach your kids these simple skills, you help build their self-esteem and people-esteem.

The Many Values of Politeness

POLITE BEHAVIOR HAS resounding effects throughout a child's life. Let him know all the benefits of good manners.

Dinner Out with Toddlers

Unlike older children, preschoolers tire quickly and react negatively to overstimulation. So expecting them to sit quietly throughout a long, formal dinner is unrealistic. Give your toddler opportunities to have make-believe dinner parties. Practice skills using puppets or dolls as the guests. Then encourage her to use these new skills at the family dinner table. When she goes out to dinner with you, keep it short and simple and provide some diversions like coloring materials or a favorite toy. Make it a happy time and comment on the things she is doing appropriately. "Did you notice how the waiter smiled when you said, 'thank you'?"

Here is a list to keep in mind and maybe to post about why old-fashioned manners can be good for your children.

Reasons to act right:

- People will like you.

- People will notice you.

- Opportunities will come your way because of your perceived maturity and competence.

- You'll feel good about yourself and have more self-esteem.

- You'll have something to fall back on in new situations where you are not sure how to act.

- It will be easier to maintain your personal boundaries in all situations, but especially in unpleasant ones or in cases where you want to say no to someone.

- Manners help you manage your feelings because appropriate behavior can save you from embarrassing outbursts.

- You can go places other people can't (fancy parties, celebrity events, the White House, trips).

This chapter has focused on helping your kids learn civility skills. These skills are best taught through modeling and logical consequences when needed. Part III focuses on the ultimate manifestation of rudeness—violent behavior. Practical suggestions for better insuring your child's safety, dealing with media violence, video games and toys, role models and heroes, and safety at school are discussed.

Dealing with the Ultimate Rudeness: Violence

8

Parents Preventing Violence

If we are to reach real peace in the world,
we shall have to begin with our children.

—GANDHI

VIOLENCE IS RUDENESS in the extreme. Violent acts show maximum disrespect for another person. The violent act can be verbal, vicious insults, for example, or physical by harming a person or the person's property. We'll begin by discussing the general nature of violence, then talk in this chapter and the next about the influences and violence your kids may face.

What Can We Do to Protect Our Kids and Ourselves from Violence?

GANDHI'S QUOTE ABOVE on the role of children attaining peace in our world reflects an attitude of positive action.

Reverend Mary Manin Morrissey of the Living Enrichment Center points out:

> "Nonviolence is not about passivity. Gandhi talked about nonviolence as a path for the courageous. Courageous literally means 'of the heart.' Therefore, the energy we direct every single day moves through the heart, and we empower others and ourselves with that energy." [1]

Of course, there will be times when nonviolent methods fail. In these situations, our kids need to know what to do. Self-defense comes in many forms. For example, knowing safe houses in the neighborhood in case kids are threatened or assaulted is one form of self-defense. Learning physical skills such as karate is another. Physical means of self-defense should be your child's last resort. Whenever physical means are used, your child is at risk for injury. Later in the chapter we'll discuss how to choose self-defense classes.

> Learning to handle adversity is an essential step to becoming a well-functioning adult.

And, of course, there may be times when we have to step in and protect our kids. But the more they learn to protect themselves, the better off they will be. We cannot be at their side in every threatening situation. Learning to handle adversity is an essential step to becoming a well-functioning adult.

The American Psychological Association and Music Television (MTV) teamed up to produce materials for kids from ages 12 to 24 on violence prevention. In a publication called *Warning Signs*, the organizations outline things kids can do about violence (see appendix, "References and Resources").

Violence in Fun and Games

IN THIS SECTION we'll discuss media with violent themes. Many of the suggestions you'll find in this chapter depend on the skills you've learned and practiced as you've read the previous chapters. In following the suggestions here, you'll need to:

• Understand the child's goal.

• Encourage.

• Listen and talk respectfully about feelings and beliefs.

• Negotiate.

• Apply natural and logical consequences.

Violence in the Media

While it's tempting to blame the media for the violence in our society, this would be an injustice. That is not to say that violent media does not share part of the responsibility, for it certainly does. The American Medical Association, the American Academy of Pediatrics, the American Psychological Association, and the American Academy of Child and Adolescent Psychiatry collectively conclude the following on media violence:

> The conclusion of the public health community, based on over 30 years of research, is that viewing entertainment violence can lead to increases in aggressive attitudes, values, and behaviors, particularly in children.[2]

The media models violence as a form of problem solving and excitement. So-called action films are bloody, violent portrayals of very disrespectful human relationships. Television plays a part, too; action cartoons and programs are meant to appeal to youngsters. And some of the music kids listen to certainly doesn't calm the savage breast.

Many video games emphasize giving points for destroying the enemy. The military uses what is called "first person shooter" games to train its soldiers and our kids have access to similar games. Some kids involved in recent school shootings have "trained" on such video games. There are computer games that are equally violent; the Web is loaded with such games. But there are also nonviolent games available.

Books, too, can have a violent theme. Consider some of the comic books that appeal to kids.

Let's examine different types of media to see how they contribute to attitudes toward violence.

Films

The rating system helps parents sort out movies that are appropriate for children. This system is not perfect nor are the people who let kids into films. Some G-rated films have a degree of violence. Kids under 17 do get admitted to R-rated films.[3]

Advertising for movies motivates kids. The Federal Trade Commission reported the media industry advertises R-rated films and M (meaning for over 17) video games on TV and in other publications that kids read.[4] If your child shows an interest in a particular film that you think is inappropriate, discuss it with him. (See "Guidelines for Media Discussions.") You may want to see the film with him and discuss it afterwards.

Television

A study from the American Academy of Pediatrics reports that children as young as two watch 16 to 17 hours of TV a week. Teens who watch TV and play video games spend 35 to 55 hours a week in a combination of these activities. On average, children see 10,000 incidents of violence on TV yearly. TV programs involve sexual content in the form of ". . . references, innuendoes, and jokes, of which fewer than 170 deal with abstinence, birth control, sexually transmitted diseases, or pregnancy." And 70 percent of TV network prime time dramas involve tobacco, alcohol, and drugs.[5] Prime time TV airs three to five acts of violence hourly, and Saturday morning cartoons feature 20 to 25 violent scenes each hour.[6]

Obviously, American kids watch a lot of TV, not to mention the type of programs. One wonders what models of human relationships and conflict resolution they are absorbing and when kids have time to interact with their family and peers.

How much TV should kids watch? Organizations like the National Parents and Teachers Association and the American Medical Association suggest a maximum of two hours a day.[7]

> On average, children see 10,000 incidents of violence on TV yearly.

How much TV does your family watch? We suggest you keep track of the hours your kids—and you—spend in front of the tube. Write it down. Also, write down the types of programs you watch.

In your family meetings, involve your children in setting the time limits and the type of programs watched. Look for programs that model good social values. If your children insist on watching some programs you consider inappropriate, watch them with the kids and discuss what's seen. Of course, you'll want to say no to certain programs, especially if you have young children in your family. V-chip technology and parental controls from cable companies can help you in this task.

Music

Preteens and teens often listen to music we adults do not consider music, but it's "music to *their* ears." Some popular music stars have crude and violent messages in their songs. Often, parents may not be aware of music the kids listen to on their

Walkmans and MP3 players. Pay attention to the type of music they buy; listen to it with them. If your children like to watch MTV, watch it with them to find out what music appeals to them.

> In your family meetings, involve your children in setting the time limits and the type of programs watched.

Video and Computer Games

The market is full of violent video games, but there are also nonviolent games like some sports games. Some nonviolent games challenge your kid's minds and can actually be helpful. Again, pay attention to the games your children want to play. You may have to do some limiting, just as you do with TV. You may also want to discuss their interest in violent games. Play the games with them and discuss them.

Books and Promotional Materials

Monitor the books your kids read just like you monitor TV, and so on. Go to the library with your children. Talk to librarians about appropriate books for your children's age. Ask their teachers. Again, if you discover your kids reading inappropriate books, read the book yourself, and talk it over.

Some promotional materials with violent themes include T-shirts, board games, and role-playing games. If your child shows an interest in these materials, find out what interests her and discuss the implications of such items.

Guidelines for Media Discussions

The suggestions here will apply to discussing any type of media we've talked about. Remember, when you discuss a film, TV program, music, game, or book, it's important to listen and respect your child's feelings and opinions. Use open questions that begin with words like "what" and how." Questions that begin with "is" (as in "Is that right?") and "do" (as in "Do you think . . . ?") tend to shut down discussion because they require only a one-word answer and kids try to guess the answer you want. Open questions allow for discussion of opinions.

Give your own opinions. Make sure your sharing of your opinion is just that—an opinion, not a lecture.

You could begin the discussion by asking, "What do you like about (film, TV program, and so on?)" or, "What appeals to you about . . . ?" You may get an answer like, "It's fun," or, "It's exciting." You could respond with, "What's fun about it?" or, "What are some other ways things can be exciting?" "How do you feel about how people are treated?" "How about how these people treat each other?" "If someone treated you this way, what would that be like for you?" Discuss other ways to satisfy the desire for excitement. What about a video sports game? Maybe it's something the two of you can play together.

Ask about what the media demonstrate about human relationships and conflict solving.

"What does this show you about how people solve problems?"

"What are some other ways people can solve problems?"

"What does this show about what men are like?"

"What does this show about what women are like?"

"What do you think about the way they show men and women?"

Include discussions about how various ethnic groups are represented in the media "What does this show say about people who are (name the minority)?" If the image is negative, point out people of a particular ethnic group who are positive models.

Ratings, Ratings, Ratings!

TV, in it's search for Neilsen ratings, is looking for ways to attract viewers. Venues which appeal to our base instincts such as so-called "reality TV" and extreme sports are being offered. These types of shows emphasize rudeness or violence. If you are a fan of these kinds of programs, consider what your kids are learning from your model.

Check the reality of the media. "How does this relate to real life?" Kids who watch a lot of violent TV may come to believe that the world is unsafe. Television exaggerates the threat of violence to the average citizen.[8]

Share your own opinions as well. Sometimes when asked to discuss your child's choice of media, you'll be met with an "I don't know" to your questions about his interest. "I don't know" often means "I don't want to discuss this." You can respectfully tell your child, "When you say 'I don't know,' I get the feeling this is something you don't want to talk about. That's okay, but I have some feelings about this material I'd like to share with you." Share your feelings. Sometimes this will open up a discussion—as long as the sharing is not lecturing. If you think you need to limit your child's exposure to such material, explain why.

The news keeps us informed, but can be frightening as well. When children hear about violent acts, they may fear such things can happen to them. Listen to their feelings. Discuss the possibilities of such violent acts happening in your neighborhood. Discuss ways to be safe. Later in the chapter we'll discuss what children can do in potentially violent situations.

Media Death and Real Death

With the exception of the news and some talk shows, much of the violence our children are exposed to in the media is make-believe. It's designed to be exciting, as in action films. This type of media not only gives kids a poor model of human relationships, but young kids don't know the difference between fantasy and reality. They'll see a cartoon character that gets "killed or seriously injured" bounce back to life. Point out to the child that this is not real. If a person is blown up, shot, stabbed, falls off a cliff, and so forth, that means he is dead and can't come back to life.

> **Young kids don't know the difference between fantasy and reality.**

Your child may have had experience with real death, such as a death of a pet. If that's the case, then you can use that experience to draw comparisons. If your child has not had experience with death, then simply explain that what she is seeing is make-believe. You can use dolls, for example, to explain the difference between real and unreal. Point out how the doll doesn't breathe, but the child does; the doll doesn't walk, but the child does, and so on.

The Internet

The Internet is a wonderful invention, giving access to a wealth of information. Almost anything can be found on the Web. While that's good news in a lot of ways, it can be bad news for your children if they enter sites where they shouldn't be. For example, violent video games can be played online. Sex Web sites can be found. Pedophiles prey on children in certain newsgroups, in chat rooms, and through e-mail. Fortunately, there is monitoring software designed to be the V-chip of the computer. Talk to salespeople at computer stores to locate current software packages.

The Helpanswers Educational Foundation (see the appendix, "References and Resources") is a not-for-profit organization that provides computer help and education to students, teachers, and has many answers to computer questions. They have many searchable articles plus a free e-mail service for questions not already answered. The following is an excerpt from an article on their Web site about protecting children on the Internet.

> Explain to your children that people they do not know well, and do not know in person, should be considered "strangers." It's okay to talk to people on the net that they do not know in the hopes of making new friends, but they should be very careful to not reveal a lot of personal information. They should immediately stop conversing with anyone who tries to get them to talk about things that make them uncomfortable, or who ask them to do things such as meet them in person. Instruct [children] to save any messages that make them feel uncomfortable and to tell the parent about them immediately.[9]

This is also a good time to discuss the concepts of "secrets." Many perpetrators are successful in convincing children to keep their actions as "just a secret between us."

As children grow older they will be interested in sex. At the present time there are many pornography Web sites. The Helpanswers Educational Foundation suggests the following regarding talking to your children about such sites:

> When [children are] old enough, it's best to acknowledge that such material exists, explain why it isn't appropriate, and let [them] ask any questions they may have, so they can perhaps understand better and not be lured by the great temptation of the unknown or, worse, the banned.[10]

There are several books on children and the Internet. Talk with your local librarian or bookstore sales representative, or search online bookstores. See also the appendix, "References and Resources."

Toys

Play helps young children learn about the world and develop skills. Toys are a large part of young children's play. The type of toys you select for your children will send different messages. Toy guns, war toys, and action figures emphasize relationships and conflict solving based on violence. Instead, choose toys that help children learn about respect, peace, and cooperation and help with developmental skills.[11]

TV advertisers make toy selection difficult for parents because kids want what they see on the commercials. This is especially true during Christmas holidays or after popular films are released where toys are associated with the films. But if you feel an advertised toy is inappropriate for your child, state your reasons and refuse to be manipulated by begging, tears, and anger. "I know you really want that toy, but we don't want violent toys in our house." After your child has calmed down, explain what these toys teach about human relationships and why advertisers are trying to sell a particular toy—the profit motive. Comment on how advertisers try to make the toys so appealing in the hope that children will be able to push their parents into buying

> If you feel an advertised toy is inappropriate for your child, state your reasons and refuse to be manipulated by begging, tears, and anger.

them.[12] Talk about other toys that you consider appropriate. Present two or three appropriate toys and ask your child which one he likes best. You can also limit TV viewing. And there are devices that drown out commercials.

Selecting Toys

Of the thousands of toys available, how do you go about selecting appropriate toys? You'll want to make sure a toy is age appropriate and fits your values. A visit to a toy store (without the kids!) can be a fact-finding mission. Some stores will have their aisles arranged by age. Talk to the staff as well.

There's an organization that rates toys, books, audio, computer software, and videos, as well as products for kids with special needs. The Oppenheim Toy Portfolio is like the *Consumer Reports* of such products for children.[13] When you visit the toy store, look for the Oppenheim seal on products in which you're interested. They publish a newsletter, an annual book on toys, books, and so forth, and are frequently guests on NBC's *Today Show*.

You can also go to the library or a bookstore for information on toys. Talk to the children's librarian. If your child's in school, talk to the teachers as well.

Some of you may be thinking: "We watched some violent movies and TV when we were kids and played with toy guns, and we aren't violent people. Why all this concern about media and toys?" Although it's true that violence has been portrayed in movies and TV in the past, and that toy guns have been around for years, it's different today. There is more media violence than in the past, it's more graphic, and there's more violence in society than when you grew up, despite recent declining statistics. And children may be more connected to media more hours a day. With the amount of violence in our world today, we need to look at what media models, the activities our children are engaged in, and what these things are teaching our kids. We need to consider what values we want our children to have.

Your Child's Role Models and Heroes

AT ONE TIME athletes were positive role models and heroes. They modeled the values of hard work and sportsmanship. Although most athletes still model these values, we also have athletes that model the worst—drugs; violence against each other, coaches, officials, and fans; and sexual promiscuity, rape, and murder. Unfortunately, the negative athletes get more press than the ones who behave themselves.

Some athletes believe they shouldn't be looked to as role models. They believe that's the job of the parents. While it's true that you are your children's primary role model, many kids look outside the family for heroes as well. An athlete's skill level is an appealing example of excellence to our children. As human beings, athletes are also responsible for their personal behavior, as everyone else is.

An athlete's behavior is also under scrutiny. Being a hero or role model—on or off the playing area—is part of the price of fame. Regarding athletes' behavior, Ron Brand, New York Yankees scout said, "All the trophies don't mean a thing if your actions don't measure up." Brand went on to comment about the background of many athletes: "Most athletes are a product of how they are being raised—too many are being raised by TV today. I'm thankful for the positive role my

> While it's true that you are your children's primary role model, many kids look outside the family for heroes as well.

The Story of Josh

Here's an example of a sports figure who embraces respect—and it pays off.

Josh Pastner was a player and coach during his undergraduate days at the University of Arizona. Josh was not your all-star basketball player; he sat on the bench and got to play only at the end of the game when the team was way ahead, but he was a great student coach and is an all-around nice guy.

Former teammate John Ash described Josh as ". . . the most famous nonplayer in the history of basketball." Yet the players depended on Josh's advice. Former Arizona players in the NBA still call Josh for advice.

Josh completed his bachelor's and master's degrees in three and a half years and is, at the time of this writing, working on his Ph.D. at the University of Arizona. He's currently serving as an assistant men's basketball coach at the university.

Josh believes, "Every day above ground is a good day," and he works at making his days good days. Josh is polite. He greets people with a smile and a

father played in modeling core values of honesty and integrity."[14]

Responsibility also applies to actors, musicians, politicians, or anyone in the public eye, because they are human beings and responsible for themselves. Politicians have the added burden of the public trust (a legal responsibility). While we don't hello. He believes in being positive and spreading his philosophy around.

Josh has a 10-step approach to life, which he shares in talks he gives to high school students. His steps are: work hard, be loyal, be proud, be enthusiastic, think positively, be honorable, be persistent, take calculated risks, don't accept excuses, and be organized.

Josh credits his parents with helping him develop this attitude. He reports that his parents had a good relationship and taught him to treat others as he would have them treat him. "Kill them with kindness," Josh says. "When someone's angry with you, don't get angry back or explain." He believes in admitting your mistakes, and even if you didn't make a mistake, realize that the other person may think you did."

"Everything is attitude," says Josh. "The glass is not half full or half empty; it's overflowing."

Josh believes that athletes who are in the spotlight have an obligation to be positive role models. "Athletes are role models whether they want to be or not," says Josh. Well, Josh is certainly a positive role model in a world filled with negative ones.[15]

expect perfection from public figures, we do expect responsibility, not outrageous behavior

When a public figure does something you consider inappropriate, discuss the situation with your kids in much the same way we outlined above for media discussions. You can ask questions like, "What do you think of that behavior?" and

"What's another way the person could have handled the situation?" Give your own opinions.

You can also tell your kids about your heroes—famous and not famous. Point out the characteristics you admire in these people and how they impacted your life. "My kind of hero is one who . . ." There is most likely a family member (or members) who made a positive impression on you—a parent, grandparent, aunt, or uncle. If you have a family album with pictures of these people, go through it with your kids while you talk about your history with these people.

> Before TV, children modeled real-life characters—parents, firefighters, doctors, nurses, teachers; today they model fantasy characters with unrealistic powers and restricted humanity.

Be sure to point out positive role models in sports, acting, music, and politics. Some celebrities host charity events, for example. Some are actively involved in charities or other good works on a continuing basis. Many athletes run sports camps for kids. In other words, give positive models equal "press" in your home.

The press is diligent in pointing out the misbehavior of our youth. But, occasionally, there will be stories on kids who engage in volunteerism and other good deeds. These kids can serve as positive role models for your kids. When you find such stories, point them out. Encourage your local media to feature the good works of kids as well as celebrities—call the news departments of TV stations or send them e-mail and contact newspaper editors as well.

Fantasy heroes, so-called superheroes, also have an affect on your children—especially young children. Macho male or female cartoon figures and TV and movie superheroes often affect the play of young children. Before TV, children modeled real-life characters—parents, firefighters, doctors, nurses, teachers; today they model fantasy characters with unrealistic powers and restricted humanity.

Help your children distinguish between real heroes and fantasy heroes. Point out that the superheroes are not real. Talk about the unrealistic nature of the acts they perform with questions such as, "What could happen if a real person did that?" Again, point out real heroes in your community.

Remember, despite the fact that your children may emulate and revere celebrities and superheroes, you are still their most important role model, their hero. Your values and behavior toward your kids and other adults influence them more than someone from afar, no matter how popular that person or character may be. You can bring them back to reality.

Parents Need to Take a Stand on Violence

YOU, THE AVERAGE citizen, need to get active. Write to your representatives; let them know how you feel about the violence in this country and what needs to be done about it. The more people write, the more our representatives listen. If we leave the lobbying up to other interests, they will win.

You can also join community, national, or international groups that are trying to make changes. There may be organizations in your community you can join. Your place of worship may want to become active. At the national level, the Children's Defense Fund and Children Now are excellent resources (see the appendix, "References and Resources").

Be sure to express your opinions to your children when violent acts are reported in the news. Your children need to know that you take a stand against violence. Silence can often be interpreted as acceptance.[16]

Making Your Neighborhood Safe

HOW SAFE IS your neighborhood? Can your children travel through your neighborhood without fear of danger? How well do you know your neighborhood? How many of your neighbors do you know? In our busy lives, how many of us know the neighbors beyond those who live next door or across the street? If you live in an apartment, how many of the other tenants do you know?

Do you know who your kids play or associate with in your neighborhood? If some of these kids have been in your house, do you know their parents? Get to know your neighbors. You can go door to door, introducing yourself, or you can host a block or building party. It may take some time and effort, but it can be worthwhile knowing the kind of people who live around you.

Is your neighborhood a Neighborhood Watch area? Do you know who's involved? You can call your local police department to find out if you are a watch area, who's involved, or how to start such a program in your neighborhood. Neighborhood Watch citizens keep well informed about their neighborhood and of any suspicious, criminal, or dangerous activities that may be occurring. Neighborhood Watch citizens can also provide safe McGruff Houses for kids to go to in emergency situations.

Some police departments sponsor citizen patrol programs. Others have workshops, information, and crime prevention programs. Check with your local police to find out what's available in your community.

Besides making sure your neighborhood is safe, you need to make sure your kids know how to ensure their own safety in the neighborhood. Have you taught them to keep their distance from strangers? Kids can protect themselves from strangers and neighborhood bullies by traveling and playing in groups.

Set up a code word in case adults approach your kids to try to entice the kids to go with them. Any person they don't know who doesn't use the code word is someone they should not accompany.

Teach your kids safe places in the neighborhood, such as neighbors they can rely on. Police and fire stations, grocery markets, banks, libraries, and schools can all be safe places where kids can ask for help.[17]

> **Kids can protect themselves from strangers and neighborhood bullies by traveling and playing in groups.**

Self-Defense

If you've taught your kids how to avoid potentially violent situations and how to negotiate or walk away, you've given them the best offense. If a situation arises where these nonviolent methods don't work, then physical self-defense may be necessary. There are many different ways children can learn self-defense. A visit to the bookstore or the Internet can supply you with materials you can share with your children. There are probably self-defense classes in your community.

We are not advising you to teach your children physical self-defense methods. You will have to make that decision yourself, based on the area you live in and your personal belief system regarding such practices. Check out the philosophy of the self-defense class you're considering. Good classes teach kids confidence and prevention, as well as protecting themselves from attackers, rather than aggressiveness and overpowering one's adversary.[18]

Finally, make sure your kids know how to be safe at home. Teach them how to dial 911 if they sense an emergency. You can begin with kids as young as four. Start with a toy telephone. Give them lines to say. Make sure they know their address. Have them practice by role-playing. You can also place on your refrigerator a reminder picture of a police car with 911 written beside it. If your kids have to be home alone sometimes, make a list of acceptable people who may come to the door or call on the phone—such as a neighbor you know well. Tell the kids to keep the phone answering machine on to screen calls. (For more resource information on child safety, see the appendix, "References and Resources.")

Safe At School?

SCHOOL SHOOTINGS—SUCH as the one at Columbine High School—over the past few years have heightened our awareness of the need to make sure our children are safe at school. While school shootings are tragic and receive considerable press, they are rare. Still, schools need to be prepared. And there are other forms of violence in schools. Harassment, fights, bullies, gangs, and kids bringing weapons to school can threaten your child's well-being and safety. How much do you know about safety at the school or schools your children attend? It's up to you to find out a school's policy and programs.

There are many things schools can do to address the violence problem. Here are some strategies that have been found to be effective:[19]

- **School monitors.** Many schools have adults monitoring the areas around the school where students tend to gather. Perhaps the most successful and cost-effective measure is to involve volunteer parents and teacher aides as monitors. The volunteers need instruction and supervision.

- **Visitor identification.** It's important for schools to know who's in the building or on campus besides students and staff. Visitors should be required to register at the office, produce identification, and carry a pass or badge. Students and staff should be encouraged to report anyone without proper identification. Asking parents for lists of people who are authorized to pick up students and requiring identification when a child is checked out of school are other safety measures being employed by many schools.

- **Consistent discipline guidelines.** School-wide and classroom discipline expectations and consequences can be communicated to the students and enforced consistently and swiftly. As you've learned in this book, consequences are most effective when kids are aware they have a choice. For example, a student who is disruptive in class has the choice of settling down and joining the classroom activities or being separated from the group (perhaps in the principal's office) until the student is ready to be cooperative.

> The correction of negative behaviors needs to be balanced with the recognition of positive acts. The more schools can focus on the positive, the more they reinforce appropriate behavior.

The correction of negative behaviors needs to be balanced with the recognition of positive acts. The more schools can focus on the positive, the more they reinforce appropriate behavior.

- **Academic standards.** Teachers need to clearly tell students what they expect from them and communicate to the students their plan for meeting these expectations. There needs to be a system for helping students who have difficulty meeting academic guidelines—extra help from the teacher, mentors, or tutors.

- **Counseling services.** Schools need to provide adequate counseling services for all students. There are too few elementary-school counselors. Those districts that have elementary counselors often spread them too thinly, requiring them to cover two or three schools. Secondary school counselors are often overloaded with too many students and too many noncounseling functions. Support increasing counseling services in your school district. Adequate counseling is money well spent.

- **Peer support.** Students can be encouraged to provide support for each other. Peer counseling programs can be set up. Counselors can train and supervise peer counselors. Kids can be encouraged to listen to friends when they are upset. Ways to involve kids who are loners or isolated at school can be discussed. Kids who feel left out can cause problems. Involving them in friendly groups can give them a greater sense of positive self-esteem. As a parent, you can reinforce these ideas at home.

> Conflict management skills can be taught on a classroom- and school-wide basis.

- **Conflict management.** Conflict is a part of life. Students need to know how to manage anger and work for resolution of differences. Conflict management skills can be taught on a classroom- and school-wide basis. In secondary schools, a group of student leaders can receive intensive training in conflict management. The team can provide peer counseling and help kids settle disputes in a nonviolent way. The teams can also train other students in their school and visit elementary schools to teach conflict management.

- **Crisis management.** When threats or violent acts occur, students need a place where they can receive counseling from professionals who know how to handle such situations. Teachers need to be informed when such events occur. Students should be encouraged to report such incidents with the assurance of confidentiality. Kids need to be taught the difference between reporting such incidents and tattling. Finally, schools need to have specific plans for what to do in the event of a crisis.

- **After-school programs.** Many parents of both sexes work outside the home. This can create latchkey kids. The hours between when school lets out and when parents get home are the time when kids are most likely to get in trouble. Check with your school as to what after-school activities are available in the school or community.

- **Parent education programs.** Kids don't come with a manual. Most parents can benefit from parent education. Groups can be offered using this book or the popular parent education program Systematic Training for Effective Parenting (STEP). (See the appendix, "References and Resources.") School counselors often lead these groups. But other school personnel such as principals and teachers, and parents who are willing to take the time to study the materials, can also lead groups.

Warning Signs

How well are the staff and students at your children's school trained to recognize students who might be at risk for committing violent acts? According to violence expert Ken Wong, there is no one single profile for kids who have committed serious school violence.[20] From what the researchers in the violence field have learned, according to Mr. Wong, kids with the following characteristics are a higher risk population for school violence:

> How well are the staff and students at your children's school trained to recognize students who might be at risk for committing violent acts?

- A history of being directly involved in violence either as a perpetrator or victim— including being abused as a child.

- Having been indirectly involved in violence through exposure to violence in the family or community, for example, observing domestic violence between parents.

- Deficiencies in what Mr. Wong calls the "3 C's": *connected*—a sense of positive belonging or community feeling; *capable*—a belief in one's abilities and potential to develop in a positive way; and *cared for*—a perception that others truly value me.

- Feelings of hopelessness and helplessness about who they or what the future holds for them.

K. Dwyer, D. Osher, and C. Warger, authors of *Early Warning, Timely Response: A Guide to Safe Schools*, published by the U.S. Department of Education, list warning signs in two categories: early warning signs and imminent warning signs.[20] The early warning signs may or may not signal a serious concern. They do give schools cause to investigate and help the child before the problems get worse. No single sign is enough as a signal for potential violence.

Imminent warning signs, on the other hand, can signal that a child "is very close to behaving in a way that is potentially dangerous to self and/or to others. Imminent warning signs require an immediate response." Once again, no single sign is enough as a signal for potential violence. "Rather, imminent warning signs usually are presented as a sequence of overt, serious, hostile behaviors or threats directed at peers, staff, or other individuals. Usually, imminent warning signs are evident to more than one staff member—as well as to the child's family."[22] (See table 6.)

> "Usually, imminent warning signs are evident to more than one staff member— as well as to the child's family."

"When warning signs indicate that danger is imminent, safety must *always* be the first and foremost consideration. Action must be taken immediately. Immediate intervention by school authorities and possibly law enforcement officers is needed when a child:

Has presented a detailed plan (time, place, method) to harm or kill others—particularly if the child has a history of aggression or has attempted to carry out threats in the past.

Is carrying a weapon, particularly a firearm, and has threatened to use it."[23]

What can you do as a parent to assist your school in implementing such safety measures? Here are some ideas from Dyer, Osher, and Warger:

Table 6   Kids at Risk for Committing Violent Acts

Early Warning Signs	Imminent Warning Signs
Social withdrawal	Inappropriate access to, possession of, or use of firearms or other weapons
Excessive feelings of isolation	
Excessive feelings of rejection	Serious physical fighting with peers or family members
Feelings of being picked on and persecuted	Severe destruction of property
Low school interest and poor academic performance	Severe rage for seemingly minor reasons
Expression of violence in writings and drawings	Detailed threats of lethal violence (The Columbine High School shooters talked about their intentions but nobody paid any attention.[24])
Uncontrolled anger	
Patterns of impulsive and chronic hitting, intimidating, and bullying behaviors	Other self-injurious behaviors or threats of suicide
History of discipline problems	
Intolerance for differences and prejudicial attitudes	
Drug use and alcohol use	
Affiliation with gangs	
Serious threats of violence	

Source: Adapted from K. Dwyer, D. Osher, and C. Warger, *Early Warning, Timely Response: A Guide to Safe Schools,* U.S. Department of Education, Center for Effective Collaboration and Practice, 1998.

- "Become active in your parent-teacher organization.

- Work with your child's school to make it more responsive to all students and families. Share your ideas about how the school can encourage family involvement, welcome all families, and include them in meaningful ways in their children's education.

- Encourage your school to offer before- and after-school programs.

- Find out if there is a violence prevention group in your community. Offer to participate in the group's activities.

- Talk with the parents of your child's friends. Discuss how you can form a team to ensure your children's safety—create an open channel for communication.

- Find out if your employer offers provisions for parents to participate in school activities."[25]

Additionally, we recommend that you:

- Be observant of your child's friends and the children in your school. Participate in activities with your children and their friends. You will learn a lot.

- Volunteer to work with school-based groups concerned with violence prevention. If none exist, offer to form one.

Helping Your Kids Cope with Fear About Violence

WITH ALL THE attention on violence, children and teens may be afraid acts of violence will touch them. Listen to your children's opinions and feelings. For example, kids who hear about school shootings are often afraid such acts can happen at their schools. Even though school shootings are infrequent, kids may still be afraid. After listening to your children's fears, you can point out how rare such shootings are. A good analogy is to compare such acts with traffic accidents. We know there are car crashes, yet we all travel in cars. Although we drive carefully, we

Reporting Threatened School Violence

The U.S. Secret Service in cooperation with the U.S. Department of Education interviewed kids who had committed school shootings.[26] While they found no single profile for these youngsters, they did find that more than two-thirds of the kids felt they had been bullied, persecuted, or injured by someone. Further, the kids planned the attack—they did not simply run amok, and they told someone of their plans—usually peers or siblings. Not all of them were loners and some were popular. With the evidence that school shooters tell people of their plans, schools need to emphasize to students that telling adults about kids who make these threats and plans is not tattling; they are saving lives, including the lives of the aggressors who often kill themselves.

would not be able to drive at all if we were continually worried we'd be in an accident.

There may be other violent incidents or threats that your child fears, such as harassment or bullying. You can encourage your child to talk to you about her concerns. The skills you learned in chapter 4—reflective listening and exploring alternatives—can help you assist your child in sharing and solving such problems. Be patient; it's hard for some kids to admit they're afraid, or kids may be reluctant to tell for fear of being labeled a tattletale. Reassure your child that expressing concerns about being harassed or hurt is not tattling, but just being smart by finding out how to protect yourself and helping to make sure that others don't get hurt.

You can ease the way for such discussions by initiating them yourself. Dr. Susan Linn, author of *How to Find Out If Your Child Is Afraid,* suggests you tell your child:

> If anyone ever threatens to hurt you, someone else, or himself, it's important that you tell me about it—even if the person tells you to keep it a secret. If you know that someone has hurt you, someone else or himself, it's also essential to tell.[27]

Another approach to getting your child to open up is suggested by Dr. Alvin Poussaint, author of *Fears About School Violence.*[28] Look for an opportunity to introduce the topic. Perhaps when watching a TV drama with your child, you might say something like:

> It's hard for some kids to admit they're afraid, or kids may be reluctant to tell for fear of being labeled a tattletale.

> Boy, the kid in that television program was really mad. . . . Do any kids you know get that angry? What would you do if you heard a kid talking about doing something violent? Or if you knew that someone in your class brought a gun or other weapon to school?

Of course, there may be some incidents your children share with you that need your attention. You may have to contact the school or other parents. If you have to do this, reassure your child that he has done the right thing by telling you. If the child begs you not to tell (he fears for his reputation or is worried this will put him in harm's way), acknowledge his feelings but stress

The Ulster Project

The Ulster Project is an example of community peace-building. The project is sponsored by Catholic and Protestant churches in Northern Ireland and in various locations throughout the United States. This project brings together Catholic and Protestant teens in various communities in Northern Ireland in a effort to gain understanding and acceptance of each other's religious beliefs and to build peace in Northern Ireland.

After training in their homeland, the Irish teens travel to various United States cities for a month in the summer. During this time they interact with American Catholic and Protestant teens, their families, clergy from participating churches, and counselors who continue the peace-building efforts. Each Irish teen stays with a host family whose teen is in the program. You may want to check to see if there's an Ulster Project in your area. It's a wonderful experience for teens and their families.[29]

that you need to take action. Assure him that you will take steps to protect him. If you are concerned word will get around that your child is the one who told, you could inform the parties concerned through an anonymous note.

In some cases the violence we fear may be overrated. In other cases it's for real. As parents, we need to be aware of the influences on our children and what we can do to minimize those influences and provide protection.

In this chapter we've explored various violence issues and how you can handle them with your kids. We've discussed safe neighborhoods, media violence, role models, and safety at school. Chapter 9 further explores the issue of violence and its impact on our children. Such potential at-risk child and teenage activities such as bullies, gangs, drugs, dating violence, and other forms of violent behavior are discussed and specific recommendations presented.

9

··

Helping Your Kids Deal with Violence in Their World

*Security comes from a feeling of being able to deal
effectively with anything life may have to offer.*
—RUDOLF DREIKURS

THIS CHAPTER WILL focus on how you can handle
tough issues that may affect you and your kids. We'll discuss the challenges of dealing with bullies, gangs, drugs, and
violence in teen dating relationships. You'll find additional information in the appendix, "References and Resources."

Bullies

BULLYING CAN RANGE from verbal harassment—such as
teasing or inappropriate sexual comments, or spreading rumors—to exclusion, stealing, and breaking property, or even

personal physical violence resulting in serious injury or death. Most kids are involved in verbal bullying at one time or another. Most kids tease others. Today's victim can be tomorrow's bully. A kid who's teased or otherwise verbally harassed will often get even. Boys tend to be direct in their assaults on others. Girls can do this, too, but they are prone to engage in spreading rumors and practicing exclusion.

Parents and school personnel may not take verbal bullying seriously. They don't see it as very rude behavior—they think it's just part of growing up. Dr. Dorothy Espelage of the University of Illinois in Urbana-Champaign has done considerable research on bullying. About teasing and name-calling she says:

> To a certain extent, there is some kind of teasing and name-calling that's going to be there, but what happens is, in schools where there is not a climate of respect, then it becomes excessive. When you have an environment where it's tolerated, where teachers turn their heads, and administrators—when it's reported to them—don't follow through, then I think it becomes excessive.[1]

The National Association of School Psychologists estimates that daily 160,000 kids don't come to school because they are afraid of being bullied.[2] This indicates that bullying—in one form or another—is a serious problem in schools. Bullying can be related to school violence especially when it takes a physical form.

What Does a Bully Look Like?

Bullies are often victims of abuse themselves. Kids who frequently bully others seek importance by picking on people. They choose to harass or assault those they perceive as weaker and unable to defend themselves. Ironically, bullies may be popular. They are often rule breakers and liars, accepting no responsibility for their behavior, showing no remorse, and often blaming the victim for the problem. They are incapable of compassion or respect for the feelings of the victim. Bullies may become violent criminals or spouse abusers.

Bullies appear to have strong self-esteem. But this is a myth: They usually feel good about themselves only when they are in power. Bullies are often victims of abuse themselves. They often come from disrespectful homes where the parents use physical punishment and are cold and insensitive. These kids learn to use physical means to solve problems. They bully to overcome their feelings of powerlessness.[3]

> Bullies are often victims of abuse themselves.

What Does a Victim Look Like?

Kids who are victims of bullies are usually anxious, insecure, cautious, and suffer from low self-esteem. They may lack social skills and friends and thus are often socially isolated. Victims may be close to their parents and may have parents who can be described as overprotective. The major physical characteristic of victims is that they tend to be weaker than their peers. They may cry easily.

Some victims will tease and fight back and come back for more even when they lose. Others will not retaliate. Kids who are frequent victims of bullies may also turn violent. Some react by becoming bullies themselves. Some victims commit suicide, others may respond with violent retaliation. Thirty percent of the victims of bullies admit they've carried weapons to school on occasion. More than half of suburban principals say that violence has gotten worse on their campuses. All of the kids recently involved as school shooters had been victims of bullies for years.[4]

Who Isn't Bullied?

Aside from some teasing, most kids aren't bullied. Kids who are confident and can take care of themselves are too much of a challenge for a bully. They have better social skills and connections. They know how to manage conflicts more effectively. These kids can be very helpful in assisting other children (victims) in settling disputes and getting help.[5]

If Your Child Is Being Bullied

Some kids may be reluctant to tell teachers or their parents about being bullied for fear the adults will get involved and make matters worse. If you notice your child physically hurt or depressed, you may want to inquire as to what is going on. If you suspect a problem, you can ask some indirect questions regarding how things go at lunch, walking to school, or riding the bus. You can inquire if there are children in the neighborhood who pick on other kids.[6]

> Kids who are confident and can take care of themselves are too much of a challenge for a bully.

If your child is being bullied, stay calm. As parents, we want to protect our children from being bullied. But we can't be with them 24 hours a day. So the best protection we can give our children is to teach them how to protect themselves. The following suggestions can help you make your child "bully-proof."[7]

- Listen to the child's feelings and explore alternatives. A bully often relies on teasing as the means to start a confrontation. Teaching your child to ignore teasing can spoil the bully's purpose. Humor can also work. "If you think I'm ugly (weird, and so on) you should see my parents." Agreeing with the bully can also defuse him. "You're right, I'm dumb." When ignoring or making such a reply, the child should walk away.

- Don't encourage fighting back. Some kids are not capable of this—the bully is bigger and stronger. Fighting also teaches our children that violence is a way to solve problems. We need to teach them that there is a way to back away from the problem.

- Look for characteristics in your child that may invite bullying. Kids who appear weak and lack confidence are often targets. Does your child slouch? Does she look afraid? Help your child see how these physical signals can invite bullying. Teach your child to stand up straight and "walk tall." The more confident your child looks—and feels—the less she's likely to be bullied. Role-play confident behavior with your child.

- Encourage group travel. The bully usually picks on a single child. A simple protective technique is to teach your children they are safer in a group.

- Although kids can handle teasing, if the problem moves to actual violence and injury, you'll need to step in. If the problem is at school, talk to the teacher, counselor, or principal. Find out their policies for dealing with bullying. If you receive no satisfaction, you may need to move up the line in the school district.

- There may be times you'll have to talk to the parents of a child who's bullying your child on school grounds, on the way home, or in your neighborhood. If you do talk to the parents, realize they may be defensive. Avoid calling their child a bully. Simply state the facts: "My son tells me that John hit him in the face and took his lunch box on the way home from school." Your focus is how to solve the problem, not labeling the child nor blaming the parents for their child's behavior.

- If it's a neighborhood problem, discuss safe solutions with other parents. Safe houses are one solution. If none of the things you've tried to do about the bullying help, you may have to involve the police if you think your child can come to serious harm.

If Your Child Is a Bully

Childhood bullies don't always grow out of it. It often becomes a lifelong behavior. Positive intervention can help. The following ideas offer some possible strategies:[8]

- Examine your relationship with the child. Are power and punishment part of your family atmosphere? In some cases the bully is a product of a permissive family atmosphere. The bully is used to getting whatever he wants. Change the relationship. Set firm and clear guidelines.

> Childhood bullies don't always grow out of it. It often becomes a lifelong behavior.

- Build the child's self-esteem. Look for ways to appreciate and encourage positive behavior. Focus on strengths.

- Listen to your child's feelings. Bullies are often angry. What might be contributing to his anger? Has he been bullied by

How Schools Can Deal With Bullying

Schools can deal with bullying by:

- Holding discussions and role plays about teasing and harassment
- Encouraging kids to speak up when they see bulling taking place, for example: "Hey, knock it off."
- Encouraging kids to tell an adult if they see physical bullying, stressing that this is not tattling.
- Providing discipline. Assigning a monitor to a bully for a while when he's out of the classroom, or keeping him in from recess for a while if the incidents happen on the playground.
- Redirecting the bully's desire for power. Responsible jobs can be found to help the bully use her power in a useful way.
- Applying some of the suggestions in the "Safe at School" section in chapter 8.
- Establishing a school-wide policy and practices for dealing with bullies.

someone else? Help him explore alternatives for dealing with anger. If necessary, seek professional help.

- Take advantage of opportunities to help her develop empathy and respect for others. If you hear of an incident where someone has been injured emotionally or physically, talk about it. "How do you think that person feels?" "What would that be like for you?" "How could someone help the person feel better?" The news, TV programs, films, and books can often provide material for such discussions.

- Look for ways to involve the child in positive activities. Focus on ways she can contribute to the neighborhood— build her people-esteem. Perhaps she can join supervised activities like sports or scouts. Your child needs new friends. Bullies often hang out with their own kind.

- Involve your child in helping out around the house. Redirect his desire for power in a useful way. Choose jobs where he can use his power and involve him in choosing the jobs. These actions will help him feel important.

- Stop all punishment. When a bully is punished, she feels she has the right to punish others. Give choices, and allow consequences to occur. For example, if your child is involved in a bullying incident that means she has chosen to spend time away from others (according to your prestated conditions for being with others).

Gangs

GANG INVOLVEMENT IS a serious problem in our communities and at times leads to violence. This problem is no longer limited to urban or ghetto areas. Gang expert Ken Wong says, "Now that gang involvement affects the lives of the middle and upper classes, we have all taken notice."[9]

There are many different types of gangs. Not all gangs are bad in the sense that they engage in illegal activity or violence. Some gangs exist solely for status and affiliation. The common denominator for most gangs is that they have no officially sanctioned status at school or in the community. Gangs have a leadership structure, a decision-making process, and methods of recruiting members. They tend to use symbolism—names and images for identification as well as colors and styles of attire. Gangs also develop rituals for initiating members and conducting business. Gangs consider themselves a family where loyalty is demanded; they also have enemies, and association with enemies is forbidden and punished. Some gangs develop a territory that they define as "theirs" and which they will aggressively defend. Those gangs that engage in illegal activity and violence are the greatest concern for communities and parents.

> Violence in the community and schools may leave kids feeling insecure, and the desire for safety and protection is understandable.

Kids join gangs for many reasons:

- To belong, to feel a part of something, to find camaraderie with others.

- To find significance, to be somebody.

- To feel safe and be protected.

These reasons are all positive. Gangs fulfill a need for kids. This need appears to be rising because of the troubled times we live in. It is more difficult for kids to experience belonging and significance in their families and communities. Violence in the community and schools may leave kids feeling insecure, and the desire for safety and protection is understandable.

Kids who are the most discouraged and operate on a sense of hopelessness and helplessness are most likely to get involved in gangs. They lack positive role models and caring adults. Too often they've been told they aren't good enough. These kids believe they have no future, have nothing to lose, and are prime candidates for violence.

Preventing Gang Involvement

You can increase the likelihood your children will not be drawn into gang membership by using what you've learned in this book. Keep the following in mind:

- Increase your son or daughter's sense of belonging by staying involved in their lives. Take an active interest in their activities and friends. Look for opportunities to maintain your ties with extended family and friends.

- Refrain from parenting that emphasizes power and control, which alienates kids from the family, making gang affiliation all that more attractive. Give kids increasing choices and incorporate their ideas and suggestions in family rules and decision making.

- Refrain from all forms of pampering. Empower your kids by allowing them to do for themselves and learn from their mistakes. Kids who are pampered develop an exaggerated sense of their own importance, along with the awareness that they aren't capable of handling life's problems on their own. From this standpoint, gang affiliation would be most appealing—enhancing status and providing support.

> Kids who believe in themselves and their own future are less attracted to what a gang has to offer and more capable of practicing refusal skills.

- Practice encouragement in your parent-child relationship. Kids who believe in themselves and their own future are less attracted to what a gang has to offer and more capable of practicing refusal skills.

What Are the Warning Signs of Gang Involvement?

Your child may be involved in a gang if he:

- Drops out of other activities.

- Changes friends from ones previously associated with and is more secretive about these new relationships.

- Breaks agreed-upon curfews.

- Changes clothing style—wearing the same attire or the same colors as a group.

- Possesses money or purchases items beyond his means.

- Keeps getting involved with school authorities or the police.

What Can I Do If I Suspect My Child Is Involved in a Gang?

There are two important objectives for parents when encountering a child involved in gang activity: creating channels of communication and supporting alternative, nongang-related activities. The following will help you accomplish these objectives.

- Be honest and respectful when confronting the problem. Share your observations, concerns, and desire to support your child. Don't be surprised if your initial response is to deny or minimize the problem. Parents have a hard time coming to terms with gang involvement. This can result in parents being judgmental and overreacting to the suspicion or knowledge that their kids are involved in gangs.

- Seek professional help. Many youth and family counselors are equipped to assist both parents and gang-involved kids. Schools and law enforcement departments can also provide useful information. See this as an opportunity to evaluate and modify your relationship and parenting style.

- Avoid power contests over gang involvement. This will only create further alienation and push your child toward the gang. Realize that within some gangs there are strong forces to hold on to gang members. This is especially true if the gang has been involved in illegal activity. It may be dangerous for your son or daughter to abruptly end gang affiliation. The safest process is often a gradual one.

- Find opportunities for stimulating involvement in activities outside of the gang. Encourage activities in which your child has a natural ability or interest.

- Realize that no matter how challenging the situation gets, your child needs your ongoing support. Exercise patience and persistence.

> Encourage activities in which your child has a natural ability or interest.

Schools can address the gang issue by establishing a curriculum which emphasizes how kids can belong in positive ways, and by providing positive activities in which kids can get involved, for example, clubs and sports. The staff can also watch for gang-related activity, and a school monitoring and visitor identification programs, as well as a dress code, should be implemented.

Alcohol and Other Drugs

DRUG USE AFFECTS judgment, reactions and self-control, and relationships.[10] For example, kids who might otherwise avoid a fight may get involved while under the influence of alcohol or other drugs. Danger also exists in the buying and selling of drugs. Conflicts among dealers or between dealers and buyers can lead to violence. Gangs are often involved in drug dealing. Kids involved with drugs may have weapons.[11]

Why Kids Use Drugs

Some of the reasons kids use drugs include:

- **Modeling.** We're a drug-taking culture. Watch TV commercials; we have medications for practically every pain or emotional problem. What message are kids getting when they see these advertisements? Got a pain or a problem? Take a pill.

  Of course, some medications are appropriate and necessary. But, our society overemphasizes drug solutions for health problems. For instance, some headaches respond to a heating pad, a cool cloth, lying down, or taking a break.

  Many emotional problems can be handled through procedures such as changing one's thought processes, meditation, talking about the problem with a good friend or professional, rather than using medication. In their book *How You Feel Is Up to You: The Power of Emotional Choice,* psychologists Gary D. McKay and Don Dinkmeyer Sr. give nonmedical ways to manage upset feelings.

> Our society overemphasizes drug solutions for health problems.

  Medications aren't the only drugs advertised on TV. Of course, beer and other alcoholic drinks are not harmful in moderation for most people. The problem is in the message they give to kids. They communicate that people who drink have fun, are "real" men or sexy women. In addition, the use of alcohol is very much a part of the social culture in many places and a rite of passage for teens.

Then there's your own drug use. How you—and others, such as relatives, who are in contact with your child—use medications and other legal substances like alcohol provides a model for your kids.

- **Availability.** Both legal and illegal drugs are easy to get. For example, younger kids get older ones to buy alcohol and tobacco. Marijuana, cocaine, crack, heroin, Ecstasy, and so on can be obtained if kids really want them. Most kids who use drugs get them from older siblings or friends at school.

  Some drugs, such as over-the-counter or prescription medications, are available around the house. Inhalants are readily available and can also be used to get a high.

- **The "Quick Fix" Syndrome.** We are an impatient society—we want what we want when we want it. We look to outside sources to make us feel good. Drugs offer a quick fix.

- **Rapidly Changing Society.** Immigration and the mixture of cultures, divorce, single parenting, and remarriage all have an impact on the stability of our society. We're also very mobile—changing locations frequently. We lose a sense of extended family, community, and belonging.

- **The Goals of Misbehavior.** Kids who take drugs gain a sense of power over their parents. The drugs are a means of defiance and can be a way to get even.

- **Gaining Peer Acceptance.** These are kids who have low self-esteem and poor decision-making skills. They tend to associate with kids who have similar problems and may also have a poor relationship with their parents. Further, alcohol and, to some extent, other drugs can lessen the discomfort teens can experience in social situations with their peers and are often a key element in teen social activities.

- **Excitement.** Some drugs, as well as hanging out with other users, may produce a sense of excitement. The very act of doing something illegal (forbidden) may be exciting.

- **Escape.** Some kids feel they can't face up to life's challenges, so they find escape from their problems in drug use. This is a form of the goal of displaying inadequacy. Drug use can also reduce the anxiety of academic, athletic, and family pressures many of our youth experience.

Helping Kids Stay Drug Free

What most parents don't realize is that drugs are not just a teen problem. Some kids as young as eight experiment with drugs. Begin teaching your kids about drugs early.

> Drugs are not just a teen problem. Some kids as young as eight experiment with drugs.

Even preschoolers notice changes in behavior due to substance abuse such as too much alcohol. "Why does Grandpa act funny when he drinks that stuff out of that big bottle?" Answer your child's questions honestly and in line with her developmental level.

As children get older, talk to them about appropriate and inappropriate use of substances and the difference between legal and illegal drugs. They also need to know that while some drugs like alcohol are legal for adults, they are illegal for children. Alcohol is the most widely abused drug in our society and is one of the "gateway" drugs for kids—it can lead to other drug use. Tobacco is the other gateway drug.

Talk to your kids about why people take drugs and what the effects of various substances are. Make sure you have accurate information. Keep current; new drugs may come along. Your police department may have publications on drugs. Talk to your child's teachers and counselors. Check out the yellow pages under "Alcoholism and Drug Abuse" and under "Treatment Centers." Use the Internet. (See the appendix, "References and Resources," for sources of alcohol and drug abuse information)

When you're watching TV with your kids and medication or beer commercials come on the screen, use the opportunity for discussion: "What are they saying about dealing with headaches (stomachaches, and so forth)?" "What are some other ways to handle pain?" "What are the people who make these beer commercials trying to tell us about using their product?" "Why do people drink alcohol?" Talk about the motivations behind advertising.

Keep lines of communication open. Answer their questions on drugs as best you can. State your opinions when necessary. Use the skills of reflective listening and I-messages you've learned in this book to have open, respectful communication.

Build your child's self-esteem through using the encouragement skills you've learned in this book, such as accepting your child, having positive expectations, and focusing on contributions and strengths. Kids with positive self-esteem and people-esteem tend to hang out with positive kids.

But self-esteem is not enough. Resisting negative peer pressure and drugs involves knowing how to make good decisions. Natural and logical consequences help children learn about decision making. When you give your children choices and expect them to accept the consequences—either positive or negative—they learn responsible behavior. By exploring alternatives for problems your child owns, you help him learn how to evaluate choices and carry through on a commitment. When conflicts between you and your child occur, exploring alternatives teaches him how to solve conflicts respectfully and peacefully.

Decision making is a developmental process. The more opportunities your children have to make choices and experience the results, the more they are prepared to deal with peer pressure.

Teach your kids to say no by talking with them about how to resist negative peer pressure. Encourage assertiveness. Create "what if" scenarios: "Suppose a stranger approaches you on the street and offers you some free (marijuana, cocaine, heroin). What could you say?" "What if your best friend says, 'Let's try some grass (alcohol, Ecstasy, crack)?' What could you do?"

Use role-playing. Sometimes you can use role reversal—have your child play the person trying to get her to use drugs and you play your child and model responses the child could give. One phrase that often appeals to kids is, "No way. If I do that, my parents will ground me forever." Some other comebacks could be, "No thanks, that stuff really messes you up," or, "I'm not really into that."

> Get to know your child's friends and the friends' parents. Plan safe, healthy, drug-free activities for your kids.

Set no-use rules. Discuss the consequences for breaking the rules. Don't threaten; just state what will happen. For example, you could say, "If you drink and drive, you'll lose your driving privileges," or, "If there's drinking or drugs at the party, you will not be able to hang out with those kids."

Get to know your child's friends and the friends' parents. If you know the people and their values are similar to yours, then the likelihood of drug use decreases. Meet with the parents and plan safe, healthy, drug-free activities for your kids.

Get to know your community. Where do the kids hang out? Kids will often frequent small establishments such as convenience stores. Sometimes the personnel in these places can spot problems. Get to know the staff.

Plan healthy, positive family activities in your family meetings. Encourage your children to participate in positive youth activities. After-school programs, youth groups at places of worship, Scouts, and sports, all can help your kids develop positive values and friends.

How Can I Tell If My Child Is Using Drugs and What Can I Do?

Some of the signs of drug abuse include a favorable attitude toward drugs; health and physical problems such as bloodshot eyes, dilated pupils, mood swings, slurred speech, coordination and concentration difficulties; changes in appearance, behavior, and friendships; a drop in grades; drug or drug paraphernalia possession; and the odor of drugs or attempts to cover the odor with things like breath mints and incense. Drug paraphernalia and odors or your child's attempt to cover them up are signs that warrant your immediate attention. You own this problem and, in this case, you may have to violate your child's privacy by searching his room or other places you think he might be hiding drugs.

It's useless to ask your child if he's using. Kids who've become involved in drugs have chosen to lie.

If you determine your child's using drugs, you'll need professional help. Check with your family doctor, a school counselor, your clergy, the yellow pages, or the resources in the appendix to find a counselor or agency in your area that works with substance abuse. Maintain communication with your child's teachers, counselors, and others who are a regular part of your child's life.

> Drug paraphernalia and odors or your child's attempt to cover them up are signs that warrant your immediate attention.

Be prepared for emergencies. Keep a list of places you can call or get to quickly such as 911, poison control, your doctor, the quickest route to a hospital near you. Sometimes you may have to take emergency procedures yourself. For example, if your child abuses alcohol, you want to be sure he doesn't become ill and inhale vomit into his lungs. Turn him on his side or induce vomiting with ipecac syrup.

A positive relationship with your children is your best defense against drugs. Avoid power and revenge contests. A close, encouraging family where kids feel they belong and are comfortable in sharing their concerns as well as their joys promotes positive behavior. When kids feel accepted, despite their mistakes and faults, they are more likely to be drug and violence free.

Check with your school to see what drug prevention programs are provided. Drug education curriculums should focus on drug information, self-esteem, decision making, refusal skills, and parent involvement. See the appendix information on recommended programs.

Violence in Teen Dating Relationships

TEEN DATING VIOLENCE is a serious and sometimes deadly problem.[12] The same patterns that are noticeable in all domestic violence relationships can occur in the early dating relationship of teenagers. The problem is serious. Studies show that 28 percent of teen relationships involve violence.[13]

What Is Dating Violence?

Dating violence is the use of physical, emotional, verbal, or sexual force by one person in a dating relationship to control, overpower, or dominate the other. Such a relationship may include name-calling, criticism and insults, control of resources, threats to isolate the person from friends and family, coercion, violent acts, stalking, and physical injury. Since more than one out of four American teens experience teen dating violence, it is an issue for parents to be aware of and be prepared for.

> Since more than one out of four American teens experience teen dating violence, it is an issue for parents to be aware of and be prepared for.

As with adult domestic violence, it is most common for boys to be the perpetrators of dating violence and for girls to be the victims. Though rare, boys can be victims of dating violence and girls the perpetrators.

Teens are vulnerable to violence in dating relationships. They are beginning the process of preparing for adulthood by becoming independent from their parents, with an increased desire to "belong" among their friends. Often this leads to an adolescent's desire for greater privacy and decreased communication with parents. Sexual and romantic feelings are emerging for the first time in the teen—and sometimes preteen—years. It is natural to reach out to peers, to wish to date, and to provide an outlet for these romantic feelings. Teens, of course, are new to the experience of dating and can make mistakes. Combine these factors with the tendency of teens to resist adult efforts to control them, and you can see their vulnerability to dating violence. This is a prevalent and challenging problem.

How Can I Help My Teen Avoid Dating Violence?

The way in which you conduct your relationship with your spouse (or partner or ex-spouse) as well as with your kids, teaches children what is acceptable and what is not. When you model mutual respect and shared decision making, kids are more likely to expect this in dating relationships. On the other hand, when controlling, demeaning, or disrespectful relationships are modeled, kids are more likely to repeat the pattern in their own dating behavior.

> The way in which you conduct your relationship with your spouse (or partner or ex-spouse) as well as with your kids, teaches children what is acceptable and what is not.

It's important to talk with your kids about what makes healthy and unhealthy relationships. Television programs, news, movies, and books that show relationships between men and women are good springboards for discussion. Discuss how men and women are portrayed and what the program, film, or book says about relationships.

Girls and Dating Violence

An indicator that your daughter may be a victim of a violent dating relationship is increased isolation from family, friends, and activities. As the perpetrator strives to be more prominent in his victim's life, he feels increasingly jealous of her outside activities and relationships and begins to exercise more control, limiting her prior relationships and activities. Why would any teen accept this increased control over her life? Dating violence relationships are very seductive. To be wanted and possessed to this extent initially feels good to the teen—increasing her sense of belonging and significance. Combine this dynamic with the perpetrator's growing criticism, and she begins to believe him and mistakenly conclude that she deserves no better.

Teen dating violence expert, Belinda Lafferty, describes the situation in this way:

> An indicator that your daughter may be a victim of a violent dating relationship is increased isolation from family, friends, and activities.

> The relationship is very much like what occurs in a concentration camp, steady brainwashing intended to alter the self-image of the dating partner and make her compliant. Add to this the real threat or acts of physical violence that exists in these relationships and the fear violence provokes, and you can understand why teen dating violence relationships are difficult to end.[14]

Parents who discover their daughter is in an abusive dating relationship are often motivated by fear and the desire to protect. They may attempt to control their daughter's behavior, forbidding any future involvement with the perpetrator. Although this may seem like a reasonable response, it can be deadly. Ms. Lafferty gives insight into why it's best for parents to avoid this approach:

Autocratic parenting is especially harmful with daughters caught up in a domestic violence relationship. First of all, the parents are duplicating the power and control tactics imposed by the perpetrator. Second, adolescents are very likely to rebel whenever parents attempt to control any area of life that is important to them. Furthermore, this approach tends to repel the adolescent further from her parents, adding to her isolation and pushing her closer to the perpetrator. This at a time when she most needs understanding and support.[15]

You can support your daughter and empower her to handle the situation by using the following approaches:

- Avoid blaming your daughter for her role in the situation. Empathize how hard it must be to have someone she cares for treat her in such a hurtful manner. Tell her you can understand how confusing the relationship is and how frightening it is to consider ending it.

- Continue to encourage your daughter by pointing out her strengths.

- Identify and help her access resources that are available to her in the community, including domestic violence hotlines and counseling services. Point out that it is sometimes easier to talk over the situation with a caring professional rather than a concerned parent.

- Obtain literature on teen domestic violence and encourage your daughter to educate herself.

- Help your daughter develop a "safety plan" in case the relationship becomes so abusive and threatening she needs to escape quickly. This plan may include numbers to call (professionals, friends, family), modes of transportation, a safe place to stay not known to the perpetrator, basic supplies (clothes, money, toiletries, cosmetics, and so on). This safety plan makes it much easier for your daughter to leave when she is ready because she has the tools and resources available to make it happen.

- Be patient. Many factors contribute to this problem and make it difficult for girls to leave their boyfriend when in a relationship involving dating violence.

These suggestions apply to a relationship your daughter either doesn't want to leave or is afraid to leave. If your daughter wants to leave the relationship but is frightened and asks for your help, you could talk to the boy's parents or the police if your daughter agrees. The legal system will require your daughter to file a complaint and possibly testify in court. She must be willing to do this or law enforcement can do nothing about the situation.

> Help your daughter develop a "safety plan" in case the relationship becomes so abusive and threatening she needs to escape quickly.

Boys and Dating Violence

Sons involved as perpetrators of domestic violence in teen relationships also need the support of parents. If you suspect or discover your son is involved as a perpetrator in a teen domestic violence relationship, the following are some suggested ways for parents to respond:[16]

- Tell your son you suspect or know about the abuse. Relationship violence feeds on silence.

- Get your child to think about his behavior. Perpetrators will usually blame the victim for their need to be abusive. Make it clear that he and no one else is responsible for his actions and they are not okay. Attempt to build empathy by discussing how his girlfriend must feel in the situation.

- Help your son understand the repetitive patterns that exist in these relationships and the consequences of his behavior and where it may lead—violence is a crime; police, courts, and detention facilities may be in his future.

- Encourage your son to get help from a professional counselor. His behavior could be an indication of a serious emotional problem.

Your son needs you more than ever. Respectful confrontation is called for, but never give up on the relationship.

> Since both men and women of all ages tend to have a distorted view of what rape actually is, teens are especially susceptible to the tragedy and misunderstanding of this serious issue.

Date Rape

Another dating violence situation teens may face is a one-incident date or acquaintance rape.[17] Date rape is another area where children may be exposed to unanticipated violence. Since both men and women of all ages tend to have a distorted view of what rape actually is, teens are especially susceptible to the tragedy and misunderstanding of this serious issue.

Date rape is the forcible, nonconsensual act of a sexual nature that occurs in a formal or informal dating or party situation. While presence on the date or at the party is consensual, the sexual contact is not.

How Can Parents Help Prevent Rape?

Parents who model mutual respect in their relationship with their teens and children increase the likelihood teens in dating or party situations will respect themselves and respect others.

According to sexual abuse expert, Debbi Halela, open communication about risks involved in dating relationships and sexual decision making helps prepare kids for dating and opens the door to communication when there are questions and problems. This discussion applies to boys as well as girls. Teens need to be aware "no" always means "no." Sometimes teens can send signals—intentional or unintentional—that can seem to be giving permission to engage in sexual activity. But if one person says no, then consent is not given.

It is important to encourage teens to communicate clearly with their date or partner about their sexual limits and to be clear that all sexual decisions must be mutually agreed on. Since many teens are assaulted in peer situations in which they were initially comfortable, encourage your child to trust her gut instincts when she begins to feel uncomfortable or unsafe.

Get to know anyone your child or teen spends time with. This is a protective factor for all high-risk behavior.

Discuss gender stereotypes. Girls too often get the message that they are supposed to be caring, nurturing, and sensitive to others' needs. When this is taken to extremes, girls open themselves to victimization. Boys often receive the message that they

> It is important to encourage teens to communicate clearly with their date or partner about their sexual limits and to be clear that all sexual decisions must be mutually agreed on.

are supposed to be strong, aggressive, and in charge of relationships. When this is taken to extremes, boys are more likely to exploit others. Help your teen to understand that equality in gender roles will contribute to healthier relationships.

You may want to encourage your daughter or son approaching the dating and party years to take a self-defense class. Such training increases a teen's confidence and encourages a mind-set that there are times to be assertive.

Establish respect for individual privacy, personal space and possessions within the family. By extending this to include respect for each family member's personal beliefs and feelings and the sanctity of each person's body, you are providing the value system needed to help teens assert their limits and avoid violating the limits of others. When kids are raised in families where saying no is honored, it will be much more natural for them to say no and accept no from peers.

It is important to educate your teen to the dangers of drug and alcohol use and abuse. If you suspect your teen is drinking or using other drugs, professional help may be needed. Teens should also be warned of the potential to be exploited though the use of date rape drugs which are commonly and unknowingly slipped into a teen's beverage. It is good advice for a teen to never accept a drink from someone they do not know or to leave a drink unattended.

If Your Teen Is a Victim of Date Rape

Be supportive! No matter what the circumstances, date rape is a horrendous invasion with significant emotional impact. Having the support of family and friends is the single most important factor in recovering from this trauma. The message that "you didn't deserve this, you are not to blame, and we are here to support you through this" is essential.

Refrain from your need to know everything. Respect your child's limits on how much she is willing to share with you. If she is unwilling to share the whole situation with you, let her know it is important to share it with someone. Encourage professional counseling with someone knowledgeable in the area of trauma counseling. Group counseling for survivors of sexual assault can decrease isolation and offer peer support, a particularly effective treatment method with teens. Both individual and group counseling can be an invaluable part of healing in the aftermath of an assault.

> Group counseling for survivors of sexual assault can decrease isolation and offer peer support, a particularly effective treatment method with teens.

If your child has been raped, it is vital that she get a medical exam as soon as possible. An exam may allow for physical evidence to be collected both for legal and medical purposes. Even if too much time has elapsed for medical evidence to be found, it is important to test for the possibility of pregnancy or sexually transmitted diseases.

Assist your child by contacting law enforcement if a medical or other professional has not yet done so. Giving a statement to a law-enforcement official can be both empowering and terrifying. In addition to parent support, the assistance of a legal advocate or a counselor can help during this difficult process.

What About Boys Who Commit Date Rape?

If your son commits an act of rape and the police are involved, he will have to face the legal consequences. Support your child: Reject the behavior, but don't reject the boy. His behavior could be the result of not taking no for an answer, being under

Table 7 Rudeness and Violence Factors and Solutions

Factor	Description	What parents can do
The Democratic Revolution	Due to the advancements of oppressed populations (workers, women, people of color), our kids are, for the first time, growing up with an "equality identity" and will not accept a one-down position.	Incorporate mutual respect into all forms of parenting: communication, discipline, problem solving and decision making.
Multicultural society	Increasingly diverse immigration results in more cultural differences and more potential for misunderstanding and conflict.	Help kids develop self-esteem and people-esteem. Teach appropriate civility skills such as manners. Help kids understand, respect, and celebrate cultural differences.
Technologically advanced society	Technological advances create greater mobility and decrease social involvement and sense of community.	Stay involved with your kids. Spend quality time. Keep family involved in the community.
Family issues and patterns	Greater family mobility; less extended family support; coercive, permissive, and pampering parenting; parental noninvolvement; troubled family situations (sibling jealousy and rivalry, divorce, neglect, abuse, addictions, domestic violence).	Practice respectful and encouraging leadership with your kids. Develop your own self-encouragement and self-improvement plan.
Media violence	Violence of TV, movies, music, video games, and the Internet desensitizes youth to violence and provides power/revenge images.	Discuss with your kids the media they are experiencing and contribute positive and corrective values. Contact your representatives and encourage them to create legislation to reduce unnecessary violence in the media.

Factor	Description	What parents can do
Gun availability	The easy access to guns creates the potential for more accidental or intentional shooting injuries and deaths.	Keep guns in a locked and secured location. Practice gun safety. Support increased gun control and gun safety legislation.
Substance abuse	Drugs and alcohol abuse are "fuels" for rudeness and violence. Some people will resort to illegal and violent means to maintain their addiction.	Monitor kids' use and possible abuse of alcohol and other drugs. When kids have a problem with alcohol or other drug abuse, obtain professional help. Take responsibility for your own drug and alcohol use. Get help when needed.
Belief systems	Emotions and behavior come from the beliefs kids develop. Particularly troublesome beliefs include: "I have no value." "I am special and deserve special treatment." "Others are against me." "To be significant, I must be powerful." "When others hurt me, I must get even."	Become a more respectful and encouraging parent. Avoid the roles of boss, doormat, and servant. Become a leader and encourager: Help kids develop self-esteem and people-esteem.
School challenges	Today's schools are larger and kids can become alienated. Some schools develop a competitive, status oriented atmosphere that encourages students to be excluded and harassed.	Get involved with your kids' school. Learn about the school's strengths and weaknesses and support positive developments. Help schools obtain the resources to work toward excellence in academic skills and people skills. Use communication, problem solving and encouragement skills to help your kids respond effectively to the challenges of school.

the influence of drugs, or deliberately deciding to rape. In any of these circumstances, he needs help. It is important not to minimize the seriousness of the situation. This could be an indication of a serious emotional problem. See that he gets counseling from a counselor who specializes in this area.

The same suggestions apply to girls who commit an act of date rape. While this is rare, it does happen.

Schools can provide curriculums which focus on the possibility of violence in relationships, including date rape. Since dating violence is a bullying situation, the curriculum needs to address the same mutual respect and power issues. The curriculum should discuss what students can do if they become involved in a dating violence relationship or are raped, and encourage teens to report abuse to a trusted teacher or counselor.

In this chapter we've discussed serious violence issues: bullies, gangs, drugs, and violence in teen dating relationships. We've given ideas on how parents and schools can help kids who get involved in these activities and how to prevent involvement. Table 7 lists factors that contribute to rudeness and violence, along with additional suggestions for things parents can do to counteract them. None of these factors alone "causes" violent incidents to happen. Each factor, however, contributes to situations characterized by extreme rudeness or violence. When a parent is able to respond to even one factor, and in that area make a constructive change in one's own family, school, or community, that parent has a positive influence on reducing rudeness and violence and increasing civility, mutual respect, and the peaceful resolution to conflict.

APPENDIX: REFERENCES AND RESOURCES

B ELOW IS A list of Web sites and organizations with information on various respect and violence issues.

Dating Violence

"Dating Bill of Rights," www.denisebrown.com/teen_violence.htm. Ideas for teens.

Dating violence, Center for Disease Control, www.cdc.gov/ncipc/dvp/datviol.htm. Search for "dating violence."

Dating violence, About.com, Parenting of Adolescents, http://parentingteens.about.com/parenting/parentingteens/mbody.htm. Search for "dating violence."

"Domestic Violence: The Hidden Crime," National Crime Prevention Council, www.ncpc.org/1safe2dc.htm.

"Rape: Information," www.zip.com.au/~korman/rape/info. Information on dating violence with links to other sites.

"Twisted Love: Dating Violence Exposed," a discussion guide for a PBS video, www.pbs.org/inthemix/educators/date_viol.html. Gives instructions on how to order the video and its use. Site also provides information on dating violence.

"What Is Dating Violence?," National Clearinghouse on Family Violence. A Canadian Web site with a wealth of information on dating violence. www.faceit.cyberus.ca/faceiteng.htm.

Drug Prevention

American Guidance Service, 4201 Woodland Road, Circle
Pines, MN 55014 (800-328-2560) has several programs
for teachers on drug prevention for kids of all ages. Call for
a catalogue or visit their Web site at www.agsnet.com.

The Partnership For a Drug-Free America has a wealth of information on various drugs and their uses as well as tips for
parents at www.drugfreeamerica.org.

Gangs

"A Parent's Guide for Preventing Gangs," LunaWeb,
www.lunaweb.com/pargang.htm

"Gangs: The New Family," NebGuide, http://ianrwww.unl
.edu/pubs/family/g1294.htm.

"What's a Parent to Do About Gangs?" National Crime
Prevention Council, www.ncpc.org/10ad2.htm.

Internet Safety

Helpanswers Educational Foundation, P.O. Box 597018, Chicago, IL 60659, (800-841-5961), www.helpanswers.com.

"Site Seeing on the Internet," Federal Trade Commission,
www.ftc.gov/bcp/conline/pubs/online/sitesee.

Media Concerns

Center for Media Education, 2120 L Street, NW, Suite 200,
Washington, DC 20037, www.cme.org.

Parents Television Council, 707 Wilshire Boulevard #1950, Los
Angeles, CA 90017, (213-629-9255), www.parentstv.org.

A Review of Research on the Impact of Violence in Entertainment Media. Federal Trade Commission, 2000. Available from www.ftc.gov/reports/violence/Appen%20A.pdf or Federal Trade Commission, CRC-240, Washington, DC 20580, (877-382-4357).

School Safety

Early Warning, Timely Response: A Guide to Safe Schools, Center for Effective Collaboration and Practice, 1998. To obtain the document by mail, contact U.S. Department of Education, Special Education and Rehabilitative Services, Room 3131, Mary E. Switzer Building, Washington, DC 20202. To obtain the document online, go to www.ed.gov /offices/OSERS/OSEP/earlywrn.html.

Reseda High School. A good model of a school safety program in the Los Angeles Unified School District. Reseda has a violence prevention program that includes the WARN program: Weapons Are Removed Now. WARN "promotes the awareness of the increase of weapons on campus and the growing danger." The program encourages students to report weapons through a special 800 telephone number. The school trains students who then go to elementary and middle schools in the neighborhood to inform them of dangers of weapons and encourage them to report weapons. For more information contact Dr. Jay Shaffer, WARN Coordinator, Reseda High School, 18230 Kittridge Street, Reseda, CA 91335, (818-342-6186).

Safe School Initiative: An Interim Report on the Prevention of Targeted Violence in the Schools. This is a special report from the United States Secret Service in cooperation with the

United State Department of Education involving interviews with school shooters to assess possible variables involved with kids who commit school shootings. The report is available online at www.treas.gov/usss/ntac. You can also contact: National Threat Assessment Center, U.S. Secret Service, 950 H Street NW, Suite 9100, Washington, DC 20223, (202-406-5470; fax, 202-406-6180).

The School Shooter: A Threat Assessment Perspective. This special FBI report is available online at www.fbi.gov/pressrm /pressre100/school.htm.

Toys

Oppenheim Toy Portfolio, 40 East 9th Street, Suite 14 M, New York, NY 10003, www.toyportfolio.com.

Violence Prevention (Bullies, Child Safety, Tolerance)

American Guidance Service, 4201 Woodland Road, Circle Pines, MN 55014, (800-328-2560), has several programs for teachers on violence prevention for kids of all ages. Call for a catalogue or visit their Web site, www.agsnet.com.

Children's Defense Fund, 25 E Street NW, Washington, DC 20001, (202-628-8787), www.childrensdefense.org

Children Now, 1212 Broadway, 5th Floor, Oakland CA 94612, (510-763-2444; fax, 510-763-1974), www.childrennow.org.

Kidscape: Keeping Kids Safe, www.kidscape.org.uk. A British site with information on bullies for parents and kids.

MSNBC, www.msnbc.com. Information for parents and teachers. Search for "bullying."

National Crime Prevention Council,
www.ncpc.org/about.htm. Comprehensive site that gives a
wealth of information on crime prevention including child
safety, domestic violence, and bullying.

Teaching Tolerance, www.splcenter.org/teachingtolerance
/tt-index.html.

The Tolerance Project, http://hills.ccsf.cc.ca.us/~tolerant

Warning Signs, American Psychological Association and Music
Television, 1999, http://helping.apa.org/warningsigns.
This is a publication for teens. Topics include: reasons for
violence; recognizing violence warning signs in others;
what you can do if someone you know shows violence
warning signs; dealing with anger; your own risk for
violent behavior; controlling your risk for violent behavior; violence against self. (For a free copy of the online
brochure, call 800-268-0078 or use the order page on
the Web site.)

Joining a Parent Study Group

IF YOU LIKE the ideas you've learned in this book, you may
want to learn more. You may want to be involved with other
parents facing similar issues with their kids, and there may be
opportunities in your area.

School counselors, churches, local counseling agencies may
run parenting groups. Make sure the philosophy of any group
you join is similar to the ideas you've learned in this book. Two
of the authors of this book, Gary and Joyce McKay, helped
create a popular parenting program called STEP, Systematic
Training for Effective Parenting. There are three levels of
STEP. Each program runs seven sessions for about two hours
per session. The programs are multimedia with videotapes,

readings, discussion, and exercises. Each program has a parent book that is available in most bookstores or online at sites like Barnes and Noble (www.bn.com) or Amazon.com (www.amazon .com) or directly from the publisher at (www.parentingeducation .com) or (www.agsnet.com). Here's a description of the three STEP programs:

Systematic Training for Effective Parenting by Don Dinkmeyer Sr., Gary D. McKay, and Don Dinkmeyer Jr. (Circle Pines, Minn.: American Guidance Service, 1997). This level is for middle childhood, about six to twelve. The text for the program is titled *The Parent's Handbook.*

Systematic Training for Effective Parenting of Teens by Don Dinkmeyer Sr., Gary D. McKay, Joyce L. McKay, and Don Dinkmeyer Jr. (Circle Pines, Minn.: American Guidance Service, 1998.) This level is for parents of preteens and teens. The text for the program is titled *Parenting Teenagers.*

Systematic Training for Effective Parenting of Children Under Six by Don Dinkmeyer Sr., Gary D. McKay, James S. Dinkmeyer, Don Dinkmeyer Jr., and Joyce L. McKay. (Circle Pines, Minn.: American Guidance Service, 1997). As the title says, this level is for parents of young children. The text for this program is titled *Parenting Young Children.*

If STEP is not available in your community, you could start your own STEP group. The Leader's Resource Guide gives step-by-step instructions on how to lead a group. The leader need not be an expert. The program is designed for study of the materials. The leader's job is to organize the group and follow the lesson guides for involving the group in a discussion of the ideas. You can obtain information about STEP by calling the publisher, American Guidance Service, (800-328-2560), or online at www.parentingeducation.com.

You may want to start a study group with *Raising Respectful Kids in a Rude World*. Again, you don't have to be an expert. You can involve the group in discussing the ideas in the book by asking participants to read a chapter or two for each session the group will meet. You discuss the chapters by using open questions such as, "What did you learn from the chapter?" "What ideas did you find helpful?" "How will you apply these ideas?"

If Your Child Is Violent

AS PARENTS, WE may be faced with a violent child. We need to know how to recognize violence in our children and be prepared to deal with it. Sometimes this will mean applying the skills you've learned in this book—to help our child learn nonviolent alternatives. At other times, it can mean seeking professional help. First, we need to be able to recognize the warning signs of violent behavior.

What Does a Violent Child or Teen Look Like?

The American Psychological Association lists several possible warning signs of violent behavior. The signs are grouped by age ranges. However, older children may have some of the signs for younger children as well those listed for their own age group. Those signs that are in italics indicate that you should seek professional help.[1]

Toddlers and Preschoolers
The child:

1. Is very active, temperamental, and fearless.

2. Often won't do what you say.

3. Is detached from parents.

4. Often watches violent TV, becomes involved in violent play, or is verbally or physically abusive to playmates.

5. *Throws several temper tantrums in a single day or many lasting more than 15 minutes; difficult or impossible to calm.*

6. *Has several belligerent, unexplained outbursts.*

Middle Childhood

The child:

1. Does not pay attention or concentrate on tasks.

2. Is frequently disruptive in class.

3. Has poor academic performance.

4. Participates in violent TV, movies, or video games.

5. Is a loner or has few friends; may be rejected by others because of the way he acts.

6. Associates with other troublesome or aggressive kids.

7. Is disobedient.

8. Doesn't care about others' feelings.

9. Gets frustrated easily.

10. *Overreacts angrily to criticism, disappointments, or teasing; blames others and may get even.*

11. *Often fights with other children at school.*

12. *Engages in animal cruelty.*

Preteens and Teenagers

The youngster:

1. Defies or ignores authority.

2. Is unconcerned about the feelings or rights of others.

3. Feels life is unfair.

4. Cuts classes or entire days and has poor academic performance.

5. *Relies on violence or threats of violence to solve problems.*

6. *Gets suspended or expelled, or drops out of school.*

7. *Fights, steals, vandalizes, destroys property, joins a gang.*

8. *Uses alcohol or drugs excessively.*

9. *Is fascinated with weapons of any kind.*

Dealing with a Violent Child

If you are experiencing violent acts from a child, you'll need to protect yourself and your other children. If the violent child is quite young, you may be able to remove her from the scene. If the child is older or if you're unable to do this without risking injury to you or the child, you may need to remove yourself and your other children from the violent child. With some kids, the police may need to be involved.

You probably have enough experience with your violent child that you can see the warning signs before an incident occurs. If so, take precautions before an incident happens.

Seeking Professional Help

IT'S TIME TO consult a professional if your child is violent with you, other children, or animals; at school; or in the neighborhood. This is especially true if your child exhibits some of the behaviors in italics in the "What Does a Violent Child or Teen Look Like" lists above.

Seek help when:

- Your child's behavior is beyond your influence.

- Your child abuses drugs.

- Your child's involved with law enforcement.

- Your child runs with a gang.

- You are unable to control your violence toward your child or teen.

- You are involved in a domestic violence situation with your spouse—either as victim or perpetrator.

There are many ways to find professionals. You can ask your school counselor, principal, or assistant principal. Your minister may know of someone. Sometimes family doctors are aware of counseling professionals. You may have a friend who's faced similar problems.

These and other organizations who represent helping professionals will either have lists of their members in your area on their Web sites or you can e-mail them from their sites to obtain lists.

American Association for Marriage and Family Therapy, www.aamft.org.

American Counseling Association, www.counseling.org.

American Mental Health Counselors Association, www.amhca.org.

American Psychological Association, www.apa.org/psychnet.

International Association of Marriage and Family Counselors, www.iamfc.org.

National Association of Social Workers, www.naswdc.org.

National Board of Certified Counselors, www.nbcc.org.

North American Society of Adlerian Psychology,
www.alfredadler.org.

There may be an ad in the yellow pages under fields of practice such as marriage and family therapists, counselors, mental health counselors, psychologists, and social workers. In addition, nonprofit agencies present in most communities provide professional counseling services incorporating a sliding fee scale for low-income families. These agencies are usually listed as "Social Service Agencies" in the yellow pages.

When you do locate professionals, interview them, and verify their credentials, years of experience, and so on. Tell them about the problem and ask if this is within their area of expertise—based on the age of the child and the behavior he is exhibiting. If not, they may be able to recommend someone else.

It is also important that the professional you find is a good fit for you and your family, that her style is one you feel comfortable with. Most communities have professionals in the area of specialty you are seeking. Don't be afraid to shop around to find the right person.

NOTES

Chapter 1

1. John Marks, "The American Uncivil Wars: How Crude, Rude and Obnoxious Behavior Has Replaced Good Manners and Why That Hurts Our Politics and Culture," *U.S. News and World Report* (22 April 1996): 66–72.
2. Don Dinkmeyer Sr., Gary D. McKay, and Don Dinkmeyer Jr., *The Parent's Handbook* (from STEP: Systematic Training for Effective Parenting) (Circle Pines, Minn: American Guidance Service, 1997); Don Dinkmeyer Sr., Gary D. McKay and Don Dinkmeyer Jr., "Examine Your Beliefs," *Leader's Resource Guide* (from STEP: Systematic Training for Effective Parenting program) (Circle Pines, Minn: American Guidance Service, 1997).
3. A favorite saying of Mac Logan, Scottish management consultant.
4. Time Warner/Nickelodeon poll as reported in: "Childhood as It Should Be," *Arizona Daily Star,* July 5, 1999.

Chapter 2

This chapter was developed with the assistance of Dr. John F. Newbauer, a Fort Wayne, Indiana, psychologist and professor who specializes in working with delinquent children.

1. John F. Newbauer, (correspondence with Gary D. McKay, 8 March 1999).
2. Alfred Adler, *The Individual Psychology of Alfred Adler,* edited and annotated by H. L. Ansbacher and R. R. Ansbacher (New York: Harper Torchbooks, 1956).
3. John F. Newbauer, 1999.
4. Don Dinkmeyer Sr., Gary D. McKay, James S. Dinkmeyer, Don Dinkmeyer Jr. and Joyce L. McKay, *Parenting Young Children* (Early Childhood STEP) (Circle Pines, Minn.: American Guidance Service, 1997).
5. John F. Newbauer, 1999.
6. Don Dinkmeyer Sr., Gary D. McKay, and Don Dinkmeyer Jr., *The Parent's Handbook* (STEP program) (Circle Pines, Minn.: American Guidance Service, 1997); Don Dinkmeyer Sr., Gary D. McKay, James S. Dinkmeyer, Don Dinkmeyer Jr. and Joyce L. McKay, *Parenting Young Children* (Early Childhood STEP) (Circle Pines, Minn.: American Guidance Service, 1997); Don Dinkmeyer Sr., Gary D. McKay, Joyce L. McKay, and Don Dinkmeyer Jr., *Parenting Teenagers* (STEP/Teen) (Circle Pines, Minn.: American Guidance Service, 1998).
7. Thomas Gordon, *P E T: Parent Effectiveness Training* (New York: NAL-Dutton, 1975); Don Dinkmeyer Sr., Gary D. McKay, and Don Dinkmeyer Jr.,

The Parent's Handbook (STEP program) (Circle Pines, Minn.: American Guidance Service, 1997); Don Dinkmeyer Sr., Gary D. McKay, James S. Dinkmeyer, Don Dinkmeyer, Jr. and Joyce L. McKay, Parenting Young Children (Early Childhood STEP) (Circle Pines, Minn.: American Guidance Service, 1997); Don Dinkmeyer Sr., Gary D. McKay, Joyce L. McKay, and Don Dinkmeyer Jr., Parenting Teenagers (STEP/Teen) (Circle Pines, Minn.: American Guidance Service, 1998).

8. Ibid.

Chapter 3

1. Jane Griffith and Robert L. Powers, *An Adlerian Lexicon* (Chicago, Ill.: The Americas Institute of Adlerian Studies, Ltd., 1984).

2. Francis X. Walton, "Teenage Suicide: A Family Oriented Approach to Prevention," *Individual Psychology,* 44, no. 2 (June 1988): 185.

3. Don Dinkmeyer Sr. and Daniel Eckstein, *Leadership by Encouragement* (Boca Raton, Fla.: CRC Press–St. Lucie Press, 1995).

4. Don Dinkmeyer Sr., Gary D. McKay, and Don Dinkmeyer Jr., *The Parent's Handbook* (STEP program)(Circle Pines, Minn.: American Guidance Service, 1997).

5. Adlerian is the term applied to those who follow the philosophy of Alfred Adler and Rudolf Dreikurs. This book is based on Adlerian principles.

6. Don Dinkmeyer Sr., Gary D. McKay, and Don Dinkmeyer Jr., *The Parent's Handbook* (STEP program) (Circle Pines, Minn.: American Guidance Service, 1997); Gary D. McKay, "Parent Education: From Self-Esteem to People-Esteem," *North American Society of Individual Psychology Newsletter,* V. 31, N. 4, pp. 3&4 July–Aug (1998).

7. Shirley King, *Teaching Tolerance: Tips on Raising Open-Minded Children* (New York: Doubleday, 1996).

8. Richard Bach*, Illusions* (New York: Dell, 1977).

Chapter 4

1. Don Dinkmeyer Sr. and Gary D. McKay, *Raising a Responsible Child* (New York: Simon & Schuster, 1996).

2. Thomas Gordon, *P.E.T.: Parent Effectiveness Training* (New York: NAL-Dutton, 1975).

3. Don Dinkmeyer Sr., Gary D. McKay, and Don Dinkmeyer Jr., *The Parent's Handbook* (STEP program) (Circle Pines, Minn.: American Guidance Service, 1997); Thomas Gordon, *P.E.T.: Parent Effectiveness Training* (New York: NAL-Dutton, 1975).

4. Don Dinkmeyer Sr., Gary D. McKay, and Don Dinkmeyer Jr., *The Parent's Handbook* (STEP program) (Circle Pines, Minn.: American Guidance Service, 1997).

Chapter 5

1. Karen S. Peterson, "Why Everyone Is So Short-Tempered," *USA Today*, 18 July 2000.
2. Gary D. McKay, *The Basics of Anger* (Booklet) (Coral Springs, Fla.: CMTI Press, 1992); Gary D. McKay and Don Dinkmeyer, *How You Feel Is Up to You: The Power of Emotional Choice* (Atascadero, Calif.: Impact Publishers, 1994).
3. Rudolf Dreikurs, *Psychodynamics, Psychotherapy and Counseling* (Chicago, Ill.: Adler School of Professional Psychology, 1967).
4. Albert Ellis, *A Guide to Rational Living* (North Hollywood, Calif.: Wilshire Books, 1998).
5. Aaron T. Beck, "Cognitive Therapy," Paper presented at the Evolution of Psychotherapy Conference, Anaheim, California (May 2000).
6. Edward Charlesworth and Ronald Nathan, *Stress Management: A Comprehensive Guide to Wellness* (New York: Antheneum, 1985).
7. Jane Nelsen, *Positive Time-Out* (Rocklin, Calif.: Prima Publishing, 1999).
8. Don Dinkmeyer Sr., Gary D. McKay, James S. Dinkmeyer, Don Dinkmeyer, Jr. and Joyce L. McKay, *Parenting Young Children* (Early Childhood STEP) (Circle Pines, Minn.: American Guidance Service, 1997); Jane Nelsen, *Positive Time-Out* (Rocklin, Calif.: Prima Publishing, 1999).
9. Amy Horton, "Teaching Anger Management Skills to Primary-Age Children," *Teaching and Change* 3, no. 3 (Spring 1996): 281–296.
10. Jane Nelsen, Cheryl Erwin, and Carol Delzer, *Positive Discipline for Single Parents*, 2nd ed. (Rocklin, Calif.: Prima Publishing, 1999); Don Dinkmeyer Sr. and Gary D. McKay, *Raising a Responsible Child*, rev. ed. (New York: Fireside, 1996).

Chapter 6

1. Poll reported on *Healthy Kids,* Fox Television, Primedia, 10 April 1999.
2. Jane Nelsen and Lynn Lott, *Positive Discipline for Teens* (Roseville, Calif.: Prima Publishing, 2000).
3. Don Dinkmeyer Sr., Gary D. McKay, James S. Dinkmeyer, Don Dinkmeyer Jr., and Joyce L. McKay, *Parenting Young Children* (Early Childhood STEP) (Circle Pines, Minn.: American Guidance Service, 1997).
4. Ibid.

Chapter 7

1. John Marks, "The American Uncivil Wars: How Crude, Rude and Obnoxious Behavior Has Replaced Good Manners and Why That Hurts Our Politics and Culture," *U.S. News and World Report (*22 April 1996): 66–72.
2. Ibid.
3. Carol McD. Wallace, *Elbows Off the Table, Napkin in the Lap, No Video Games During Dinner* (New York: St. Martin's Press, 1996).
4. Peggy Post, "What to Teach Your Child About Courtesy," *Good Housekeeping* (March 1997): 32–36.

5. Letitia Baldridge, *More Than Manners!* (New York: Simon & Schuster, 1997).

6. Carol McD. Wallace, 1996.

7. Ibid.

8. Alex J. Packer, *How Rude! The Teenagers' Guide to Good Manners, Proper Behavior, and Not Grossing People Out* (Minneapolis, Minn.: Free Spirit Publishing, 1999).

9. Ibid.

10. Ronald D. Williamson and J. Howard Johnson, "Responding to Parent and Public Concerns About Middle Level Schools," *National Association of Secondary School Principals Bulletin,* 82, no. 559 (September 1998).

Chapter 8

1. Mary Manin Morrissey, "Nonviolence," Living Enrichment Center, http://lists.isb.sdnpk.org/pipermail/cyberclub-old/1999-June/000579.html (28 June 1999).

2. "Health Groups Directly Link Media to Child Violence," Cable News Network, Time Warner, www.cnn.com/2000/HEALTH/children/07/26/children.violence.ap/index.html (26 July 2000).

3. "FTC Targets Entertainment: Report Accuses Industry of Marketing Violent Games, Movies to Kids," ABC News Internet Ventures, http://abcnews.go.com/sections/us/DailyNews/mediaviolence000911.html (11 September 2000).

4. Ibid.

5. "Study: 'Electronic Baby Sitter' Overexposes Youth to Sex, Violence," Cable News Network, Time Warner, www.cnn.com (6 January 1999).

6. Mary K. Reinhart, "Health Agencies Decry Media 'Toxins'. " *Scottsdale (Arizona) Tribune,* 27 July 2000.

7. Milton Chen, "Television as a Tool: Talking with Kids About TV." www.childrennow.org.

8. G. Gerbner, "The Man Who Counts the Killings; Violence on Television*," The Atlantic Monthly* (May 1997): 86–101.

9. "How Can I Protect My Children on the Internet?" Helpanswers Educational Foundation, www.helpanswers.com/tutorials/protect.html. (1997-2000).

10. Ibid.

11. Nancy Lee Cecil, *Raising Peaceful Children in a Violent World* (San Diego: Lura Media, Inc., 1995).

12. Ibid.

13. *Zina On Line Magazine,* Women's Net of Western Pennsylvania, 333 Boulevard. of the Allies, Pittsburgh, PA 15222, www.womensnet.com/oppenheim.htm.

14. Ron Brand (interview by author Daniel Eckstein, 18 May 2000).

15. Kristen Davis, "A Day in the Life," *Arizona Daily Star*, (Tucson, Arizona, 11 March 2000) (and an interview with Josh Pastner by authors Gary and Joyce McKay, 14 April 2000).

16. Janice Cohn, *Raising Compassionate, Courageous Children in a Violent World* (Atlanta, Ga.: Longstreet Press, 1996).

17. Paula Statman, *On the Safe Side* (New York: HarperPerennial, 1995).

18. Ibid.

19. Mary Hatwood Futrell and Lee Etta Powell, *Measures to Ensure School Safety,* ERIC/CUE, ERIC Clearinghouse on Urban Education, Office of Educational Research and Improvement, U.S. Department of Education, 1996. http:// eric-web.tc.columbia.edu/monographs/uds107/preventing_measures.html# conflictresolution; Chester R. Robinson and James O. Fuller, *How Can We Help Make Schools Safe for Children?* ERIC Clearinghouse on Counseling and Student Services, ACCESS ERIC, Office of Educational Research and Improvement, U.S. Department of Education, 1997. www.uncg.edu/edu/ericcass/violence /docs/safschl.htm; K. Dwyer, D. Osher, and C. Warger, *Early Warning, Timely Response: A Guide to Safe Schools*, U.S. Department of Education, Center for Effective Collaboration and Practice, 1998. www.air-dc.org/cecp/guide.

20. Ken Wong, (interview by author Steven A Maybell. 11 April 2000), Ken Wong, M.S.W., is Violence Prevention Coordinator, Youth Eastside Services, Bellevue, Washington.

21. K. Dwyer, D. Osher, and C. Warger, *Early Warning, Timely Response: A Guide to Safe Schools*, U.S. Department of Education, Center for Effective Collaboration and Practice, 1998. www.air-dc.org/cecp/guide.

22. Ibid.

23. Ibid.

24. "When the Killers Warn Us," Report on study in the *New York Times,* 10 April 2000, www.abcnews.go.com /onair/DailyNews /killers000410.html.

25. K. Dwyer, D. Osher, and C. Warger, 1998.25. Ibid.

26. *Safe School Initiative: An Interim Report on the Prevention or Targeted Violence in the Schools.* (U.S. Secret Service, Washington, DC: U.S. Department of the Treasury, October 2000), www.treas.gov/usss/ntac. (See appendix for information on this report.)

27. Susan Linn, "How to Find Out If Your Child Is Afraid," Family Education Network, 1999. http://familyeducation.com/article/0,1120,1-9754-0-2,000.html.

28. Alvin Poussaint, "Fears About School Violence," Family Education Network, 1999. http://familyeducation.com/article/0,1120,1-600-0-1,00.html.

29. Contact the Ulster Project at 14560 Beechwood, Milwaukee, WI 53005; (262) 786-8267; www.ulsterproject.org.

Chapter 9

1. As quoted in "Most School Children Take Part in Bullying," by Ann Quigley, *Journal of Early Adolescence,* Reuters Limited, Thrive Partners, August, 1999, www.thriveonline.com/ health/news/RB/1999Jul13/10.html.

2. Nathan Seppa, "Keeping Schoolyards Safe from Bullies," *APA Monitor,* October 1996, www.apa.org/monitor/oct96/bullies.html.

3. Ron Banks, "Bulling in Schools," ERIC Digest, 1999, www.accesseric.org:81 /resources/parent/bullying.html; Nathan Seppa, "Keeping Schoolyards Safe

from Bullies," *APA Monitor,* October 1996, www.apa.org/monitor/oct96/bullies.html.

4. Joyce L. McKay, "Bullies and Bullying," in *Leader's Resource Guide* (STEP program) by Don Dinkmeyer Sr., Gary D. McKay, and Don Dinkmeyer Jr. (Circle Pines, Minn.: American Guidance Service, 1997); Nathan Seppa, "Keeping Schoolyards Safe from Bullies," *APA Monitor,* October 1996, www.apa.org/monitor/oct96/bullies.html; Sherryll Kraizer, *Dealing with Bullies* (The Levi Company, 1996–1999). www.sass.ca/bully.htm; "Bullied to Death," Investigative Reports (New York: Arts and Entertainment Network, 20 April 2000); Ron Banks, "Bulling in Schools," ERIC Digest, 1999, www.accesseric.org:81/resources/parent/bullying.html.

5. Sherryll Kraizer, *Dealing with Bullies* (The Levi Company, 1996–1999). www.sass.ca/bully.htm.

6. Sara Emerson Shea, "Do You Know the Signs of Bullying?" *Contemporary Pediatrics,* MSNBC, www.msnbc.com/news/114505.asp.

7. Joyce L. McKay, "Bullies and Bullying," in *Leader's Resource Guide* (STEP program) by Don Dinkmeyer Sr., Gary D. McKay, and Don Dinkmeyer Jr. (Circle Pines, Minn.: American Guidance Service, 1997); Steve Rhodes, "How Kids Can 'Bullyproof' Themselves," *USA Weekend,* 20-22 March 1998, www.usaweekend.com/98_issues/980322/980322bully_proof.html.

8. Joyce L. McKay, "Bullies and Bullying," in *Leader's Resource Guide* (STEP program) by Don Dinkmeyer Sr., Gary D. McKay, and Don Dinkmeyer Jr. (Circle Pines, Minn.: American Guidance Service, 1997); Sara Emerson Shea, "Do You Know the Signs of Bullying?" *Contemporary Pediatrics,* MSNBC, www.msnbc.com/news/114505.asp.

9. The "Gangs" section was prepared with the assistance of Ken Wong, M.S.W., Violence Prevention Coordinator, Youth Eastside Services, Bellevue, Washington, in an interview by author Steven A Maybell, 18 November 1999.

10. The "Alcohol and Other Drugs" section was prepared using the following sources: Joyce L. McKay, Don Dinkmeyer Sr., and Don Dinkmeyer Jr., *Drug Free 2: A Drug Use Prevention Program for Grades 4-6* (Circle Pines, Minn.: American Guidance Service, 1992); Joyce L. McKay, "Drug Prevention," in *Leader's Resource Guide* (STEP program) by Don Dinkmeyer Sr., Gary D. McKay, and Don Dinkmeyer Jr. (Circle Pines, Minn.: American Guidance Service, 1997); Don Dinkmeyer Sr., Gary D. McKay, and Don Dinkmeyer Jr., *The Parent's Handbook* (from STEP program) (Circle Pines, Minn.: American Guidance Service, 1997); Joyce L. McKay, "Drug Awareness," in *Leader's Resource Guide* (from STEP/Teen) by Don Dinkmeyer Sr., Gary D. McKay, Joyce L. McKay and Don Dinkmeyer Jr., (Circle Pines, MN: American Guidance Service, 1998); Don Dinkmeyer Sr., Gary D. McKay, Joyce L. McKay and Don Dinkmeyer Jr., *Parenting Teenagers* (from STEP/Teen) Circle Pines, Minn.: American Guidance Service, 1998); Joyce L. McKay, "Drug Prevention Activities for Parents of Young Children," in *Leader's Resource*

Guide (from Early Childhood STEP) by Don Dinkmeyer Sr., Gary D. McKay, James S. Dinkmeyer, Don Dinkmeyer Jr. and Joyce L. McKay) (Circle Pines, Minn.: American Guidance Service, 1997); Gary D. McKay, Joyce L. McKay, and Don Dinkmeyer Sr., *STEP for Substance Abuse Prevention* (Circle Pines, Minn.: American Guidance Service, 1990); Don Dinkmeyer, Sr. and Gary D. McKay, *Raising a Responsible Child* (New York: Fireside, 1996).

11. Chandra Hawley, "Drugs and Violence in the Schools," *Teacher Talk* (Bloomington, Ind.: Indiana University Center for Adolescent Studies, 30 June 1997), http://education.indiana.edu/cas/tt/v2i3/drugs.html; Diana H. Fishbein, "Differential Susceptibility to Comorbid Drug Abuse and Violence," *Journal of Drug Issues,* 28, no. 4 (1998): 859–890.

12. The "Violence in Teen Dating Relationships" section was prepared with the assistance of Belinda Lafferty, M.A. CMHC, Teen Domestic Violence Program Supervisor, Youth Eastside Services, Bellevue, Washington in an interview by author Steven A. Maybell, 19 October 1999.

13. "Dating Violence, Young Women in Danger," Paper by Los Angeles Commission on Assaults Against Women, as reported by Children's Safety Network, Newton, Mass., April, 1998.

14. Belinda Lafferty, 1999.

15. Ibid.

16. Ibid.

17. The "Date Rape" section was prepared with the assistance of Debbi Halela, M.A., CMHC, Sexual Abuse Program Coordinator, Youth Eastside Services, Bellevue, Washington, in an interview by author Steven A. Maybell, 10 January 2000.

18. Debbi Halela, 2000.

19. Ibid.

20. Ibid.

Appendix

1. American Psychological Association, 1996. www.apa.org/pubinfor/apa-aap .html.

INDEX

ABOUT THE AUTHORS

••

Gary D. McKay, Ph.D., licensed psychologist, is the coauthor of 11 books and parent and teacher education programs including the STEP series, Systematic Training for Effective Parenting, the world's leading parent-education programs. Former teacher and counselor, Dr. McKay has conducted workshops in human relations, parent education, and anger management throughout North America and Europe.

Joyce L. McKay, Ph.D., certified professional counselor, is the coauthor of seven books and parent education programs including Early Childhood STEP and STEP/Teen. Dr. McKay is a former teacher and counselor who has conducted workshops in parent education, career counseling and guidance, drug abuse prevention, sex equity, and human relations throughout North America and Europe.

The McKays are diplomates in Adlerian psychology (North American Society of Adlerian Psychology). They are parents and grandparents and live in Tucson, Arizona.

Daniel Eckstein, Ph.D., is president of Encouraging Leadership Inc., Scottsdale, Arizona. He is also an adjunct faculty member for Capella University, Minneapolis; Ottawa University, Phoenix; and the Adler School of Professional Psychology, Toronto. Dr. Eckstein is the author or coauthor of 11 books, including *Leadership by Encouragement* and *The Theory and Practice of Life Style Assessment.* He is a diplomate in counseling psychology (American Board of Professional Psychology) and in Adlerian psychology (North American Society of Adlerian Psychology). Dr. Eckstein lives in Scottsdale, Arizona.

Steven A. Maybell, Ph.D., has over 25 years of experience as a counselor, teacher, and parent educator. He is a certified marriage and family therapist, clinical social worker, and a diplomate in Adlerian psychology (North American Society of Adlerian Psychology) and professional psychotherapy (International Academy of Behavioral Medicine, Counseling and Psychotherapy). Steve is currently the clinical director for Youth Eastside Services in Bellevue, Washington. He and his wife, Debbie, are the parents of two grown sons. They live in Kirkland, Washington.

The authors offer presentations and workshops on *Raising Respectful Kids in a Rude World* and the STEP programs. Contact information for scheduling a presentation or workshop:

Drs. Gary and Joyce McKay: 520-885-8197; e-mail: gjmckay@cmti-w.com

Dr. Daniel Eckstein: 602-469-5608; e-mail: deckstein@juno.com

Dr. Steven A. Maybell: 425-827-3485; e-mail: stevem@youtheastsideservices.org